The Red Web

An underground political history of
the United States from 1918 to the
present time showing how close the
government is to collapse and told
in an understandable way.

by Blair Coán

THE AMERICANIST CLASSICS

Published by WESTERN ISLANDS ★ BOSTON ★ LOS ANGELES

To My Mother
Helen Blair Coán
Who loved the truth and
taught me to fight for it.

THE RED WEB

Copyright, 1925, by Blair Coán
All rights reserved

Manufactured in the United States of America

Introduction to the Americanist Classics edition
copyright © 1969 by Western Islands
Belmont, Massachusetts 02178

CONTENTS

The Americanist Classics

. . . reaches for its manuscripts to every corner of the earth, and to every era of man's culture. For the ideals represented by America at its best have been acclaimed alike by the Roman Cicero two thousand years ago; by the Frenchman Bastiat a hundred years ago; and by the Korean Syngman Rhee only yesterday.

. . . is published for readers of every clime and color and creed, and of every nationality. An American or a German or an Egyptian or a Japanese or an Australian; a Catholic or a Protestant or a Jew or a Mohammedan or a Buddhist; each alike can be or become a good americanist, in the fundamental meaning of that term which these volumes will strengthen and support.

. . . seeks to make readily available, in a uniform and inexpensive format, a growing series of great books that define many battle lines in the long war between freedom and slavery. The first fully recorded engagement in that war was between the constructive forces of Athenian individualism and the destructive forces of Spartan collectivism. Those prototypes find their recurrent spiritual reincarnation today in the bitter contemporary struggle between the americanist and the communist systems.

For the americanist, always and everywhere, education is the basic strategy, and truth is the vital weapon. It is the purpose of this series to supply searchlights and alarm bells, and weaponry and the will to win, for those who believe that Bryant's admonition must be heeded in every age:

> "Not yet, O Freedom! close thy lids in slumber, for thine enemy never sleeps."

INTRODUCTION TO THE AMERICANIST CLASSICS EDITION

In republishing *The Red Web,* by Blair Coán, we hope to be able to set straight the record of the most maligned Attorney General and the most vilified President in American history and in so doing inform and awaken patriots as to what has been happening to our great nation so that they can more effectively fight the enemy who is now not only within our gates but in possession of the citadel!

Harry M. Daugherty ably served his country and two Presidents, Warren G. Harding and Calvin Coolidge, for three years as the fifty-first Attorney General of the United States. He successfully reorganized the Department of Justice and conducted the beginnings of a highly effective war against bolshevik terrorists and revolutionaries. But instead of being rewarded for his dedication and devotion to duty, he was subjected to a gigantic frame-up and massive smear. Blair Coán undertakes the task of vindicating Daugherty by telling the true story of the frame-up of the Attorney General and by showing how totally false were the charges.

Coán points out that although the Communists wished for the destruction of Daugherty, the frame-up of the Attorney General was carried through for them by the machinations of what Coán calls parlor pinks, who we believe can be more accurately referred to as *Insiders.* These are conspirators, such as Harry Hopkins, Alger Hiss and Harry Dexter White, who are infinitely more sophisticated and intelligent—and infinitely more dangerous—than the street revolutionaries. The *Insiders* operate in the top social, political and financial circles of a nation; their goal is the destruction of all governments, religions, and morals, by any means, so as to enthrone themselves as masters of a new world order. Their method of operation is to use their bolshevik goons at the bottom to implement and "justify" their own extension of power and control further and further down the bureaucratic pyramid until they establish total government, which *is* Communism.

These *Insiders* are presently responsible for the no-win war in Vietnam, the building of bridges to the East, the increasing surrender of American sovereignty to the United Nations, the usurping of legislative power by the Supreme Court, and the financing of revolution in our cities with government funds. In the 1920's, they were in positions of considerable influence and power, but at a lower echelon than today. They then included such men and women as

Newton D. Baker, Charles P. Steinmetz, Sidney Hillman, Jane Addams, Norman Thomas, Walter Lippmann, Christian Herter, John Foster Dulles, Allen Dulles, Amos Pinchot, Burton Wheeler, Felix Warburg, Carrie Chapman Catt, Jacob Schiff, Stuart Chase, Scott Nearing, Thomas Walsh, Clarence Dill, Felix Frankfurter, William C. Bullitt, Lincoln Steffens, John Dewey, Jack London, Theodore Dreiser, and Rexford Tugwell. The reader may ask why these illustrious men would join such a conspiracy. The answer is quite the reverse of the question: These men *became* illustrious primarily because they *were* part of the Conspiracy.

When the *Insiders* decided to "get Daugherty," they were not launching a campaign of personal revenge. Rather, their real purpose was to ruin Daugherty so completely that his defeat could be used as a means of discrediting the whole Harding Administration. And their success in this dual attack along with the resulting weakening of the Coolidge Administration, and especially of the then pro-Americanist Justice Department, were extremely important steps in bringing the *Insiders* to the top and controlling levels of American society.

The *Insiders* used on Daugherty one of their most effective, although then little understood weapons: the destruction of their opposition through a fraudulent and rigged trial, either before a court of law or a Congressional committee. After poisoning public opinion by a carefully developed campaign of smears and rumors, the *Insiders* arrange for their victim to be put on trial (either physically or by inference) on some pretense even more phony than their previous charges. When the rigged tribunal finds the person guilty, as is decided even before the first day's sitting, all of the smears, no matter how incredible, receive a legal stamp of approval. The *Insiders* then use the false verdict as a means also to discredit their opponent's associates, supporters, social order, government, and/or principles. This is precisely the technique used against Daugherty and, in later years, it was used with equal viciousness and, unfortunately, with equal success against Senator Joseph R. McCarthy.

Deadly as this weapon is, it is only effective as long as good citizens refuse to become involved. If enough patriots are willing to stand up for the truth and expose the treasonous actions of the *Insiders,* the conspiracy of these malevolent enemies of all that America represents will crumble, almost overnight, like a house of cards. It is our hope that *The Red Web* will serve as an important and effective educational tool in the fight to preserve our country and civilization.

Thomas J. Haas

INTRODUCTION

ONE of these days the inarticulates of the qualified American electorate are going to awaken from their lethargy and find voice. When they do they are going to get sufficiently aroused to go to the polls on an election day and in a strikingly emphatic manner repudiate every politician afflicted with liver complaint, softening of the brain or flexibility of the spine. The result of this will be a new quality of leadership, patterned after an old one once revered; distinguished for intestinal stamina, frankness and dependability, and exemplified in word and deed by such men as Washington, Lincoln, Webster, Harrison, Cleveland, McKinley, Knox, Sherman, etc., etc.

This accomplished, the recent frame-up against the government and the people of the United States of America by the reds, the pinks and the yellows of domestic and imported politics may, perhaps, be atoned. But in the meantime, to talk about our phenomenal prosperity; to harangue about our position as leader among the nations of the world; to discourse on life, liberty and the pursuit of happiness; to sing about the red, white and blue; to celebrate the Fourth of July and Constitution Day, and to offer reverently quoted excerpts from the writings and addresses of George Washington, the Founding Fathers and Abraham Lincoln, may be, in some instances, a thankless though high-minded task, but in most instances is nothing more than a lot of tommyrot.

It is time, right now, to get down to cases about this thing we hear called "the red menace." In doing so, about the first thing to be said is that the one real menace is a lot pinker than it is red; the pinks—parlor, bedroom, bath and bathless—are a greater peril to the national security of the American republic and its people than the reds; and even the pinks would not be so very menacing were it not for the yellows, the pussy-footers, the tread-easies, the oh-I-wouldn't-do-that-ers of American politics—the men in high places, official and otherwise, who fear to perform the duty they owe the patient and inarticulate majority because to do so means a bean-shooting barrage from the noisy and organized minorities who specialize in open letters, telegrams, resolutions, and cheap oratory about the "downtrodden peepul" whom they neither love nor represent, either in theory or in fact.

Armistice Day, 1918, had scarcely passed into history; American troops at the front in France were not yet on their way back to native soil; the treaty of peace with the foreign foe was yet to be negotiated, drafted and signed, when the frame-up, of which this book is the story, had its beginnings. From time to time since then, the United States has had its taste of civil war—abortive, to be sure, but war none-the-less, and the sponsors and promoters of it have not yet acknowledged themselves wholly beaten. Whether they are or are not entirely and permanently subdued now depends upon how far and how long the American people may be disposed to go in their toleration of soft tactics, pussy-footing and compromise on the part of politicians and public officers occupying positions of dominance in national and international affairs.

If the people of the United States are not yet fully awake to the frame-up perpetrated against them and their government, they are sure to be awakened to it sooner or later, and when this comes the reds and pinks most conspicuously implicated will not be alone in the morgues for the politically deceased, because the mangled political remains of a notable galaxy of liverless Republicans and over-bilious Democrats will occupy slabs in the same or very proximate oblivion.

The pages of this book, the reader will find, state plain things plainly, not merely about the reds, but about the pinks and the yellows who have lent themselves, consciously or unconsciously, deliberately or unknowingly, to one of the most colossal plots against a government and a nation's people since the world began to put its history on record. These pages, the reader will find, are many of them shocking, some of them thrilling, not a few of them next to incredible, but all of them are loaded with facts in support of this demonstrable truth: that the people of the United States, their government and their Presidents, since the war "to make the world safe for democracy" was fought, have been deliberately and unconscionably tricked by the mob-minded apostles of that very "democracy," aided, abetted, goaded and, in some instances, financed by the red oligarchy of Moscow and its American addicts and dupes.

Herein is told the story of the attempt to assassinate Mitchell Palmer, Attorney General in the Cabinet of Woodrow Wilson; the record of the facts in the relentless assault upon Harry M. Daugherty, Attorney General in the Harding and Coolidge Cabinets, and the attempted crucifixion of Harlan F. Stone, Mr. Daugherty's successor. But it is not said or argued that Mr. Palmer was framed, or that Mr. Daugherty was framed, or that Mr. Stone was framed. These men—Palmer, Daugherty, Stone—were, so far as they were individually concerned, figures solely incidental. It was President Wilson who was framed—and President Harding and President Coolidge; it was the American government that was framed—and the American people, and the public press of the country upon which the American people depend for the truth they seek as the basis for the formulation of intelligent opinion.

The inspiration for this frame-up was criminal; the soul of it was alien-fed treason; some of the engineers of it were ex-convicts, and others were criminals not yet apprehended and convicted; but it has to be admitted that the most of those concerned were dupes, misled tools and sycophants in mentally delicate health.

There was a time, in the course of American post-war history, when the red menace was indeed a menace, when the red web might have been, when seen, something at which to shudder. But today the red web is pink, and only the threads of its origin are red.

H. M. DAUGHERTY
ATTORNEY AT LAW
150 EAST BROAD STREET
, COLUMBUS, OHIO

June 1, 1925.

Mr. Blair Coan,

      Chicago, Ill.

Dear Mr. Coan:-

     With the distinct understanding that I am in no sense interested, either financially or as your collaborator, in the book you propose to write regarding events leading up to and culminating in the Senatorial investigation of the Department of Justice in 1924, I herewith comply with your request for a copy of a certain letter written by Gaston B. Means, as well as copies of certain affidavits made by him. You are at liberty to use these documents in connection with the affidavits you have obtained from certain other of the witnesses before the Brookhart Wheeler Committee.

     In publishing these affidavits you will, of course be confronted by the suggestion that they were made by persons unworthy of belief. The fact remains, however, that the affiants are the same persons relied upon by the senatorial committee.

     It may be that one day in the future I shall consider it incumbent upon me to make public certain very important inside phases of the investigation above referred to, and what preceded and attended it. For the present, however, I am indifferent about the matter, as I do not consider that my administration of the Department of Justice needs any defense other than its record of accomplishments.

                Very sincerely yours,

CHAPTER I

FROM MOSCOW TO MEXICO TO MONTANA

MEXICO is today, was yesterday, and will be tomorrow the most fertile incubator of bolshevik revolution on the American continent. For this and one other reason I choose it as the scene for the prologue of this story of an intrigue that had, and still has, for its ultimate goal the overthrow of republican government in the United States of America. The other reason is that it was in Mexico, in the spring time of 1922, that I learned what I know with greater certainty now than then; it was in Mexico that I learned that which, incredible, perhaps, in 1922, became obvious with time and realization.

When I went to Mexico in the spring of 1922, the subject matter of this book, or of this chapter of it, was furthest from my mind. While I had spent some fifteen years of my life as a newspaperman, and had acquired a pretty good knowledge of humankind in general and of men who make governments or endeavor to unmake them, the government of Mexico and the politics of Mexico were merely of incidental interest to me. I was not concerned with newspaper stories that had been written or with any that I might write, and the only investigation I had on my program was of a strictly business character. I went to Mexico as a representative of the Essanay Film Company. The purpose was to find a market for the motion pictures which the Essanay Company was manufacturing. The mission was a failure. There was no market, at any rate no safe or profitable market, for them, and of course the details of the prospective enterprise are of no concern here.

So, although I went to Mexico to get motion picture contracts and came back to the United States empty-handed in that respect, yet I did bring back what I thought was a pretty good newspaper story. For, however far a newspaperman of experience may stray from the profession of his first choosing, he is bound to see newspaper stories along the way even if they are furthest from his intent. The story I got never saw the light of print until two years afterward, my efforts in its behalf with editors of my acquaintance proving of no avail, and I'm obliged to admit that the full import of the story had not percolated my own intellect until those two years had passed.

My story was that the red hand of Moscow was not only concerned with manipulations for control of certain of the big labor organizations of the United States and with the promotion of strikes, sabotage and various forms of violence for the disruption of industry, but that the intellects controlling it had conceived a way in which to make this same red hand influentially felt in the American congressional elections of 1922. In short, my story was that reds and pinks with red sympathies would be candidates for congressional office in a number of states where radical theories had acquired a foothold of some strength, and that a number of these, masquerading either as Republicans or Democrats, stood a very good show of being elected.

"Somebody has been kidding you," said one Chicago newspaper editor of my acquaintance, when I explained the information I had come upon and sought an arrangement for the publication of an article or a series of articles bearing upon the question.

"And anyway, even if the story is true," another told me, "it would be folly to print it at this time. Nobody would believe it."

He was probably right, as to this last statement. I know well enough now how slowly the truth of it is dawning upon the minds of some very brilliant men in politics, both Democrats and Republicans, even now when every prophetic phase of the story stands forth in the light of subsequent events.

On March 4, 1922, I was in New Orleans, and bound for Mexico. An old friend of mine there was the port captain whom I had known while employed on the staff of the *Picayune*. It was at his suggestion that I made the trip to Tampico aboard an empty tanker.

"You'll enjoy the experience," he said, and I thought I

would—and did, since the port captain arranged for me the luxuries of the captain's cabin aboard ship.

Tampico! The second port in America, second to New York City, it had been, because of the vast shipments of Mexican oil. But what I found upon this visit was little short of an intolerable stench pot. Unless the place has been cleaned up since then, which is not at all likely, it is either the dirtiest hole in the world or in second place for that distinction at any rate.

The odor of Tampico smote my nose before we were within six miles of port. The captain of the tanker laughed at my comments about it, and said:

"The worst is yet to come, son. Wait till you get ashore."

And between then and the time I got ashore I profited by his advice on what to do when we made port.

"There is nothing but graft there," he said. "I know you're no greenhorn, but watch your step or they'll take all you've got away from you before you get to your hotel."

My first trouble was at quarantine. I had my samples of films with me. The customs officer told me the duty on the films would be $180.

"For forty pesos ($20) I let them in for you duty free," he eagerly informed me, and at once I sensed the itching palm.

"Nothing doing," said I. "When I get to Mexico City and show these pictures, the authorities might take them away from me. I'll have to have the regular custom's receipt."

"That cost you 360 pesos, but you may be plenty safe to take these films along with you without any receipt. That cost you only forty pesos."

I refused. I insisted upon a duly executed receipt for $180, preferring not to have my films later confiscated and myself, perhaps, lodged in jail on a charge of smuggling. My preference was a source of much chagrin to the grafting customs officer.

The tanker docked about three miles from the passenger docks. For twenty pesos I got my baggage conveyed in a motorboat to the docks for passengers.

Aboard the tanker I had been warned, "Don't attempt

to take your own grip to your hotel. If you do, when you get there it will be taken away from you in all likelihood and mutilated if not destroyed. These bolsheviks, who run these Mexican labor unions, tolerate no scabbing against the baggage-smashers."

I went to the Imperial Hotel, a couple of blocks from the docks. My single piece of hand baggage was carried to the hotel by a native for a charge of a peso and a half. Another carried my trunk there for three pesos. That was the union scale of wages, I was informed, and I learned subsequently that it is a rule of the union that baggage carried by the owner thereof shall be and of right ought to be confiscated and destroyed.

Of course these incidents, just referred to, are of small importance so far as this story is concerned, but they are instances of the general condition of petty graft and open robbery in a place where the apostles and disciples of bolshevism and communism hold sway—where, as I learned, agents and tools of the Red Internationale were dominant, both popularly and officially.

It was at the Imperial Hotel that I first met Smith, an American of Scandinavian nativity or extraction. It was a natural acquaintance, because both of us were from "the States." And, of course, we hadn't been together a great while when Mexico became the topic of conversation.

"Who runs things in this town, anyway?" I asked him.

"We do."

We? This was not exactly clear. I pressed him for enlightenment.

"Why, we, the workers—the proletariat," he proclaimed with some show of eloquence.

Ah, how interesting! Here was a reminder of an old newspaper acquaintance of mine in Chicago who required little or no provocation to be sent into flights of oratory about the woes of the proletariat and the wonders of socialism. I wondered if Smith was like that. No, he was not. But I saw soon enough that he wouldn't object to converting me to something if he got the slightest encouragement.

"Of course, I'm a Communist," he informed me with evident pride, and explained that he was engaged in Mexico in the promotion of communism, and that Tampico at the time was virtually controlled by the revolutionists of that faith. He talked a great deal about communist principles, the Russian revolution, the soviet government of Russia, Karl Marx, Lenin, Trotsky, and other popular heroes of the modern world radical movement, not overlooking Debs, Sinclair, Foster, "Big Bill" Dunne, Ruthenberg and sundry others whose names are familiar to the initiated.

This man called Smith had come from Mexico City to Tampico, as he frankly revealed to me, on a mission connected with the organization of railroad workers. Speaking almost as though he thought I ought already to be aware of what was going on in the world along this particular line, he told me about the destruction of the Tampico railway station which had then but recently occurred.

"All the lesser oil operators have been driven out of this section now," he said, "and we'll be getting rid of the big fellows, too, in time. It's already costing them so much to operate they can't make any money that amounts to anything."

Interesting indeed, thought I!—and my new acquaintance was the soul of frankness. He delivered himself so eloquently of the Russian government and of the great organization for propaganda of the Third Internationale, I concluded, with the hope of influencing me toward his millenial hopefulness, but his connection with actual violence there in Tampico seemed to me to be nothing about which to boast so openly.

"Oh, I'm perfectly safe," he told me. "When you belong to the majority, you're safe enough down here. Besides, if they send any troops down here from Mexico City, we'll probably convert them, too."

A new railroad station was in course of construction in Tampico while I was there. Not long after I left, it was destroyed as was the old one, and troops, which Obregon did send there to maintain order, joined the rebels, helped burn the station, and participated in a subsequent celebration of the event.

My acquaintance with Smith was resumed and improved later on in Mexico City. His "mission" to Tampico had not been concluded when I left there. Upon my taking leave of him, he gave me a bit of advice on traveling. It was to this effect:

An upper berth is rather to be chosen in a sleeping car in Mexico than a lower berth. Bullets are too frequently penetrating the glass windows, before which the lower berths are laid out. It's much safer in an upper berth.

So, taking Smith's tip, I traveled to Mexico City in an upper. There were two day coaches, a sleeper and a special car for soldiers escorting the train. From Tampico to Mexico City was a forty-eight-hour run. The speed limit was twelve miles an hour. It was one of the trains on one of Mexico's government owned, government operated railways.

Arriving in Mexico City I found a station porter already firmly attached to my hand luggage. My trunk, roped and sealed by a government agent, I ordered sent to the Regis hotel. The porter tossed my grip into a taxicab and directed me peremptorily to enter. I did so and was driven to the hotel—by two taxi drivers.

Curious thing about these taxicabs, I found out, in Mexico City. They are all Fords, but that is not the curious thing. It is this: Each cab has a driver and an assistant driver. This makes robbery of a visiting foreigner so much more simple. Driving foreigners out upon the plateau to rob them, and not infrequently to murder them, appears to have been a flourishing side-line in the "union" of taxicab drivers. At any rate, when I was there protests had been received by the Obregon government from foreign countries whose subjects had been robbed, murdered, or both, so the Mexican president decreed the taxicab drivers and their assistants would be required to register with the police. They refused, and announced there would be a "general strike" (favorite bolshevik weapon) if any attempt was made to enforce the decree. The decree was withdrawn, and a new one issued. Under its terms, the drivers must obtain "good conduct cards," have their pictures taken for identification purposes and make solemn pledges not to engage in lawlessness. Again refusal by the drivers. Obregon insisted. Defiance from the taxicab banditti.

The Mexican congress was in session. Obregon was making a speech to the congress. The taxicab drivers and assistant taxicab drivers, 400 or 500 in number, marched in a body to the capitol, tore up cobblestones from the street and proceeded to hurl them through the windows. The legislators did not seem to mind this so very much, but when one of the stones hit Obregon on the nose it incensed him and a squad of soldiers under command of a sergeant was dispatched to disperse the rioters. An attempt was made by the troopers to disperse the crowd without the use of firearms, but this failed, and one of the taxicab drivers was shot. Then there was a real riot, and the soldiers came out second best, with the commanding sergeant placed under arrest on a charge of murder. He was awaiting trial on the charge when I left Mexico City.

The funeral of the dead "comrade" was a spectacular event. He was given full bolshevik honors. Carried to the grave on a truck, his casket was draped with a red flag, and his comrades marched in a long and noisy procession, with shouts of "Long live Lenin and Trotsky! Long live the Communist Internationale!" Down the Avenue de Juarez went the procession until the headquarters of the governor of the federal district was reached. Here a halt was called. The governor was called upon to make a speech of eulogy of the dead. He refused. But he was dragged from his office to the street in short order and made the speech, whether he liked it or not.

By order of the chiefs of the taxicab drivers' organization, traffic was commanded to be suspended during the funeral, but somehow traffic seemed not to halt, and 200 policemen were detailed to stop the procession instead. This move was equally unsuccessful, for the police got the worst of it, and the dead "comrade's" funeral cortege proceeded, not peacefully but victoriously.

Most of the facts here stated I got from Olson himself.

Olson? Yes. His name was Smith in Tampico, but in Mexico City it was Olson.

I had been in Mexico City but a few days when I was stricken with a fever and confined to the hotel. The food in that insanitary hole, Tampico, had evidently knocked me out—as it had many another foreigner who has tarried there. I ran into Smith in the Regis hotel while I was convalescing. He now told me his name was Olson.

To some of his "comrades" he introduced me, and I made mental note of the fact that sometimes he was referred to by them as neither Smith nor Olson, but Redfern. Of course, as I have found out since, this was not a mere isolated case of bolshevik use of several names for one individual. Among the comrades it is an accepted part of the system of operation, and a great convenience—for use of one name indicates one thing, use of another something else, and use of another something else again. At the time, I made no attempt to get from my acquaintance an explanation of his abundance in nomenclature. It was my impression that such curiosity might not be considered good form. So, in Mexico City we shall know him as Olson—the name he gave me on better acquaintance, and probably the name he was born with.

Having now become quite chummy with Olson, arguing with him to draw him out, conceding to him by way of encouragement to his confidence, I seemed to have inspired him to discuss things with me in ever greater frankness than he had down in Tampico. He told me the new railway station at Tampico had been destroyed, that the railroad workers' organization had been responsible for it, that he had been in Tampico in the interests of that organization and that the organization was controlled by the Communists and that they and he were well supplied with funds which came to them from Russia.

The Communists were belaboring the Obregon government on every occasion. Olson told me the railroad strikes were financed with money from Moscow.

"It is only a question of a few months when de la Huerta will have control of this government," are almost the exact words of Olson.

"But," I said, "how did you induce the railroad workers and the waterworks employes to strike so you would get this hold upon the country you were aiming at?"

"Easy enough," was the reply. "We promised them more money, and kept the promise by giving it to them." He laughed, and said in a half-confidential manner: "Let the poor fish have the money for a while. We'll take it away from them."

I suppose I must have had at least twenty conversations with Olson. He had no hesitancy about telling me he was one of the many agents of the Moscow government in Mexico, regularly employed and well paid. Russia, in seeking recognition of foreign governments, lays a great deal of stress upon the claim that the soviet government should not be confused with the Third Internationale—that what the Third Internationale does the soviet government of Russia cannot be held accountable for. But the personnel of the two are the same, and anyone who knows anything at all about either is aware that the difference between them is a sham and a pretense.

"We've got this country now," this agent of Moscow told me, referring to Mexico. "It's only a question of time, and maybe the time is not so remote, either, when we'll have the same control, in effect, across the Rio Grande. We're going into the elections this year in the United States for all we're worth. We've got to get the right sort of representatives elected to Congress."

Remember this was in March of 1922, a congressional election year.

"Our campaign is in the Western states," he said, "where we can work on the farmers as well as on the industrial workers. Montana is an especially promising state. We are going to get men into Congress, if we can, with the courage to show up the conditions in the government under the capitalist system."

Now, I was not at all familiar with Montana politics, and Olson's particular mention of Montana carried no special meaning to me at the time. Had he mentioned names of prospective candidates they would have meant little to me then. Had he mentioned any other state than Montana, it would have had as much meaning to me then. But the point is, he did mention Montana particularly, and the significance of that statement becomes vivid in the light of a prophecy later bearing the appearance of having been realized.

Olson told me there already were a number of men in the American Congress favorable to "the cause"; that whenever and wherever possible, "the cause" was being carried into the American labor organizations, the pacifist groups, the universities, the women's clubs, the churches and the schools; that a great fund was available for the promotion of "the revolution" among the youth of the nation and for the conduct of schools for spreading the communist doctrine among children; that the program of operation was of Russian origin, and that the financial support for it came in no small measure from Moscow.

Now, I could tell you a lot about my personal experiences in Mexico, of personal views of revolutionary outbreaks, of conditions prevailing in this land of chaos, but adventures of travelers in Mexico are more or less passé. I've told what is of present importance—these prophetic confidences of my communist friend, Olson, alias Smith, alias Redfern.

There was a direct connection between those prophetic confidences and subsequent history both in Mexico and in the United States. Olson predicted the overthrow of the Obregon government, and the ascendancy of de la Huerta. The prediction, from the bolshevik viewpoint, was a bit over-optimistic. But Huerta's revolutionary coup, although a failure, did take place only two years later. And when Huerta's success became evidently impossible, the reds, including the Moscow agents, turned to Calles, and Calles became president of Mexico. The attempted crucifixion of Calles by the bolsheviks who helped to place him at the head of the Mexican government is current history.

CHAPTER II

FIRST PETTERS OF THE SNAKE

THERE are those who have openly charged or conveyed the impression that President Woodrow Wilson brought bolshevism to the United States, but this is an unjust accusation. Whatever the fault, so far as President Wilson is concerned, it may be laid against every other petter of the bolshevik snake in America during Mr. Wilson's time and since. It is not too charitable to say that Mr. Wilson's part in bestowing altruistic love-pats upon the slick back of the reptile was due to the war President's professedly indiscriminate love for all mankind, his colossal inability to discern the difference between sheep and wolves in sheep's clothing, and his own misfit and un-American political philosophy. The same ignorance that inspired Mr. Wilson to utter such plain and unadulterated nonsense as "to make the world safe for democracy," in stating the reasons for the entry of the United States into the World War, was no doubt responsible for his saying, early in 1918, when the Russian bolsheviks were preparing to betray their own country and the Allies at Brest-Litovsk, that they were working "in the true spirit of modern democracy," that they were the "voice of the Russian people," and that the voice was giving utterance to ideas of right "with a largeness of view, a generosity of spirit, and a universal human sympathy which must challenge the admiration of every friend of mankind." The quotation is from Mr. Wilson's address to Congress, January 8, 1918.

The Brest-Litovsk treaty between the Russian bolsheviks and Germany was made on the 3rd of March, 1918. There already had been ample evidence before the world that while the czarist overthrow of March, 1917, opened the way for a genuine participation in the war against Ger-

11

many, under the Kerensky government, the subsequent
counter-revolution under Lenin meant the end of Russia
as a factor in the defeat of the Central Powers. Long
before Brest-Litovsk, it was clear the bolshevik rule of
Russia was almost anything but "democracy"; it was plain
that, in fact, it was the most determined sort of autocracy. But when these bolsheviki accomplished their triumph in November, 1917, it was hailed by no less a
person than Mr. Wilson as a manifestation of "the new
day." And yet, when Mr. Wilson's vision had been somewhat cleared in September, 1918; when he had been able
to see the error of his earlier conclusions with regard
to the bolsheviki, and had been obliged to admit that
the rule of the bolshevists was a "campaign of mass
terrorism," he remained too blind to see that love-pats
on the slick back of a snake tend not to subdue it or
make it gentle or harmless.

In the early days of the peace conferences at Paris and
Versailles, the red snake of Russia was admitted to what
became known as the Prinkipo conference. To this conference President Wilson appointed, as his representative,
one George D. Herron.

"We have become accustomed during these past six
years," said Nicholas Murray Butler of this appointment,
"to the President's fondness for surrounding himself with
intellectual and political midgets; but we have heretofore
been spared anything so shocking as this appointment,"
which Dr. William A. Quayle, Bishop of the Methodist
Church, referred to as "the most disreputable appointment ever made in the United States."

Herron was an avowed apostle of world revolution, a
socialist who had said: "I have no expectation that the
present kind of civilization can be amended—it can only
be ended * * * It is already too late to reform society
in America. It is no longer a question whether you will
have a socialistic revolution. It is only left to you to de-
cide what kind of revolution you will have."

Mr. Herron may not have been, exactly, representative
of American traditions and ideals, but his was a soul
not out of harmony with those of two others of Mr.

Wilson's commissioners of the time, Messrs. Lincoln Steffens and William C. Bullitt.

Nothing came of the Prinkipo conference, of course, except further assurance that the bolsheviks were bent not upon peace, but upon world revolution. The World War had ended, and peace was the purpose of the great statesmen foregathered in Europe. But that peace was not the purpose of the bolsheviks, the Prinkipo fiasco made conclusively clear. Upon President Wilson, however, the bolsheviks continued to look as their advocate, and he had so many reds and pinks gathered about him as his personal advisers both during the war and during the period of peace discussions that it is small wonder they did so look upon him.

Notwithstanding the bolshevik offensive against Poland; notwithstanding Lenin's bold words, "Germany forms the important link in the revolutionary chain, and the success of our world revolution depends to the greatest degree upon Germany"; notwithstanding the bolshevik chaos visited upon Hungary; notwithstanding the bolshevik propaganda drives already started and bearing fruit in Asia; notwithstanding innumerable evidences that the oligarchs of Russia were engaged in a determined effort to spread discontent and sow the seed of class rule in all countries; who but President Wilson made a tour of Europe, and, to the delight and the cheers of the emotional mobs that greeted him, delivered himself of such glittering "democracy" speeches as to make the wild-eyed apostles of world revolution chuckle with satisfaction?

Italy, subsequently saved from wreck and ruin and bolshevik chaos only by the stern hand of the Fascisti, was fertile ground for the bolsheviks when President Wilson appeared there on his speech-making expedition. The hotbed of socialism in Italy was Milan, and it was there that President Wilson reached the heights of his popularity abroad when he said: "Here in Milan, where I know so much of the pulse of international sympathy beats, I am glad to stand up and say that that pulse beats also in my own veins." The working classes, he had just told his hearers, "by their consciousness of community of interest and spirit, have done more, perhaps, than any other influence to establish a world which is not of nations, but is the opinion, one might say, of mankind."

President Wilson may not have meant precisely what they thought he meant, but he was talking internationalism as against nationalism, and that was what they wanted to hear. The bolshevik doctrine, the socialist doctrine, is one of internationalism, and the hope of its triumph rests upon the destruction of nationalism.

President Wilson, in his ignorance—an ignorance constantly nurtured by the pinks and red sympathizers who were his advisers, men like Herron, Steffens, Bullitt, Norman Hapgood, Charles Edward Russell, George Creel and innumerable others—was an unconscious ally of bolshevism abroad during his speech-making expeditions in Europe, for he was repeatedly appealing to the emotions of the crowd, inevitably appealing to the people as against their governments, endlessly prating about "democracy" and "internationalism," and constantly enthroning "peoples" and deprecating governments. He was one of the first and foremost petters of the bolshevik snake.

Unwittingly, perhaps; doubtless misled by his radical-minded advisers, the advance agents of the new socialist revolution and the new program of the pinks in the United States, Mr. Wilson's vision was so obscured that, to him, the true character of the head the bolshevik monster was then preparing to raise in America was invisible. In his blindness, therefore, and prompted by his own misconceptions of the spirit of America, President Wilson was the outstanding bolshevik dupe of his time, and contributed a share, proportionate with his prominence, in granting to bolshevism the toehold that later became a foothold and, soon thereafter, only short of a stranglehold upon the government of the United States.

"He [President Wilson] was as helpless to meet the menacing situation in America as he was to meet the appalling disaster which he had invited in Europe," says Ernest W. Young, LL.M., in a chapter on "Russia and Bolshevism," in his book *The Wilson Administration and the Great War*.

"Originating," Dr. Young continues, "in the perversion of the developing revolution in Russia which he had failed to recognize in its real character, it [Russian bolshevism] swept eastward and southward into farther Russia and Asia, sank Hungary in the slough, grasped Italy in its tentacles, struck at Poland, sought Germany, aimed at France and England, and reached out toward America. The attempt to starve and freeze Winnipeg to its knees; the attempt to overthrow civil government in Seattle; the plan to starve the people of the United States in the 'outlaw' railroad strike and to freeze them into submission in the coal strike; the steel strike, directed by a horse-shoer who had never worked at a steel plant; the planned dynamiting of the home of the Attorney General of the United States and many others in nine eastern cities at one time; the constant demand for higher wages among highly-paid employes regardless of the burden it placed upon the shoulders of those outside of their particular class; the fostering of class spirit, particularly of the obstructionist or destructionist kind—these were symptoms manifested during President Wilson's incumbency that never had been seen before in like manner in the history of America. Its blow was aimed at so-called capitalism and at the very foundations of civil government itself."

It is to be noted, at this point, that Mr. Wilson himself became alarmed over the consequences to which he had been no puny contributor.

"Let us be frank about this solemn matter," he said in a message to Congress in December, 1919. "The evidences of the world-wide unrest which manifest themselves in violence throughout the world bid us pause and consider the means to be found to stop the spread of this contagious thing before it saps the very vitality of the nation itself."

But Mr. Wilson yet held to the view that to make a snake behave one must deliver oneself of soft words in the ears of the reptile, pat it gently on the top of its flat head, and pretend that the milk of human kindness is the food that makes it tame and harmless. Compromise and concession continued to be his policy; he called conferences and settled industrial disputes without settling anything; he dickered with reds, counselled with pinks, agreed with yellows and pussy-footers, and evidently reached the end of his career firm in the belief that he was himself a true apostle of "the new freedom," an inspired agent in advance of the millenium.

Duped and intimidated by organized radicals, through the Department of Labor where Louis F. Post was their outstanding champion, as well as through other channels, President Wilson had lent himself to prevent the execution of the dynamiter, Mooney; he had tolerated the notorious communist and revolutionary propagandist, Robert Minor, son of a Texas federal judge, as representative of George Creel on a mission to Russian in 1918; he had not interfered when, by some strange processes operating in Washington in 1919, this same Minor was permitted to escape punishment for intrigues with Lenin and Trotsky following his arrest by American military intelligence officers after a French secret service officer had interrupted a confab he was having in a Paris cafe with Lincoln Steffens, one of President Wilson's advisers and confidants.

The effrontery of Ludwig C. A. K. Martens, unrecognized but none-the-less officially designated representative of the Lenin-Trotsky government in the United States with credentials signed by the soviet foreign minister, George Chicherin; his opening of headquarters in New York City with a large official staff, and his public appearances as a frank advocate of sovietism, were precedent to Mr. Wilson's appearance before Congress in December, 1919.

Throughout his incumbency, both before and after his address to Congress in December, 1919, President Wilson maintained a peculiarly inconsistent attitude with respect to the intrigues of the red radicals and to other forms of disloyalty and anti-Americanism. There were occasions when he gave encouragement to stern and uncompromising methods of dealing with the menace, but usually such occasions were followed by a yielding to the counsels of his pink and pussy-footing advisers and to the clamor of organized groups engaged in the correlated "causes" of pacifism and radicalism. Mitchell Palmer's bold stand against the reds, after he had become Attorney General in 1919, had little if any sympathy or actual encouragement from his chief in the White House. Newton D. Baker's softness of heart toward the reds and disloyalists, while Secretary of War, was as well known as his seemingly inherent pacifism; and William G. McAdoo's vast following of the sundry shades of red and pink, to whose support he looked in his fight for presidential nomination in 1924, was won for him by his subservience as a dupe of the radical movement while serving as director general of the railroads.

While strikes and threats of strikes in the steel, coal and transportation industries were bringing the country to the brink of that state of stagnation which makes bolshevik power possible, and while the agents and disciples of Lenin and Trotsky were boldly and brazenly carrying on their propaganda in press and public gatherings, even within the very shadow of the White House and the Capital, President Wilson found himself almost inextricably embarrassed by his own utterances and actions, so that he could not take a firm stand with conviction and, as is ever the case, he could not dispel the menace with soft words.

Of these first petters of the snake, Ole Hansen, in his *Americanism versus Bolshevism*, published in 1919, very aptly said: "The government started, stopped, started again, conciliated, pandered, and generally pursued a skimmed-milk policy. Argument was tried, kindness, public statements appealing to patriotism, and this to a class of men who know but one argument, force; who think kindness is weakness, and who have no patriotism."

"Listen to me carefully," Trotsky said to Colonel Raymond Robins, before the Central Powers had been brought to the end of their string in 1918. "Follow me step by step. We have started our peace negotiations with the Germans. We have asked the Allies to join us in starting peace negotiations for the whole world on a democratic basis—no forcible annexations, no punitive indemnities, and a full acceptance of the principle of self-determination of all peoples. The allies have refused to accept our invitation. We still hope, of course, to compel them."

Compel them? The phrase was a bit strong, thought Colonel Robins, and when he gave voice to his curiosity on this point, Trotsky replied: "By stirring up the comrades in France and in England and in America to upset the policy of their governments by asserting their own revolutionary socialist will."

An obvious and frank confession that not only England and France, but the United States, were honeycombed with "comrades" of the Russian red dictators, and that it was the business of these "comrades" to do the will and wish of the bolshevik oligarchs of Russia. It may be true that they overestimated their power then; it may be true that they overestimated their power in the years that followed; it may be true, also, that they overestimated their power to carry out so grand a coup as they hoped for in the United States in 1924. But the purpose, nevertheless, is evident, or should be evident, to the thinking mind. If the bolsheviks aspired at the outset to bolshevize the world, which they did; and if they have not given up that aspiration, which they have not, then they have been striving assiduously from the outset to bolshevize the United States.

It was long the boast of the I. W. W. that the bolshevik revolution in Russia was planned in Seattle, Washington, United States of America, when Lenin and Trotsky were in that city en route to Russia. This boast may or may not be true. But whether or not it is, what is true is that the bolshevik activities in the United States were very definitely organized and in operation almost simultaneously with the ascent of Lenin and Trotsky to power in Russia. This was during the Wilson administration.

"We still hope, of course, to compel them," said Trotsky to Colonel Robins, as quoted above.

How?

"By stirring up the comrades in France and in England and in America to upset the policy of their governments by asserting their own revolutionary socialist will."

To upset the policy of their governments!

Certainly. Not merely in its relation to the World War or to the peace that followed it, but *ever and thereafter* until such governmental policies have been so upset or so weakened as to make the international socialist revolution possible and the "dictatorship of the proletariat" a subsequent actuality!

CHAPTER III

THE BASE IN MOSCOW

THE overthrow of Czar Nicholas II, of Russia, occurred on the 15th of March, 1917. Upon the abdication of Nicholas, authority was vested in a provisional government constituted by the Duma. The overthrow of Nicholas was not the result of a red revolution. It was rather pink than red. It came about very largely because of the failure of Russia, under the Czar, to meet its responsibilities in carrying on the war "to make the world safe for democracy." The Russian armies had been driven out of Poland and Galicia in 1915, for want of ammunition. The apostles and disciples of "democracy" were stirred by these disasters. General Brusilov's drive in 1916, eased the situation somewhat. But the premier, Boris V. Sturmer, a hater of "democracy" and a pro-German, began negotiations for a separate peace with Germany, which again stirred the elements of revolt, and the "pink" revolution of March, 1917, was the result.

Prince Lvov became premier, and the Cabinet was composed of Constitutional Democrats, with the exception of Kerensky, the minister of justice, who was a Moderate Socialist. The new government set out at once to bring about the recovery of Russia's position as a force in support of the allied cause against the Central Powers, but in doing so it also endeavored to put into practice such democratic policies as free speech, the right to strike, universal suffrage, general amnesty for all political prisoners and exiles, and various other reforms on the program of the pink revolutionaries. The bolsheviki, whose leaders were not for reform but for complete socialist revolution, at once were at war with the new government and took full advantage of the privileges and liberties extended by the pinks.

19

Instead of meeting the machinations of the bolshevik leaders with a firm stand, the pinks entered upon a policy of compromises which weakened their government and made its fall inevitable. Kerensky became minister of war, in the progressive deepening of pink toward red; the exiled bolshevik leader, Lenin, returned from exile, by way of Berlin; disgust, despair and disloyalty became prevalent in the army. Kerensky sought to handle the army with persuasion, but the bolsheviks had beaten him to it, and he realized too late that soft words do not tame tigers and that caresses on the flat head of a poisonous reptile do not make the fangs of the snake less poisonous.

With the Duma abolished by the All-Russian Congress of Workmen's and Soldiers' Delegates, meeting in Petrograd, Kerensky found himself virtually abandoned by his fellow pinks, and as premier he sought to meet the chaotic situation by showing a firmer hand. The realization of his and his colleagues' mistakes, however, was too late.

President Wilson, meanwhile, had sent his special mission to Russia, headed by Elihu Root. The mission reported back to Washington August 12th, and George Creel's Committee on Public Information informed the public that the mission "was able to announce firm hopes of a speedy restoration of internal harmony and military efficiency" on the part of Russia. It is to be noted that the Root mission included a galaxy of American reds and pinks, chosen by President Wilson at the suggestion of other reds and pinks. The "firm hopes" had begun to fade within three weeks. Kerensky and the military leadership were at odds early in September. Another three weeks, and a democratic congress, called by the Central Council of Workmen's and Soldiers' Delegates, met in Moscow, demanded a "Temporary Council of the Russian Republic" to act until the constituent assembly should meet in December and made other demands which Kerensky felt himself obliged to reject. As the weeks passed, the Russian army continued to meet defeat after defeat in the field, while the following of Lenin grew stronger and stronger in its influence. Kerensky's fall and flight occurred on November 7th, less than three months following the "firm hopes" report from the Root mission.

Lenin, who had been in Berlin, and Trotsky, who had been sojourning in the United States, carrying on a revolutionary propaganda campaign with headquarters in New York City, were now in control as leaders of the bolshevik, or red, revolution.

There appeared in the *New York Times,* November 18, 1917, a summary of Lenin's views on government, based on a pamphlet by him written in the form of a catechism.

"We represent the class-conscious proletaries, hired laborers and the poorer portion of the rural population," said Lenin. "We stand for socialism. The workmen's councils must at once take the necessary practical steps for the realization of the socialistic program. They must immediately take over the control of the banks and capitalistic syndicates, with a view to nationalizing them; that is, making them the property of the whole people * * *."

"We advocate a republic of councils of workmen, soldiers, peasants, etc. All the power must belong to them. * * * Should the peasants immediately take possession of the private lands? Yes; the land must be seized immediately * * * What color is our flag? Red, for the red flag is the flag of the universal proletarian revolution."

It has been noted that Lenin had been in Berlin during the latter part of his exile from Russia. But to say that, upon his return to Russia, he acted as a German agent in behalf of victory for the Central Powers over the Allies is to state the case inaccurately. Lenin was not interested in the defeat of Germany. Unquestionably he spoke truly when he said: "We took German money to make a Russian revolution. Then we will take Russian money to make a German revolution." The attempt to make good on this prediction subsequently took place, and to deny that the bolsheviks had an important part in the fall of the Central Powers before the Allies is to deny them the credit—if you want to call it that—that is their due.

The treaty of Brest-Litovsk was made between Germany and the bolshevik government of Russia March 3, 1918. The German revolution began early in November. It did not run the full course Lenin had expected or

hoped, to be sure, but that was no fault of his, nor of
Karl Leibknecht, nor of Rosa Luxemberg. And Zinoviev,
president of the Communist Internationale, says now:
"Turn now to Germany. Take the years of 1918-23. The
German proletariat in that period fought for revolution.
The fight went on, not in a steady, rising line, but with
interruptions, severe losses and so on. Taking the European labor movement as a whole, the severest losses were
suffered by the German proletariat during this time. But
what do we observe today in Germany, a country passing
through the zone of a certain stabilization of capitalism?
*   *   * Considerable sections of the working class of
Germany have retained their courage, have not lost
stamina and under most difficult conditions unhesitatingly
are following the Communist party."

The German revolution of November, 1918, opened a
series of rapidly-moving events of vast importance. The
German kaiser abdicated and fled the country. The Germans agreed to an armistice, and this began on the 11th
of November. The subsequent course of events, so far
as Germany and the peace negotiations are concerned,
bears no special importance to this volume, and so I pass
from it to other matters. But not without making note,
that what happened in Germany, with the part played
therein by the bolsheviks, also happened in Austria and
Hungary, and in Bulgaria; and that the part the bolsheviks played was in conformity to well-laid plans for
the promotion of the "world revolution,"—plans that have
since been greatly extended and have not, in purpose,
been altered, no matter what changes in method have
taken place.

Exiled, like Lenin, from Russia, Trotsky went first to
Berlin, then to Switzerland, then to France, then to Spain,
coming thence, by way of Cuba, to the United States.
January, 1917, finds him in New York City. The revolution
in Russia was then in the making. While in New York
Trotsky published a socialist newspaper and engaged, otherwise, in socialist propaganda and in activities in furtherance of the international "working class revolution." Associated with him were the left wing socialists of the
United States.

The United States entered the war against the Central

Powers April 6, 1917. That month witnesses an especial
impetus in the activities of the left wing socialists. The
right wing socialists, the chief difference between which
and the left wing is that they are of the parlor type
who hate the inside of jails, determined to "stand by
the government." By that they meant not to oppose the
government, openly at any rate, in the war against the
Central Powers. In cooperation with Trotsky, then unquestionably working in complete harmony and understanding with Lenin and the bolshevik organization and
program, the left wing functioned during the early months
of American participation in the war, and when Trotsky
had gone back to Russia to join Lenin in carrying out
the coup of November, 1917, the work he had helped
to get under way in the United States continued throughout the remainder of the war. Almost simultaneous with
the German revolution of 1918, which precipitated the
armistice, a communist propaganda league was formed in
Chicago. Subsequently there resulted, in New York City,
February, 1919, a definite organization of the left wing
section of the socialist party, with an ultra radical platform, which was adopted by many of the locals of the
socialist party and all of the Slavic federations in the
country.

In March, 1919, the Communist party of Russia had
issued a call for an international congress to organize a
new Internationale—now known as the Third Internationale. The left wing socialists of the United States sent
S. J. Rutgers as their delegate. A Russian convention,
designated, "the Convention of the Russian Socialist Federations in America, or the Fifth Regular Convention of
Federations of Russian Branches of the Communist Party
of America," was held in Detroit, Michigan, in August,
1919. The convention adopted resolutions of greeting to
the communist convention, called to convene in Chicago
in September, that year. Simultaneously, then, there were
organized in Chicago the Communist Labor party and
the Communist party of America, subsequently merged
and now the illegal, underground foundation of the Workers' party and sundry related organizations whose operations and connections will be explained further on in the
pages of this volume.

"In the period prior to 1917," said Zinoviev, addressing the 1925 meeting of the enlarged executive committee of the Comintern in Moscow, "the working class in each country fought isolately. Not in a single country during that period was a single more or less decisive victory of the proletariat recorded. What is the position today? Today, the international proletariat has achieved more or less conclusive victory in one country. I mean the Union of Soviet Socialist Republics, representing a sixth part of the globe." Whereupon he goes on to explain that in every other country the bolshevik organization has been extended, and that the operation of the international organization are achieving conspicuous results. The quotation is from a translation of the address of Zinoviev, printed in the June, 1925, issue of the *Workers' Monthly,* official organ of the communists in the United States, published in Chicago.

So, while "the working class in each country fought isolatedly" in the period "prior to 1917," subsequent to that time, and even before the red revolution in Russia under Lenin although to far greater extent since, the "class war" evolved into definite international proportions, with a clearly defined system of coordination. "It is of extreme importance," quoting again from Zinoviev's address, above referred to, "that the international working class fighting against the world bourgeoisie, have a *base,* have a sort of revolutionary rear."

This *base,* as Zinoviev somewhat superfluously explains, is Russian, with staff headquarters in Moscow. The battlefronts are many, notably the Far East and the Near East, the Balkans, Mexico, but also Germany, France, England, other continental countries, not excluding the United States.

How this "class war," this international socialist revolution, is being waged we shall see. How it has been waged in the United States since the establishment of the base, with general staff headquarters in Moscow; how it has succeeded and wherein it has failed, the readers of this book want to know. Their curiosity shall be fully satisfied.

CHAPTER IV

TEMPORIZING WITH TERRORISM

DISCUSSING what he called "the widespread condition of political restlessness in our body politic," President Wilson, in his message to the first regular session of the Sixty-sixth Congress in December, 1919, said: "The causes of this unrest, while various and complicated, are superficial rather than deepseated. Broadly, they arise from or are connected with the failure on the part of our government to arrive speedily at a just and permanent peace permitting return to normal conditions, from the transfusion of radical theories from seething European centers pending such delay, from heartless profiteering resulting from the increase in the cost of living, and lastly, from the machinations of passionate and malevolent agitators. With the return to normal conditions this unrest must rapidly disappear."

One of the outstanding suggestions as a remedy for "this unrest," offered by the President in this same address to Congress was "genuine democratization of industry." In making it, Mr. Wilson but repeated the suggestion that it is that of the bolsheviks themselves, and but echoed the essence of his attitude toward economic problems as set forth in his *The New Freedom,* a collection of addresses to which the radicals of the country have gone for ammunition from the day it came off the printing presses. What the President proposed as the remedy, in addition to "the return to normal conditions"—a circumstance at once impossible with "a genuine democratization of industry," as Soviet Russia so eloquently testifies today—was what the reds had been clamoring for. It was nothing more nor less than sovietism, the evolutionary steps from which can be nothing short of industrial mobocracy first, and finally industrial autocracy.

The particular "condition of political unrest" to which President Wilson referred consisted of the manifestations of that year, 1919. The year was just drawing to a close. It had been a particularly auspicious year for the promoters of violence in behalf of the "working class revolution." Mr. Wilson's administration was in virtual panic over the situation. By turns it had been temporizing with the radicals, on the one hand, and using "strong arm" methods, on the other, but if there was any one policy the more generally adhered to, it was the policy of temporizing, vaporizing, coaxing, promising, compromising and petting. This was so because it was the natural inclination of Mr. Wilson throughout his administration to be as pink as possible, and because the President had surrounded himself, all during his presidency, but more particularly during the war and immediately thereafter, with a crowd of advisers that was as fine a collection of reds, pinks and yellows for which the most optimistic boosters of revolution in the United States could hope.

There were occasions, to be sure, when President Wilson seemed to get a flash of the proportions and proximity of the menace of red radicalism, and on these occasions he grew petulant, impatient, downright enraged, and did something to make the bolshevik reptile strike at him directly. On such occasions, a modern Mirabeau might very justly have said to him: "You have turned loose the bull, and now complain that he gores you."

While the administration, at the close of this hectic year of 1919, was in a state bordering on palpitant panic, the public, too, was in a state of sweat. Men whom other men called "alarmists" expressed the fear that the United States was "on the brink of a class war." But, in fact, these alarmists were far too mild. They didn't know, at least they didn't begin to tell, the half of it. We were not "on the brink" at all. We had been "on the brink" for quite a time, but the brink had long since been passed, and "class warfare" was on in earnest, with nearly all the heavy artillery and almost all the generals familiar with the trench and poison gas methods of attack on the side of the bolsheviks.

This war had not even waited for the World War to cease, to state the truth of the matter, when our own and imported bolshevik allies in the cause, with Moscow the base of operations and the seat of the general staff, were doing their full share throughout the final year of the World War. The field of operations was the world, and 1918 was not by any means free from sanguinary engagements on that battlefront that was and still is the United States of America. But in 1919, when the bolsheviki had accomplished much to their liking in Hungary, in Germany, in Italy, and on sundry other battlefronts, and when they had almost put down counter-revolution in Russia, thus giving them more time, energy and money to give to the job of revolting in the United States, we experienced in this country what might be termed a banner year and a full crop of red flag warfare of the most violent character.

Since there is not a year in which strikes of some greater or less magnitude do not figure in American industry, it would not be true to say that bolsheviks and bolshevik sympathizers were at the bottom of all the strikes that occurred in the United States during the year 1919. But it is in perfect harmony with truth to charge that a great many of them, some of very large proportions, were of bolshevik origin; that bolsheviks and soviet-lovers participated in and agitated every one of them, and that whenever and wherever possible, agents, dupes and tools of the Russian oligarchs capitalized, exploited and promoted them in the interests of the so-called working class revolution.

The day Victor Berger, the Milwaukee socialist leader, was convicted, January 9, 1919—although this is no related coincidence, particularly, the strike of the marine workers at the port of New York was begun. The general strike at Seattle, to support striking shipbuilders, took place on the fourth of February. The nation-wide strike in the building trades began two days later. The New England telephone workers went on strike April 20th. On May 14th there took place the Chicago milk-drivers strike—a strike the milk-drivers won within two days and after a precarious condition developed, particularly in hospitals and among the infant population of the city. Strike riots in Toledo, Ohio, resulted in two deaths and many injuries on the third day of June. Commercial telegraphers in the south-east struck June 5th. The strike of Detroit carmen occurred on the eighth of June. Two days later there took place the general strike of telegraphers, of which the walk-out of June 5th was the prelude. The street-car men of Boston went on strike on the 18th of July. Surface and elevated carmen in Chicago struck eleven days later.

August first marked the beginning of the strike of the railroad shop workers, and five days later fourteen railroad unions made demands for wage increases. Carmen in Brooklyn went on strike August 6th. New York actors struck the day following, and less than a week later the actors' strike had spread to Chicago. New York traction workers went on strike August 17th. The next few days were marked by especially violent riotous demonstrations, notably at Hammond, Indiana, and Cudahy, Wisconsin, to which places troops had to be sent. The 24th of August the Pacific coast railways were tied up by strikes. Transportation strikes had become so serious that President Wilson, August 25th, ordered wage increases to the shopmen, and issued an explanatory statement to the public pleading for an industrial truce. The President's wage proposal and his appeal for a "truce" were both spurned by the railway shopmen's chiefs.

On the same day that three men were killed in strike riots at Hammond, Indiana, where troops had been sent, because the police had been unable to control the situation, the unionized police force of Boston went on strike. State troops were called to Boston the next day, when seven persons met death in riots due to the strike of policemen. On the day the great steel strike began, September 22nd, two persons were killed and many others were hurt in riots which the reds precipitated in the Pittsburgh region. Many newspapers and other periodicals were forced to suspend publication in New York City October 1st because of the strike in the printing trade.

The pay office of the Anaconda Copper Mining Company, at Butte, Montana, was dynamited in July, and in August the home of Oscar Lawlor, former United States attorney, of Los Angeles, and the colliery of the Lehigh and Wilkesbarre Company, at Wilkesbarre, Pennsylvania, were wrecked by bombs.

Serious strike riots occurred at Gary, Indiana, in connection with the steel strike October 5th, and the next day federal troops were sent to Gary, East Chicago and Indiana Harbor. The New York harbor was completely tied up by strikes by October 10th. Four days thereafter came forth the order, effective November 1st, for the nation-wide strike of soft coal miners. The order came on the heels of President Wilson's summoning of the conferees for his subsequently famous but futile industrial conference, from which the "labor bloc," so-called, withdrew when it found it impossible to dominate the conference. The conference very quickly thereafter dissolved.

Pleadings, temporizings and compromisings, resorted to by the government, were of no avail against the coal strike threat, the coal miners' union chiefs declining any and all offers. Experiencing one of his periodical lapses from an attitude of patience and tolerance for the bedevilments at the hands of radical agitators, who were playing no minor role in the warfare in the coal industry, President Wilson became so enraged on October 25th that he denounced the proposed coal strike as "a crime," and said the government would use every means to frustrate it.

While the international congress of working women and the international labor conference—sideshows of the League of Nations—were taking place in Washington, and innumerable red and pink delegates thereto were chuckling with satisfaction every time they passed the White House, the President was wrestling with "this condition of political unrest." He was striving to keep up with his Attorney General, A. Mitchell Palmer, who, notwithstanding the limitations put upon him by administration policy, had been sufficiently active in defending the country from the "machinations of passionate and malevolent agitators," of which Mr. Wilson so petulantly complained later on, that pink apologists for red tactics and the "liberal" press of the country denounced him as a "labor baiter." Of course, to a pink or a "liberal," anyone who indicates anything more militant than mollycoddling towards bolsheviks, particularly, and the industrial blight generally, is a "labor baiter." However, the red agitator knows much better.

As per schedule, and crime or no crime, the coal strike began November 1st, the day after the government had obtained before Judge Anderson, of the federal court, at Indianapolis, an injunction forbidding it. On the 8th of November, Judge Anderson ordered the miners' leaders to call off the strike by November 11th. The next day the executive committee of the American Federation of Labor pledged its "full support" to the strikers. The strike order was cancelled, as per Judge Anderson's order, November 11th, but the strike did not end, nevertheless, and the end of November found President Wilson both panicky and chagrined because the administration's efforts to end the strike by negotiation had completely failed and the strikers' chiefs had refused to return to work at wages which had been increased fourteen per cent. Fuel Administrator Garfield, in consequence, began functioning as in wartime on the 1st of December, simultaneously with the opening of a second "industrial conference."

The second conference accomplished an armistice in the "class war" as manifested in the coal strike, and in the middle of December it was announced, on behalf of President Wilson, that "the coal strike is settled as the government wanted it settled." But it was a long, long way from being a settlement. As a treaty of peace, it was of less subsequent authority than the World War armistice, for it failed to settle anything. In fact, the peace is yet to be made, not merely in the coal industry, but in the "class war" as a whole.

Let it here be noted, that the Department of Justice, all this time, was the most abused branch of the government. Congress was bombarded with protests from organizations big and little and of all shades of red, pink, yellow and peagreen—protests against this "labor baiter," Palmer, and against the courts whose decisions in cases tallied with the contentions of the Department of Justice whenever and wherever prosecutions were undertaken. How the reds, the pinks and the putty-colored protagonists of "the new freedom" hated Palmer, and Judge Anderson, and Judge Landis!—and the sundry others who stepped forth to perform their public duties without apol-

ogy to the Society for the the Prevention of Cruelty to
Burglars, Pickpockets and Bomb Tossers—hated them and
plastered them with abuse, just as later, for the same
reason, they hated, abused and harassed Judge Wilkerson, Daugherty, Stone and, now, Sargent. Attorney General Palmer may not have nursed any wounds inflicted
by the missles of the reds and their sympathizers, but he
must have been peculiarly well armored if the abuse
heaped upon him in the Senate and House—not for his
inhumanity toward the reds, but for his "softness"—did
not hurt, when he was forever conscious of the fact that
whatever of softness did mark the conduct of the Department of Justice in this respect was the sign of the hand
of Wilson and not that of the hand of Palmer.

Palmer was down on the lists for destruction, along
with many others, in the bomb plots that were a part of
the "condition of political unrest" in 1919. On the 2nd
of June, the Attorney General's home in Washington was
blown up with a bomb, fortunately without damage to
Mr. Palmer, himself. Two reds who had planted the
bomb were themselves blown to such small bits that identification was impossible. The same day, the home of
Representative L. W. Powers, of Newtonville, Massachusetts, was wrecked by a bomb; destruction of the rectory
of Our Lady of Victory, Philadelphia, was attempted, and
a bomb placed at the Frankfort arsenal failed to explode;
in Pittsburgh, houses were damaged by bombs intended
to exterminate Judge Thompson and Police Inspector Si-
bray; the home of Judge C. C. Nott, in New York City,
was wrecked, and two persons were killed by the explosion; the home of Justice A. F. Hayden, Boston, was
bombed, and an attempt to wreck the home of Mayor
H. L. Davis, of Cleveland, failed. At Paterson, New Jersey,
and East Orange, New Jersey, minor bomb explosions
occurred.

Subsequent to these outrages, William Gibbs McAdoo,
whom the radicals of the country strove in 1924 to make
the Democratic nominee for President, was quoted in the
press as having excused the bomb plots as due to "ignorance of Americanism." He said later his remarks had
been "misinterpreted"—an alibi that is familiar in all
newspaper offices.

At Franklin, Massachusetts, dynamite had been planted at the American Woolen Mills, in March. Four men were killed in this explosion. In January, at Philadelphia, bomb outrages had occurred; the homes of Justice Van Moschzisker, Acting Superintendent of Police Mills, and others being wrecked. The conviction of the forty-six I. W. W.'s in Sacramento, California, for the dynamiting of the home of Governor Stephenson, had occurred in January. The Brownsville, Pennsylvania, municipal building had been wrecked by a bomb May 2nd, this date and May 1st —the bolshevik "May Day" holiday—marking a number of bombing operations on the part of the makers of revolution.

The mails also had been used for the dissemination of missives of violence for the defenders of the "old order" against that of the "new." This system was a part of the May Day program. A bomb intended for Attorney General Palmer at that time was intercepted in the mails, as were bombs mailed to Ole Hanson, of Seattle; to Senator Overman, Senator King and F. R. Nebeker. Senators Overman and King had been particularly strong in their demands for Senate investigation of bolshevik propaganda and activity, and were active in having such an investigation made. Mr. Nebeker had prosecuted the Chicago gang of I. W. W.'s before Judge Landis. The bombs intercepted had been held up in the mails because of insufficient postage. One sent to ex-Senator Hardwick reached its destination, exploded, and wounded Mrs. Hardwick and her daughter.

Between the occurrence of the outrages of the first part of May and those of a month later, Frederick C. Howe, President Wilson's immigration chief at New York City, presided at a "Justice for Russia" meeting in New York, where denunciation of the United States government was as vociferous as the pleas for "justice" for the bolsheviki were fulsome.

Generally soft, but not always, the Administration, in February, had made a gesture toward ridding the country of alien enemies of the bolshevik stripe, when fifty-four reds apprehended in the West were ordered deported. An immediate howl against this "injustice" was raised by the radical and "liberal" crowds. Radical factions in the International Association of Machinists were joined by other organizations in a fight in behalf of the deportees. Some of them were, in due time, deported, but others were released on parole as a result of the bombardment of protests from reds and pinks, and twelve of them later were released unconditionally, everyone of them returning to the ranks of the red army of propaganda and violence from which they had been taken.

Among the loudest of the protesters was Louise Bryant, wife of the communist and soviet agent, John Reed, and Albert Rhys Williams, an officially designated propagandist for Soviet Russia in the United States. They held in Washington but one of the innumerable pro-soviet mass meetings held all over the country—meetings of praise for the new saviors of mankind and champions of liberty, Lenin and Trotsky, and of denunciation of the United States and of all Americans who failed to perceive the virtues of the radical gentry and the system of government they headed and dominated.

Taking it all in all, the year 1919 was a great year for strikes, "class war" violence, bomb outrages, and bolshevik propaganda; it was the year Glenn E. Plumb, pro-soviet counsel for the railroad brotherhoods, presented his famous plan—the Plumb Plan—for nationalization and "democratization" of the railroads, a plan which he subsequently expanded with the proposal for its application to all industries in the United States. It was the year the railroad brotherhoods and the railway department of the American Federation of Labor sought to impose this socialistic scheme upon the country by strikes and threats "to tie up the railways so tight that they will never run again." It was the year the notorious Ludwig Christian Alexander Karlovich Martens, born in Russia of German parentage and confessedly a lifelong revolutionist engaged in that profession in both Russia and Germany before coming to America, was appointed soviet "ambassador" to the United States, established headquarters at 110 West Fortieth Street, New York City, and installed an extensive staff of American and alien reds. It was a banner year for "the widespread condition of political restlessness in our body politic," as President Wilson described it as the year drew to a close.

The President told Congress that the causes were "superficial rather than deep-seated." It is possible he was only whistling to keep his courage up, but it is more probable that his conclusion was that of a peculiarly superficial mind or the result of an ostrich-like disinclination to look disturbing actualities in the face.

Superficial? The Sub-committee of the Senate Foreign Relations Committee, directed by the Senate to "investigate the status and activities of one Ludwig C. A. K. Martens, claiming to be a representative of the Russian Socialistic Soviet Republic," brought out a wealth of proof to the contrary.

"Revolution, not reform," was Lenin's message to his agents in the United States and elsewhere. "Organize the workers of the world, including the American, in one fraternal union; crush all resistance, using terror if necessary."

Lenin admitted to Colonel Raymond Robins, who testified to the fact before the Senate Committee, that it was his ambition to overthrow the United States government. Solicitor Lamar of the Post Office Department, submitted to the committee a memorandum in support of the charge that a plot existed among the various radical groups in the United States to overthrow the American government and establish a bolshevik republic, and alleged the Department of Justice was in possession of evidence that more than 8,000 labor unions in the country were controlled by red radicals pledged to give aid to the revolutionary program.

Albert Rhys Williams admitted to the committee of the Senate, when called to the witness stand, that he was a soviet agent, and that he had been sent to the United States by the red chiefs of Russia to promote soviet propaganda, and that 25,000 ex-residents of the United States were office-holders in the government of the bolsheviki in Russia. John Reed, who died later in Russia, where the reds erected a monument to his memory, admitted to the committee that he, too, was in the employ of the soviet government and that he had planned a propaganda bureau—he called it an "information bureau" —to be financed with money raised among wealthy American women whose names appear in the bolshevik "sucker list."

"Ambassador" Martens first came to the United States in January, 1916. A short time before the United States entered the World War, Martens joined Leon Trotsky in New York City. Trotsky and Gregory Weinstein were the editors of the Russian socialist paper, *Novy Mir*, and Martens was a contributor and a member of the editorial board of the paper which was one of the organs of the Socialist party of the United States. These facts came from the lips of Martens, himself, when he was examined by Senator George H. Moses before the Senate sub-committee investigating his status and activities.

"The paper belonged to a society," said Martens, "the so-called Russian Socialist Publication Society, and I was a member of this Society and was elected on the editorial board of the paper."

Both Martens and Weinstein remained with the publication after Trotsky left New York to join his comrade, Lenin, in Russia to carry out the coup which resulted in the overthrow of the Kerensky government and the establishment of the so-called dictatorship of the proletariat. When Martens established the soviet "bureau" and began publication of another weekly paper, an official publication of the "bureau," called *Soviet Russia*, in January, 1919, Weinstein became his personal secretary and general office manager. Weinstein, as well as Martens, was a Russian citizen. Another Russian, Santeri Nuorteva, was secretary of the "bureau," and his assistant was Kenneth Durant, an American, whose prior employment was with George Creel on the staff of the American Committee on Public Information.

Abraham Heller, of Russian birth, a New York manufacturer, a director of the Rand School of Social Science, which George Herron, President Wilson's representative and eulogist, had established with the Widow Rand's money, was director of the commercial department of the soviet "bureau." Owing to his connections and activities later on, when "Comrade" Martens had been obliged to depart the shores of the United States—particularly as bearing upon events in 1922—"Comrade" Heller will appear as a figure in a later chapter of this book. Evans Clark, organizer of the Labor Bureau, Inc., and a vice president of the League for Industrial Democracy, born in New Jersey, was "Comrade" Martens' director of information and publicity. Another of George Creel's former deputies, an Englishman, Wilfred E. Humphries, was associate director of the publicity department. He had been in Russia in 1917-18 with the Y. M. C. A. International Committee, and delivered lectures from February until December, 1919, favorable to the "new freedom" inflicted upon Russia and the world by the bolsheviki.

Morris Hillquit, who added to his own fame and detracted nothing from the fame of Messrs. Robert M. La Follette and Burton K. Wheeler when he became one of their campaign managers in the presidential campaign of 1924, was the director of the legal department of the soviet "bureau." The managing editor of the "bureau's" house organ was an American, Jacob W. Hartman, an instructor in languages and history in the College of the City of New York from 1901 to 1919, who subsequently collaborated with Caleb Harrison and others in organizing the Friends of Soviet Russia. Of Hartman, Harrison and the Friends we shall hear more in chapters dealing with events of a later period.

"Ambassador" Martens, revealing the names of the members of his official staff during his testimony before the Senate committee, said the staff was thirty-five in number. Those just mentioned were the principal ones of those whose names figured in the evidence. The cost of maintaining the "bureau," Martens told the committee, was about $10,000 a month, the money being supplied, he testified, by the Russian government which transmitted it "mainly by couriers from Russia."

We are still talking about that hectic year, 1919, which President Wilson referred to as a "widespread condition of political restlessness," the causes of which were "superficial" rather than "deep-seated"—that year of bomb outrages, of strikes twice as numerous and many more times as riotous and as serious otherwise as ever before in American history; that year of the Plumb plan for "industrial democracy" and of radical railway labor leaders' threats to force it upon the country; that year of "ambassador" Martens and the official soviet "bureau"; that year of strenuous effort at crystallization and coordination of revolutionary forces within the United States to act with the same forces in other countries for the achievement of "revolution, not reform," quoting Lenin, "using terror if necessary."

This was the year of the first congress of the Communist (Third) Internationale, the call for which, released by "rosta," official telegraph agency of the bolsheviki, February 24th, contained invitations to various organizations throughout the world, including the I. W. W. of America, the Socialist Labor Party of America and the "left wing" faction of the Socialist Party of America. The Socialist Labor Party of America, represented by one Boris Reinstein, gave its sanction to the issuance of the call, "Comrade" Reinstein attaching his signature on one of the dotted lines under that of "comrades" Lenin and Trotsky.

"The present is the period of destruction and crushing of the capitalistic system of the whole world," read the call, "and it will be a catastrophe for the whole European culture should capitalism with all its insoluble contradictions not be done away with. The aim of the proletariat must now be immediately to conquer power. To conquer power means to destroy the governmental apparatus of the bourgeoisie and to organize a new proletarian governmental apparatus."

"The dictatorship of the proletariat must be the occasion for the immediate expropriation of capital and the elimination of the private right of owning the means of production, through making them common public property. * * * The establishment of a workmen's government and the concentration of economic functions in the hands of the organs of the proletarian dictatorship are the most essential aims of the day. In order to protect the socialist revolution against external and internal enemies, and to assist the fighting proletarists of other countries, it becomes necessary to entirely disarm the bourgeoisie and its agents and to arm the proletariat."

"The most important task of the present moment for the conscious and honorable workmen of all countries," said a manifesto from the congress, addressed to the "proletariat" of all lands, "is to strengthen the soviet, to increase their authority, and to intimidate the government apparatus of Russia."

"The Great Communist Internationale was born in 1919," said a May Day proclamation from the executive committee of the Internationale. "The Great Internationale Soviet Republic will be born in 1920."

CHAPTER V

THE REPTILE CHANGES ITS SPOTS

"THE Great International Soviet Republic will be born in 1920!"

Such was the hope expressed in the bolshevik May Day proclamation in 1919. Realization of the hope fell considerably short. The campaign of violence, by which revolutionary mass action was hoped for in the United States —a nation which the bolsheviki call the one remaining bulwark of capitalism—failed to accomplish its purpose.

Notwithstanding the wobbling and temporizing of the Wilson Administration, Attorney General A. Mitchell Palmer continued to kindle the fires of hatred for himself among the reds by his relentless warfare upon the forces of radicalism which had made the year 1919 well-nigh a nightmare for orderly government in the United States.

"During the latter part of 1919," said Secretary of State Charles E. Hughes, summarizing a bit of history in his report of sensational facts submitted to the sub-committee of the Senate Committee on Foreign Relations of the Sixty-eighth Congress, "the Department of Justice submitted to the Department of Labor a large amount of evidence on the Communist Party of America. This resulted in the issuance of a large number of warrants of arrest for deportation hearings. The cases were based upon the theory that the Communist Party of America advocated the overthrow by force and violence of the government of the United States and, therefore, its officers and members who were aliens, were subject to deportation as being members of an organization proscribed by the immigration laws.

"The situation had become so acute and the spread of ultra-radicalism so broad," continued Secretary Hughes, "that by the end of 1920 most of the states had passed laws against anarchy, criminal syndicalism, sabotage, red flag demonstrations, and organizations advocating the use of force or violence in a political or economic program."

Of course the most notable of the cases at the time was that of the soviet "ambassador" Martens, against whom a mass of evidence had been obtained by the Department of Justice which turned it over to the Department of Labor. The sub-committee of the Senate Committee on Foreign Relations of the Sixty-sixth Congress, whose investigation of bolshevik propaganda was touched upon in the preceding chapter, had continued its hearings in 1920, and the result of these hearings was a recommendation that Martens, instead of being recognized by the government, be deported as an alien engaged in the promotion of propaganda and activities subversive to orderly government in the United States. The deportation order was issued in December, 1920. The Russian government, meanwhile sensing defeat of its efforts to foist itself upon the United States as a government and obtain the recognition of Martens as its "ambassador," issued orders "withdrawing" Martens and closing the "embassy" in New York City.

Among the first personages of prominence to arise, in the face of the overwhelming mass of evidence of the subversive purposes of Martens and the crowd he had assembled about him, and to protest against the deportation order, was United States Senator Joseph I. France, of Maryland, who had made a trip to Russia and came back primed to join with the reds in their demand for recognition by the State Department of the soviet government of Russia and of Martens as the Russian envoy to the United States. Senator France had been elected to the Senate as a Republican. In the Senate he was one of Senator Robert M. La Follette's supporters and admirers, and was a member of the national council of the People's Legislative Service, the La Follette propaganda bureau directed by the radical, Basil M. Manly. Of the People's Legislative Service we shall hear considerably more later.

Throughout 1920, as well as in 1919, the government faced an onslaught of appeals for the recognition of Russia under bolshevik rule and of abuse for the failure to heed the appeals. The Amalgamated Clothing Workers were insistent that the bolshevik government be recognized and that Martens be received on a diplomatic plane. According to evidence presented to the New York State Legislative Committee investigation of red activities in New York, the Amalgamated Clothing Workers' organization was linked with the Communist party of America. The Socialist party of the United States went on record as demanding the recognition of Russia by the American government, as did the Committee of Forty-eight, headed by J. A. H. Hopkins, another organization and individual occupying conspicuous parts in events of subsequent interest and importance. The national convention of the Socialist party, held in May, 1920, delivered itself of lusty cheers for the Russian soviets, and nominated Eugene V. Debs—then in the Atlanta federal prison—as its candidate for the presidency. Debs responded to the bestowal of this honor by declaring his party should support "the revolution" with all its power. Recognition of Martens by the State Department was "demanded" by the New York State Socialist party in July, 1920, and radical organizations of all shades joined in the cry for the recognition of Russia and its "ambassador" and participated in the demand for the scalp of the "labor baiter," Attorney General Palmer.

"Victory" for the proletarian cause in the United States in 1924 was the prediction of Debs, as the Socialists sent a special mission to Russia in 1920. "Recognition of the soviets," was the cry of the radical factions controlling the International Association of Machinists, whose President, William H. Johnston, a socialist, was secretary-treasurer of Senator La Follette's People's Legislative Service, and became the leading spirit in the Conference for Progressive Political Action and its campaign of 1924 to make La Follette and Wheeler President and Vice-President.

A particularly bitter attack upon Attorney General Palmer for the raids and arrests directed by the Department of Justice against the reds in 1920 was made by the National Popular Government League early in 1921, as the Wilson administration was drawing to a close. This organization, sponsored, among others, by Jackson H. Ralston, whose connection with the attempted impeachment of Attorney General Daugherty in 1922 will be discussed later, subsequently promoted the circulation of a book, *The Deportation Delirium of 1920,* by the radical assistant Secretary of Labor in the Wilson Administration, Louis F. Post.

Ralston had appeared for Assistant Secretary of Labor Louis F. Post in an investigation of Attorney General Palmer by a sub-committee of the House Committee on Rules in 1920, an investigation that fell flat, and then presented to a sub-committee of the Senate Committee on Judiciary, in January, 1921, the charges preferred by the Popular Government League. In the conduct of these proceedings, Senator Thomas J. Walsh, of Montana, enacted the role of "prosecutor" of the Attorney General and ate a considerable quantity of fire in his endeavor to make a case against Mr. Palmer. By the time the Attorney General got through with his accusers, who had charged him with violations of law in the conduct of his campaign against the reds, it appears that he had them on the run, and this investigation fell as flat as the earlier one.

Attorney General Palmer, however, submitted to a Senate Committee a report in defense of the Department of Justice that was so loaded with evidence of red revolution, with its pink and yellow approval and applause, that his conduct of warfare against bolshevik propagandists and plotters was fully justified in the eyes of patriotic American citizens.

When the Harding administration came into power in March, 1921, the Communist Party of America, operating under strict supervision of and discipline laid down by the Communist Internationale headquarters in Moscow, was functioning and had been functioning illegally, or "underground," as the communists are inclined to characterize the operations. To quote Secretary Hughes' explanatory communication, accompanying the mass of evidence he submitted in 1924 to the sub-committee of the Senate Committee on Foreign Relations: "There was in existence during that period of time within the Communist party certain factions, but for all practical purposes the Communist movement was united in its ultimate aims and ends, the differences that existed being limited largely to personal leadership. The Communist Internationale was finally moved, by the differences existing among the various factions, to pass upon the question of unity and to cement the communist movement within the United States in 1920 and 1921."

As the result of and in compliance with orders from Moscow, a unity convention was held in May, 1921, unity of the factions within the Communist party itself accomplished, and a revised program and constitution adopted. The revision of the program recognized and confessed the blunders of 1919, which led to retaliatory measures on the part of the Federal Department of Justice and the legislatures of the various states. The recognition of these blunders, the realization that a program almost exclusively devoted to violence could lead nowhere, particularly with the Wilson administration supplanted by one less afflicted at the top with pink sympathies, tolerance and "watchful waiting," prompted the formulation of plans for a change of tactics.

Heretofore, political or parliamentary action on the part of the Communist movement itself had been scoffed at, and every effort devoted to organization for revolution by force and violence. Now, however, it had been determined that, although forceful overthrow of the American government should be the ultimate aim, it was necessary first so to weaken the government by a process of "boring from within" that operations of a violently revolutionary character might be carried out with less resistance by the government itself. The new scheme of operations, then, became one that subordinated force and violence to political or parliamentary revolution.

Said the revised *Program and Constitution of the Communist Party of America:*

> The proletarian revolution comes at a moment of economic crisis precipitating a political crisis. The politico-economic crisis causes a collapse in the capitalist order. * * *
> The proletarian revolution is a long process. It begins with the destruction of the capitalist state and the establishment of the dictatorship of the proletariat, and ends only with the complete transformation of the capitalist system into the communist society. * * *
> Every class struggle is a political struggle. The object

of the class struggle which inevitably develops into civil war, is the conquest of political power. * * *

The Communist party of America recognizes that the revolutionary proletariat must use all means of propaganda and agitation to win over the exploited masses. One of these means is parliamentary activity. * * *

The American bourgeois state was quick to recognize the communist parties in America as its historic and deadly enemies. It employed all its power in a vicious onslaught against them. Being outlawed, the communist parties reorganized as underground, illegal parties. Thus, for the present, the Communist Party of America, is prevented from participating in the elections under its own name. * * *

The Communist Party of America will support with all its power every movement for the liberation of the oppressed colonial peoples of the United States. The Communist party will fight against the economic aggression of American capitalists upon the populations of the weaker American republics. * * *

"In the United States of North America, where, on account of historical circumstances, there was lacking a broad revolutionary movement even before the war, the communists are still before the first and simplest task of creating a communist nucleus and connecting it with the working masses," said Lenin, Radek, Bukharin, Trotsky, Zinoviev and Kamenev in their *Theses on Tactics,* submitted to the third congress of the Comintern. (Comintern is the short word for Communist Internationale.)

The present economic crisis, which has thrown five million people out of work, affords a very favorable soil for this kind of work. Conscious of the imminent danger of a radicalized labor movement becoming subject to communist influence, American capital tries to crush and destroy the young communist movement by means of barbarous persecution. The Communist party was forced into an illegalized existence under which it would, according to capitalist expectation, in the absence of any contact with the masses, dwindle into a propagandist sect and lose its vitality. The Communist Internationale draws the attention of the Communist party of America (unified) to the fact that the illegalized organization must not only serve as the ground for collecting and crystallizing the active communist forces, but that it is the party's duty to try all ways and means to get out of the illegalized condition into the open, among the wide masses. It is the duty of the party to find the means and forms to unite these masses politically, through public activity, into the struggle against American capitalism.

The Communist party of America, therefore, to carry out the mandate of the Comintern to form a so-called legal political organism in the United States, organized what was known as the American Labor Alliance in the summer of 1921. This organization soon afterward became what is now known as the Workers' party. This transformation led to another split in the leadership of the organization which required the further services of the Central Executive Committee of the Comintern to straighten out.

For the guidance of the reorganized and re-unified communist movement, now destined to practice a dual system of operations—one illegal and "underground", the other in the open—the Comintern transmitted from Moscow a program bearing the title, *Concerning the Next Tasks of the Communist Party in America.*

A few quotations from this "thesis" prepared by the executive committee of the Comintern are both interesting and enlightening:

> In order to assist the American comrades in working out and formulating their line of action, the Executive Committee of the Communist Internationale proposes for their examination, the following main points: *   *   *
>
> *   *   * The general elections in which hundreds of thousands of workers take part, cannot be rejected as being merely a peaceful movement with which the communists will have nothing to do. Further, certain mass organizations which not only are not communistic, but are not proletarian in composition, must be utilized by communist strategy for the benefit of the proletarian class struggle. As for instance, the existing mass movement of small farmers (who are, in a sense, semi-proletarian), and even movements of middle class farmers under some circumstances. *   *   *
>
> *   *   * The fighting proletarian is to be led from one stage to another in the revolutionizing process by means of suitable slogans. *   *   *

* * * Communist demands for immediate concessions to the workers are formulated, not to be "reason-
able" from the point of view of capitalism, but to be rea-
sonable from the point of view of the struggling workers,
regardless of the state's power to grant them without
weakening itself. Thus, for instance, a demand for payment out of the government treasury, of full, union-
standard wages for millions of unemployed workers, but
damaging from the point of view of the capitalist state
and the capitalist wage competition which the state demands.

We suggest a few examples of the type of demands
that may be made. * * *

Favoring a close alliance between the United Mine
Workers of America with the Railroad Brotherhoods and
all other unions for common action to raise the standard
of living of all workers in both industries. * * *

For the immediate recognition and unrestricted trade
with Soviet Russia. For the reestablishment of postal
agreement with Russia.

And so on.

Advising the communists to participate in all general
election campaigns, municipal, state, congressional and
presidential; counseling that they conceal their underground apparatus to better advantage and develop it more
effectively "within the outer framework" of legal campaign organizations and election activities; suggesting that
"of course, the Communist party can develop upon labor
organizations" and can "even launch a legal revolutionary
Labor party"; declaring that "a legal press" and "organized groupings of sympathizers within the trade unions"
are imperative, the "thesis" from Moscow continued:

* * * The government of the United States will
not now permit a "Communist party" to exist but it is
compelled to permit "parties" to exist in an otherwise
almost unrestricted variety, for the purpose of its own
preservation. * * * The state attempts, wherever it
can, to exclude a truly proletarian revolutionary party
from this public field. It attempts first to exterminate
the revolutionary party, if possible, or second, to terrorize
and corrupt the revolutionary party into subservence to

capital law which makes revolution impossible, or third, at least to confine the revolutionary party's operations to the narrow sphere that can be reached secretly.

A Communist party must defeat all these attempts. It must not be exterminated. It must unequivocally refuse to obey capitalist law, and must urge the working class to the violent *destruction of the entire legal machinery*. (Italics added.)

"Destruction of the entire legal machinery!" That is something for the reader to remember.

The Communist, official organ published "underground" by the Communist party, had this in its issue for September, 1921:

Comrades, conditions known to all of us and at present beyond control make it impossible for us to go into an elaboration of the details involved in our plans.* * *

Suffice it to say that our Central Executive Committee is not pledged to any iron-clad formula as to our machinery for country-wide work. We frankly recognize that the form is a matter mainly dependent upon the prevailing party and outside conditions.

And in another place, same issue:

The Communist party of America has now reached a point where a change of tactics [the change noted above] is an absolute necessity. This change is vital not only to the party but to the progress of the entire American labor movement. The mountain did not go to Mahommet, so Mahommet must go to the mountain. The masses do not and will not come to our underground organization, so we must organize above and carry our agitation on a legal basis.

In December, 1921, the first convention of the Workers' party, built upon the foundation laid by the American Labor Alliance and organized to function as the "open" or "legal" branch of the illegal and underground Communist party of America, was held in New York City. "The resumption of trade relations with Russia, and the recognition [by the United States government] of the

Soviet Republic," continued to be a foremost and vital plank of the party program.

This gathering marked the preliminary preparations for the participation by the red radicals in the congressional elections of 1922.

CHAPTER VI

A BULWARK OF ORDERLY GOVERNMENT

As has been already quite clearly indicated, the thorn in the side of bolshevism in the United States throughout 1919 and 1920 was the Federal Department of Justice under the generalship of A. Mitchell Palmer. To discredit and cripple the Department of Justice were imperative to whatever degree of success the red radicals hoped to attain, for the simple reason that the breakdown of orderly government in all of its functions is surely the natural consequence of a breakdown of that arm of the government the function of which is the maintenance of domestic tranquility by the enforcement of law and the safeguarding of order which laws and law enforcement are intended to insure.

"Destruction of the entire legal machinery," was the communist aim, as set forth in the "thesis" from the Comintern, quoted in the previous chapter. To be sure, the word "destruction" was preceded by the word "violent," in the advice to the American reds transmitted to them from Moscow, but demoralization must necessarily precede destruction, whether the destruction be accomplished by violence or by milder means.

Now, let it not be understood by the reader that the writer of these pages has it in mind, for a single instant, to suggest that anyone other than the criminal bolshevik agents themselves entertained the thought or desire to promote violent revolution in the United States.

United States Senator Joseph I. France, of Maryland, spoke at a mass meeting in New York City early in January, of 1921, in protest against the ousting of the soviet "ambassador," Martens; later in that month he bitterly assailed Mr. Palmer's conduct of the Federal Department of Justice; after the Harding administration came into power and Harry M. Daugherty became Attorney General, he participated in a debate in Carnegie Hall, New York, with Senator King, of Utah, a staunch opponent of the reds, and advocated United States recognition of Soviet Russia, and so stirred up did the reds attending the debate become that they rushed the stage from which the debate was delivered.

But it is unthinkable, of course, that Senator France at any time entertained any thoughts in common with the bolshevik program for civil war against constituted authority in the United States. Wholly regardless of his consciousness of the fact, however, and wholly regardless of whether he ever realized it afterwards, the Senator from Maryland was giving aid and comfort to enemies of the American republic—enemies who had no scruples of any kind against the overthrow of the American government and the establishment, in its stead, of a reign of bolshevik chaos by any means at all possible to them.

The same is to be said of Senator Thomas J. Walsh, of Montana, who "prosecuted" Attorney General Palmer before the sub-committee of the Senate Judiciary Committee. The same is to be said about the many others who figure prominently in this narrative because they have enacted roles as "dupes" of red radicalism since the bolsheviks mastered Russia, and of innumerable others equally misled but too inconspicuous to warrant identification.

It is perhaps well for Mr. Palmer that his obligations to his country, as the chief law-enforcing officer of the federal government, came to an end with the termination of the Wilson administration. What would surely have been his fate, had not a change of administration come to his rescue, fell to the lot of another man.

President Harding had no sooner selected and installed the Attorney General of his Cabinet, Harry M. Daugherty, than the guns that had been bombarding Palmer were turned and levelled upon his successor, Mr. Daugherty. This would have been true, had the appointee to the Attorney Generalship been any other man fit and big enough for the job. It would have been true had the

man been anyone but a mollycoddle or a Morris Hillquit
—and, of course, had it been the latter the bombardment
would have been from another quarter.

The guns were turned, sighted and levelled at Daugherty, but the bombardment, at any rate that of the heavy
artillery, did not begin at once. There was considerable
sniping throughout 1921, and at frequent intervals the
"resignation rumor" was put into circulation as a sort of
feeler of the new Attorney General's sense of security.
The quality of Daugherty was not so very well known
outside of Ohio, at first; and it was not known for a
certainty among the natural enemies of the Department
of Justice that he was not something of a mollycoddle
upon whom mild tactics might have sufficient influence to
make the use of poison gas and high explosives unneces-
sary. So that, except for the sniping and bush-whacking
and minor attempts at intimidation, the heavy artillery
destined ultimately to open up on him remained virtually
inactive. The first few months of the new administration
were notable chiefly for the propaganda use that was
made of a "general amnesty" campaign directed at both
President Harding and the Attorney General.

The "amnesty" campaign was, of course, nothing more
or less than a propaganda campaign in the interests of
the radical movement. The prime factors in the General
Defense Committee, functioning in Chicago, and in the
American Civil Liberties Union, headquarters in New York
City, were then and are now far less concerned, sen-
timentally, with the fate of individual "political prisoners"
than they were and are in the establishment of a principle which they always call "free speech" but which is,
in fact, freedom to advocate destructive revolutionary acts
without danger of unpleasant consequences to the advo-
cators.

Prof. Paul Frederick Brissenden, formerly of the faculty of the University of California, later of the faculty
of Columbia University, described as having "traveled extensively through the industrial regions of the country
as a special agent for the United States Department of
Labor," and the author in 1919 of a book entitled *"The
I. W. W: A Study of American Syndicalism,"* wrote a

pamphlet for distribution by the General Defense Committee after the "amnesty campaign" had been waged for a time upon the Harding administration. *Justice and the I. W. W.* was the title of it. One of the professor's arguments in behalf of the I. W. W. was that "its members would stack up not unfavorably with 'the Founding Fathers' who, as is well known, urged the unlawful destruction of property by the destruction of tea and by the burning of stamped paper." What the professor overlooked, however, was the fact that the "Founding Fathers" were quite aware that discovery and arrest at the hands of the officers of King George would involve highly unpleasant consequences, of which they were not only cognizant but which they were entirely prepared and willing to experience. It is quite probable, in fact, that Nathan Hale, for one, would have scoffed at even the suggestion of amnesty or of the organization of a defense committee in his behalf.

The pamphlet referred to, extensively circulated by the General Defense Committee, which also staged a number of demonstrations in Washington and brought delegations of "pickets" to do duty at the gates of the White House, contained, in addition to the animadversions of the distinguished professor, a particularly vitriolic attack upon the Attorney General, reprinted from the *New York Call,* a socialist newspaper.

As already suggested, the reds who were the most passionate and industrious workers for the professed objects of the General Defense Committee and the American Civil Liberties Union were interested considerably less in obtaining freedom for so-called "political prisoners" than they were in using the "amnesty campaign" as a smoke-screen for their agitation of class warfare. Had President Harding issued a decree of general amnesty, releasing at one swoop the entire mob of criminals whose freedom from the federal jail houses was demanded by the amnesty campaigners, the props would have been knocked completely from under the campaigners in this particular line. But even that would not have quieted them. They would simply have concentrated their energies in some other direction for the demoralization of government, particularly the legal branch of it. The fact that some of the prisoners on their lists were released by the President, upon recommendation from Attorney General Daugherty, was gall and wormwood to them. Particularly was their hatred of Attorney General Daugherty kindled by the release, in December, 1921, of Eugene V. Debs, and nothing angered them more than the magnanimous attitude of the Attorney General in his consideration of the case of Debs. For Debs in jail, reasoned they with not a little merit, was a far greater revolutionary propagandist himself, dressed in his cloak of "martyrdom" and "suffering" for the cause of the proletariat, than he ever had been or ever could be running at large. At heart, the reds would greatly have preferred that none of their "martyred comrades" received compassionate consideration by the Attorney General or the president. President Harding commuted the sentences of twenty-seven "politicals" on Christmas Day, 1921, but there remained in prison 114 others, for which the reds among the amnesty campaigners were truly grateful because, so long as there was one still in jail, they and their campaign had legs to stand on.

It was not long after the coming in of the Harding administration that the reds, and the misled pinks and parlor bolsheviks, who indulged them with both moral and financial support, encountered the reality that the Attorney General was no mollycoddle and that, furthermore, unlike Mr. Palmer, he had the full and unqualified support of his President. So, as in the case of Palmer, they began working upon the other end of Pennsylvania Avenue—the Capitol end—finding sympathetic ears among "dupes" that had served their purposes in the previous administration and among bollweevil politicans more concerned with the promotion of partisan and personal interests than in either honesty in government or ethics in politics.

Among those selected as a medium through which to bombard the Department of Justice, by way of the United States Senate, was Senator William E. Borah, of Idaho, who had played a sort of second fiddle to Senator Walsh, of Montana, during the investigation of the complaints of the National Popular Government League against Attorney General Palmer, and who, also, had revealed some

sympathetic tendencies with respect to the soviet government of Russia. Senator Borah was the recipient, early in
February, of a telegram from Harry Feinberg, I. W. W.
journalist and lawyer, representing the General Defense
Committee, charging Attorney General Daugherty with
using the Federal Department of Justice as "a center
for anti-labor propaganda." Although this telegram in
itself may not have got anywhere in particular, it served
admirably as a wedge, full advantage of which was taken
in due time, and Senator Borah as a public advocate of
the "cause" of the "politicals" was exploited by the General Defense Committee along with Representative George
Huddleston, vice-chariman of La Follette's People's Legislative Service, the public utterances of both being published
in pamphlet form for distribution as part of the continua-
tion of the "amnesty campaign."

The "amnesty campaign" continued, by the way, long
after other campaigns of a more direct character had been
instituted against the Harding-Coolidge administration of
the government generally and the Department of Justice
particularly, and when the propaganda had been "sold"
to the press of the country and all but thirty-two of the
so-called "politicals" had been relased, the *New Republic*,
highbrow journal of the pinks and parlor bolsheviki, ob-
served:

> The act of amnesty by which President Harding re-
> leased twenty-seven political prisoners serving sentence
> under wartime laws will be received with satisfaction
> tempered with indignation. What two years ago would
> have been a bold and generous declaration of good will
> appears now as a delayed, grudging and rather cowardly
> measure of reparation. The President has bowed for
> two years to the truculence of the American Legion and
> the malevolence of his Attorney General. * * * The
> campaign must go on.

The propagandist basic purpose of the "amnesty campaign" became the more apparent when fifty-two members of the I. W. W. had declined to make application
for individual clemency. These men were serving terms in
the federal penitentiary at Leavenworth, Kansas. Subsequent to the filing of a petition with President Harding

by the General Defense Committee in July, 1922, the prisoners attached their signatures to "an open letter" to the President, the letter being, of course, not so much for the enlightenment of the President as for the purpose to which it was put—namely, publication as a pamphlet for circulation on a large scale as part of the general radical campaign of propaganda against the government and, particularly, against the Department of Justice.

"Freedom of speech," as viewed ever by the red radical, is freedom to advocate, without limit of any kind whatsoever, any doctrine that is, on the face of it, subversive to existing government and subservient to any and all causes inimical to "capitalist society" regardless of how violently destructive such doctrines may be. It is that "freedom of speech" and "freedom of the press" which led to the conviction of the communist, Gitlow, whose sentence was recently upheld by the United States Supreme Court, and which led to a great many other arrests, convictions and prison sentences of equally dangerous reds whose fate has met with the approval of the American courts which have made it clear that there is, after all, at least a slight distinction between "freedom" and "license."

"We feel we owe it to the loyal men and women outside of these walls who still believe in freedom of speech, assemblage and the press, to remain steadfast and uphold these ideals even at the cost of continued incarceration," said the martyred ones in their "open letter" to President Harding. The letter went on:

We can not do otherwise than refuse to recant. We must continue to refuse to beg for a pardon which in common justice ought to have been accorded to us long ago. * * *

Because of Mr. Daugherty's action in giving out false information about our cases [any and all information given out by the Attorney General being labeled as "false" by the amnesty campaigners] we have little confidence in his motives or of those in the Department which he heads. Frankly, we are fearful that applications for clemency would give the Attorney General an opportunity to make a gesture of fairness, by releasing some of us and holding the rest to serve out the savage sentences imposed by the courts.

It is pretty generally known that to intelligent wage-workers and to students of social science that the Industrial Workers of the World is a labor union, and not a mere anti-war nor anti-militaristic organization. Its avowed object is to create among the disinherited workers a spirit of solidarity similar to that enjoyed by the employing class, which at present owns and controls practically all of the earth and the machinery of production. The purpose of this solidarity, as stated in the preamble of the I.W.W., is "to enable the workers to carry on the everyday struggle with the employing class and *to carry on production when capitalism is overthrown.*" [Italics added.] * * * We believed in 1917, and we believe now, that the present social and economic order is wasteful, planless, chaotic and criminal. We are frankly dissatisfied with this arrangement of things, which we call capitalism. We seek to replace it with a well-ordered and scientifically managed system in which the actual producers will own, democratically control and have access to the earth and machinery of production of goods for the benefit of the many instead of the enrichment of the few.

Continuing, the prisoners held themselves up as "martyrs" to the "White Terror," a name given by the Russian bolsheviki to all forms of opposition to the "Red Terror" which they imposed upon Russia and now seek to impose upon the whole world; and concluding, they declined in any way to repent or to recant their adherence to and continued participation in the so-called "working class revolution" for the overthrow of capitalist society and of existing government in the United States.

During all this period, during a period of actual crises far more potentially perilous to the stability of the American republic than the mass of patriotic citizens of these United States have so far been brought to realize, the bulwark of orderly government was, as is always the case when the country is presumably upon a peacetime footing, the Federal Department of Justice. When the Federal Department of Justice does not or can not function efficiently, with the interests of its client, the government, foremost in the mind of its chief officer, the country is in peril. If the importance of the Department of Justice to national stability ever was demonstrated, it was in the year 1922, the history of which it is the purpose of the writer to review in some detail. But before that, let us turn back a bit, once more, and have another look at 1921 and some political events of that year that are significant in their relationship to history that unfolded afterward.

CHAPTER VII

BIRDS OF A FEATHER

THERE can be no better place than right here to impress a point that is important in reaching an understanding of a relationship which the Left Wing of radicalism, that is to say the Moscow-managed faction marching unreservedly under the banner of the Third (Communist) Internationale, bears to the Right Wing. The Right Wing has the same objective but with a presumably less violent program for accomplishing it. There are factions, of course, within each of these so-called "wings"—factions frequently at odds with one another both as to tactics and as to personnel of leadership . . . . but with these we need not be concerned, any more than we are ever concerned with factions within either the Republican or Democratic parties when such factions remain faithful to the fundamental principles and precepts outlined in the respective party programs or platforms.

As the Socialist party of America, now professing to be the Right Wing, and therefore more or less viewed with contempt by the Left Wing, has always had its factional fights which have made national conventions of the party more or less tempestuous until one faction or another was able to mobilize support sufficient to obtain for it control of the party machinery, so also has the Left Wing, made up of the Communists, the I.W.W., the Socialist Labor party and defections from the Socialist party, had its series of factional fights since the ascendancy of Sovietism in Russia. Attention already has been called to the fact that the Comintern of Moscow has heretofore been obliged to take a hand in ironing out these factional troubles, and such is the case again as this is written. The Communist organization that was unified during the political campaign of a year ago, 1924, has since split into two

factions, one headed by William Z. Foster, and the other
led by Charles Ruthenberg. While this is being written,
there is in the United States an emissary of the Communist
Internationale whose business it is to reunite these two
factions and once more set the Communist U-boat fleet
upon a more definite course of destruction. But, notwithstanding factional controversies within either of the
"wings" of the radical movement, and not withstanding
the differences existing between the two "wings," differences due as much to jealousy of power felt among leaders
as to controversy over tactics—what is important to understand is that the objective of both "wings" and of all
factions of either of them is a common one.

There are two major political parties in the United
States, the Republican party and the Democratic party.
Fundamentally, the differences between these two parties
are not great. Notwithstanding these differences, and
whether great or negligible, the common objective of both
of them is the administration of government in the United
States in conformity to civilized standards of good order
and in compliance with the provisions of the federal Constitution.

There are two principal minority organizations, to one
or other of which a number of lesser ones adhere with a
greater or lesser degree of loyalty. There are the Workers,
or Communist, party (Left Wing) on the one hand, and
the Socialist party (Right Wing) on the other. The differences between the two are even less than the differences
between the Republican and Democratic parties, and the
objectives of each of them are the same as those of the
other, namely, the overthrow of capitalism, and the destruction of the republican form of government provided
by the federal Constitution, the termination of private
property rights, the "dictatorship of the proletariat" and
the establishment of the international socialist common-
wealth. These are statements of fact that are incon-
trovertible, statements of fact irrevocably established by
socialist textbook explanations of socialism and by the entire history of the socialist movement since the *Communist Manifesto* of Karl Marx and Frederick Engels.
Any avowed socialist, whether he be of the "Left Wing"
or the "Right Wing," who disputes these statements of

fact or attempts to equivocate concerning them is either a hypocrite and a liar or he is not a socialist by conviction and hasn't even a freshman's knowledge of socialist theory or of socialist history.

As set forth in a previous chapter, it was in the summer of 1921 that the Communists determined upon a change of tactics, decided to "come into the open" and participate in a parliamentary political program.

A gathering of the leaders of the Socialist party was held in April, 1921, in Chicago, at which meeting public announcement was made of the endorsement of the Third (Communist) Internationale and the soviet government of Russia by the socialists. The national convention of the Socialist party was held in Detroit in June, of the same year, and at this convention there were stormy debates over the question of officially affiliating with the Comintern. The convention voted not to affiliate, but it refused to repudiate party members favorable to and giving their endorsement to the Comintern.

Morris Hillquit, of New York, who had been officially connected with the bolshevik "embassy" in New York under "Ambassador" Ludwig C. A. K. Martens, and who subsequently became one of the campaign managers for Senators La Follette and Wheeler in their campaign for the presidency and vice-presidency, introduced a resolution providing for the first step on the part of the Socialist party toward a coalition of radical revolutionary forces for political action. The introduction of this resolution which was passed by the Detroit convention, was subsequent to the similar step taken by the Communists in contemplation of their program for political action. Whether this was mere coincidence, I am not prepared to say, but it seems a bit difficult to believe that minds bent upon achievement of an ultimate and common objective should run in very much the same direction, each entirely unconscious of the proximity of the other.

"The task of reconquering and maintaining our civil rights and liberties and securing substantial measures of economic relief can be accomplished only through the united and concerted action of all progressive, militant and class-conscious workers, industrial and agricultural, in the United States," said the Hillquit resolution as reprinted in the socialist newspaper, the *New York Call,* June 28, 1921.

"Be it Therefore Resolved, that the Incoming National Executive Committee be instructed to make a careful survey of all radical and labor organizations in the country, with a view of ascertaining their strength, disposition and readiness to cooperate with socialist movement upon a platform not inconsistent with that of the party and on a plan which will preserve the integrity and economy of the Socialist party."

"Resolved, that the National Executive Committee report its findings with recommendations to the next annual convention of the Socialist party."

The broad inclusiveness of the resolution—"All radical and labor organizations" denotes its scope—made it imperative that the National Committee take into account the "Left Wing" organizations (Communists) as well as those of the "Right Wing." Had it then been intended not to cooperate with or not to seek cooperation from the communists, it would appear certain that the resolution should have given expression to exceptions to that effect.

At any rate, the "survey" by the National Executive Committee of the Socialist party presumably was made during the months following, for a coalescing of radical forces in conformity with the plan indicated by the Hillquit resolution soon took place. The representatives of "progressive, militant and class-conscious workers" of the "industrial" group assembled in Chicago in February, 1922, and almost simultaneously there assembled in Chicago also representatives of the "progressive, militant and class-conscious workers" of the "agricultural" group.

William H. Johnston, long known as a socialist and as a socialist candidate for political office, was there to mobilize the "industrial" group. He was and is president of the International Association of Machinists; had been a lecturer in the radical Rand School of Social Science, New York; was a member of the National Advisory Committee, National Labor Alliance for Trade Relations with the Recognition of Russia; was a member of the National Council of the League for Industrial Democracy (formerly the Intercollegiate Socialist Society); was secretary and treasurer and a member of the executive committee of the

La Follette People's Legislative Service; was vice-president of the People's Reconstruction League; was a member of the board of directors of the Labor Publication Society; was a member of the Executive Committee of the American Civil Liberties Union, and was a soviet sympathizer who took an active part in the movement to obtain official recognition of "Ambassador" Martens by the United States and to prevent the deportation of the distinguished and officially designated representative of the soviet government.

The mobilization of the "agricultural group" was in the hands of Benjamin C. March, managing director of the so-called Farmers' National Council; managing director of the People's Reconstruction League, and press agent for the Plumb Plan League.

While the "industrial" and "agricultural" groups were mobilized separately, when they had been assembled they combined and held their conference jointly. Leading spirits in the conference were "Comrades" Morris Hillquit, Victor Berger, Otto Bramstetter, Bertha Hale White and Daniel W. Hoan, all conspicuous personages in the socialist movement. The gathering was marked by a number of highly inflammatory speeches, denunciatory of the American government, and larded with fulsome praises for the virtues of the soviet regime in Russia. A political program was determined upon, providing, among other things, for a scheme of "boring from within" the Republican and Democratic parties, and avoiding as far as possible, for strategic reasons, too much use of the words socialist and socialism. It was a socialist program that was contemplated, but it was agreed that expediency demanded its being carried out under a different name.

Pending another conference to be held later, a committee of fifteen was named to carry on the affairs of the coalition. Besides Hillquit, Johnston, March and others on the committee, there was Jay G. Brown, of Chicago, whose name is mentioned here particularly that it may be remembered by the reader when the communist connections of this committee-man are gone into later.

This was the termination of "isolated action" by the socialists and other red radicals. It was the beginning of the Conference for Progressive Political Action, of which we shall, of course, see and hear a great deal more in due time.

In the meantime, the Federal Department of Justice, under the generalship of Harry M. Daugherty, had further enraged the reds and stirred up the sympathetic protests of the pinks, first by instituting in February, 1922, an inquiry into the conduct of Russian famine relief, and second by issuing, in March, a warning against acts of violence instigated by the reds during the coal strike which was then in progress.

Evidence was developed by the investigation of Russian famine relief by the Department of Justice, and subsequently made a part of the record of the hearings of the sub-committee of the Senate Committee on Foreign Relations, Sixty-eighth Congress, purporting to reveal the true character of an organization known as Friends of Soviet Russia, ostensibly organized to help finance relief for famine sufferers in Russia; but, in fact, according to the evidence uncovered by investigators, engaged mainly in financing and conducting bolshevik agitation and propaganda in the United States.

It is, of course, beyond dispute that the soviet government of Russia and the Third Internationale were then and still are engaged in a very real and entirely manifest warfare upon the United States government, as upon many other governments, and that the purpose of this warfare is to overthrow the constituted government of this country and supplant it with a socialist government to be made a part of the contemplated international socialist federation under the dictatorship of the proletariat. So that, by its very name—Friends of Soviet Russia—the organization in question was composed of individuals who were pro-soviet and, therefore, by the very nature of things, anti-American.

"Ambassador" Martens before his enforced departure from our shores, had established a publication called *Soviet Russia*, and this "house organ" of the bolshevik embassy in New York City became the subsidized organ of the Friends of Soviet Russia. Later the name was changed to *Soviet Russia Pictorial*. The publication became the official organ of the Friends of Soviet Russia in February, 1922, and has been the medium for pro-bolshevik and anti-American propaganda ever since.

At the time of the investigation by the Department of Justice, the list of officers and directors of the Friends of Soviet Russia included such well known communists as Elmer T. Allinson, Dennis E. Batt, Ella Reeve Bloor, Jack Carney, William F. (Big Bill) Dunne, Max Eastman (recently excommunicated), J. Louis Engdahl, William Z. Foster, Caleb Harrison, Ludwig Lore, Alfred Wagenknecht (alias A. B. Martin), Robert Minor, Edgar Owen, Upton Sinclair, Rose Pastor Stokes, Hewlett M. Wells, H. M. Wicks, and Albert Rhys Williams. But in addition to these, others were J. O. Bentall, veteran of the Socialist party of America; Jay G. Brown, a member of the "committee of fifteen" previously referred to in connection with the formation of the Conference for Progressive Political Action; Elizabeth Gurley Flynn, notorious I.W.W. and socialist agitator; H. W. L. Dana, former Columbia University professor, active in the American Civil Liberties Union and the League for Industrial Democracy; Helen Keller, the deaf and blind woman, long a radical writer and agitator; Charles P. Steinmetz, "electrical wizard," long active as a socialist; Paxton Hibben, a captain in the Officers' Reserve Corps and secretary of American Relief Committee for Russian Children, and a well known admirer of Soviet Russia and a public advocate it in its behalf and in its defense.

According to general report found among other documents bearing upon activities of the Communist party, of which the Friends of Soviet Russia was, in fact, an arm, thousands of locals of all the important labor unions in the United States were officially affiliated with the Friends of Soviet Russia, and also affiliated with the central labor bodies—Central Labor Councils and Federations of Labor —in Chicago, Detroit, Seattle, Tacoma, Minneapolis, Portland, Oregon, Trenton, New Jersey, Denver, Ogden, Utah, Mansfield, Ohio, Richmond, Virginia, Bedford, Connecticut, Binghampton, New York, Rockford, Illinois, San Diego, California, New York City, and Washington, D. C.

The machinations of the avowed bolsheviks in the coal strike, their promotion of violence and the destruction of mining machinery, were exposed by investigations made by the Federal Department of Justice. The red campaign against the Department of Justice became more and more militant and defiant in character. The red campaign against this branch of the administration of government was not merely defended by the pinks and the new political coalition, originated by the Socialist party and brought into definite form as the Conference for Progressive Political Action, but it was applauded and echoed and helped in every manner possible. The program of violence, in which the communists were the most active factors, had the moral support of the leading spirits in the "Right Wing" of the radical forces aligned against the government, and the political program of the "Right Wing" had the moral and active support of the leading spirits in the more inflammatory "Left Wing."

The reds were preparing to use the pinks for their own ends, and the pinks were only too willing to use the reds for theirs.

After the "coalition" of February, 1922, under the name Conference for Progressive Political Action, in which radicals of many shades from deep red to ripe pink were marshalled, the "committee of fifteen" functioned with fine effect. First among the organizations to affiliate in this coalition were the "Big Four" Railroad Brotherhoods; the railroad crafts, including the United Brotherhood of Maintenance of Way Employes and Railway Shop Laborers, the International Association of Machinists, the International Brotherhood of Blacksmiths and Helpers, the Steel Metal Workers, the Brotherhood of Railway Electrical Workers, the Brotherhood of Railway Car Men, the International Brotherhood of Boiler Makers, the Order of Railroad Telegraphers, the Brotherhood of Railway Clerks, the International Brotherhood of Stationary Firemen and Oilers, and the Brotherhood of Railroad Signal Men.

Other affiliations were from the United Mine Workers, the Amalgamated Clothing Workers, the Farmers' National Council, the Non-Partisan League and elements of the Farm-Labor party which subsequently became the Federated Farm-Labor party under almost complete dominance of communist leadership. A. C. Townley, the famous Non-Partisan Leaguer, who was imprisoned in Minnesota for seditious utterances, was instrumental in obtaining the Non-Partisan League affiliation, and he was one of the prime movers in bringing about the "coalition." It was the Townley system of stealing party names and "boring from within" which the communist, William Z. Foster, borrowed and used with such good effect in the labor unions, that the Conference for Progressive Political Action adopted. The system was one of well known fruitfulness to Senator Robert M. La Follette in Wisconsin, and to the pink politicians of North Dakota and elsewhere.

An affiliation not to be overlooked was, of course, that of the People's Legislative Service, which Senator La Follette had organized and set up in Washington to be "On Guard for the People," as the motto of this pink institution for uplift expresses it. The director of this organization was and is one Basil M. Manly, a socialist and for years a radical lobbyist in Washington, and the author of literature sufficiently red to warrant circulation by the Rand School, New York City. Senator La Follette was the chairman of the executive committee; Congressman George Huddleston, of Alabama, the vice chairman; William H. Johnston, secretary-treasurer, and W. G. Lee, Warren S. Stone, Mabel C. Costigan, other members. This same William H. Johnston, as secretary-treasurer of the People's Legislative Service, and the president of the International Association of Machinists, was the one who took the job of "mobilizing" the "industrial" groups for the "coalition" of radical forces for political action in accordance with a program laid down by the Socialist party under the provisions of the Hillquit resolution of June, 1921. The versatility of William H. Johnston, as an office-holder in the radical groups, has already been indicated, but special attention to two or three of these official connections may well be directed at this time.

As a member of the National Committee of the American Civil Liberties Union "Comrade" Johnston was an associate and co-worker with such well known communists, socialists and reds as Elizabeth Gurley Flynn, William Z. Foster, Helen Keller, Scott Nearing, Seymour Stedman, Norman Thomas, and Roger M. Baldwin, the last named being the director of the Union and himself an ex-convict, having been convicted and imprisoned for draft-dodging during the war. As a member of the National Council of the League for Industrial Democracy, formerly the Intercollegiate Socialist Society, we find "Comrade" Johnston at work with as fine a collection of communists, socialists, reds and pinks as any one organization could wish to boast of, including the I. W. W. apologist and defender, Professor Paul E. Brissenden, heretofore quoted; Evans Clark, who had served as one of "Ambassador" Martens' press agents; Upton Sinclair, Morris Hillquit, Alexander Trachtenberg, Prince Hopkins, Norman Thomas, and the Hapgood Brothers, Norman and William.

As the Conference for Progressive Political Action controlled from beginning to end by socialists, and originating from the initiative of the Socialist party, as expressed in the Hillquit resolution, was the direct link of alliance between the "Right Wing" reds and pinks of the La Follette organization, the People's Legislative Service, so the People's Legislative Service was the direct link of the radical "coalition" of the reds and the pinks with the Legislative branches of the United States Government, the Senate and the House of Representatives. William H. Johnston, secretary-treasurer of the People's Legislative Service and co-worker with some of the country's best known communists and socialists in the American Civil Liberties Union and the League for Industrial Democracy, became the directing head of the Conference for Progressive Political Action which was organized to carry out a Socialist party program in 1922, that by the oddest coincidence—if such it was—ran almost directly parallel with the program of altered tactics determined upon by the Moscow directed communists through the medium of their "legal" Workers' Party.

The People's Legislative Service supplied an imposing personnel of active workers within the Council of the Conference for Progressive Political Action, as put into operation in 1922. For, besides "comrade" Johnston and "Comrade" Manly, there were Warren S. Stone, grand chief of the Brotherhood of Locomotive Engineers; Joseph A. Franklin, president of the International Brotherhood of Boiler Makers, Iron Ship Builders and Helpers of America; former Congressman Edward Keating, editor of the extremely radical weekly paper, *Labor* published across the street from the Capitol in Washington; E. J. Manion, president of the Order of Railroad Telegraphers; Frederick C. Howe, President Wilson's radical immigration commissioner at New York and long known as a radical propagandist, I.W.W. defender and apologist, and a special writer for the daringly red news service, the Federated Press; and sundry others.

With Senator Joseph I. France's connection with the People's Legislative Service and his pro-soviet utterances, the reader is already familiar. At the time under discussion, Senator Wheeler and Senator Brookhart, later to become members of the Executive Committee of the People's Legislative Service, were not members of that organization, but Senator Ladd, of North Dakota, and Senator Norris, of Nebraska, were members of the National Council of the People's Legislative Service, as was Senator David I. Walsh of Massachusetts, and these members of Congress, Joseph D. Beck, Wisconsin; Edward E. Brown, Wisconsin; William J. Burke, Pennsylvania; Ross A. Collins, Mississippi; James A. Frear, Wisconsin; Oscar E. Keller, Minnesota; James M. Mead, New York; John M. Nelson, Wisconsin; Edward Voigt, Wisconsin.

It would be getting ahead of the story, somewhat, to discuss the Labor Defense Council now, an organization of communist origin, but it ought here to be mentioned—with further details held in reserve for a later chapter—because the chairman of the Executive Committee of the Conference for Progressive Political Action and secretary-treasurer of the People's Legislative Service, which organizations have just been under discussion, was so closely associated with the chief actors in the Labor Defense Council. For one thing, one of the members of the Executive Committee of the Conference for Progressive Political Action—none other than Jay G. Brown, twice mentioned heretofore—was chosen for the National Committee of the Labor Defense Council, serving with such other close associates of chairman Johnston in other organizations, as Roger Baldwin, Elizabeth Gurley Flynn, and Paxton Hibben. Other members of the National Committee of the Labor Defense Council were Eugene V. Debs, later a highly distinguished figure in the Conference for Progressive Political Action, and the Detroit communist editor and writer, Dennis Batt; and cooperating with the Council were four leading communists, Earl R. Browder, William F. (Big Bill) Dunne, William Z. Foster and Charles E. Ruthenberg. The National Secretary of the Council was William Z. Foster, and cooperating, also, were some of the country's most justly renowned pinks and parlor reds, such as the Reverend John Haynes Holmes, the Reverend Percy Stickney Grant, the Reverend Norman Thomas, Mary Heaton Vorse, Francis Fisher Kane, etc., etc.

Verily, it doth seem strange that, if these birds were not of a feather, they should have flocked so frequently together.

CHAPTER VIII

THE CONSPIRACY OF 1922

"WHAT shall be done with the railroads?"

This was an engrossing question in the last years of the Wilson administration. William G. McAdoo, as director general of the railroads under wartime governmental control, had made for himself a vast political following in the railroad brotherhoods, but in consequence of the governmental operation of the railways $18,000,000,000 worth of privately owned property was brought to a state bordering on ruin, due to political mismanagement and extravagance. The experience was one of great profit to the employes of the roads, but it was one of tremendous loss to the American public and to the owners of the lines. Government operations in 1918 entailed a loss of no less than $266,000,000, and the loss in 1919 was even greater than that.

The question, "What shall be done with the railroads?" was readily answered by the railroad brotherhoods themselves. Why should they surrender to its owners $18,000,-000,000 worth of property that was proving such a boon to themselves?

Whether the general counsel for the organized railway employes, Glen E. Plumb, got his idea from the newly instituted system of running affairs set up by the bolsheviki in Russia, I am not prepared to say. I do not even take the responsibility of hazarding a guess on that point. The idea may have been entirely original with him, and just another of the "coincidences" peculiar to the "trend of the times." However that may be, Representative Everett Sanders, of Indiana, now secretary to President Coolidge, can not have been far wrong when, writing to George W. Greenleaf, secretary of District 72, International Association of Machinists, in October, 1919, he said of the Plumb plan: "This is not government ownership but the Russian soviet system with slight variations. Of course, the nationalization of the railroads would only be the opening wedge. Street railways, coal mines, steel mills, automobile factories, lumber mills, leather factories, clay plants, and every large industry would have to follow as a natural law of economics. In fact the proponents of this measure recommended that this nationalization scheme be used as to other like industries whenever the employes desire."

A league to "put over" the nationalization scheme of Plumb, himself a publicly acknowledged admirer of the genius of Lenin *et al*, who had set up sovietism in Russia, had been organized in February, 1919. Throughout that year, when the administration was being bedeviled by agitation, intimidation and violence at the hands of the reds, with plenty of encouragement from the pinks, and in time thereafter the Plumb Plan League was an industrious institution, striving with all its might, and with none too particular scruples as to the means employed, to bring about this "opening wedge" to the nationalization of American industry.

Samuel Gompers, in spite of his firm claims to "conservatism" and his denial of susceptibility to "radical influence," received the distinction of being the "honorary president" of the Plumb Plan League. The president was the grand chief of the Brotherhood of Locomotive Engineers, Warren S. Stone, later destined to become the treasurer of the camouflaged Socialist party, the Conference for Progressive Political Action. The vice-presidents of the League were the presidents, acting presidents and other high officials of the various unions of railway employes. Bert M. Jewell, acting president of the Railway Employes' Department of the American Federation of Labor, and J. J. Forrester, grand president of the Brotherhood of Railway and Steamship Clerks, Freight Handlers, Express and Station Employes, were members of the league's executive committee.

Never before nor since was such pressure brought to bear upon a Congress of the United States as was brought to bear by the railroad brotherhood officials, through the Plumb Plan League and other agencies, to pass the Plumb plan for solving the problem presented by the plight of the well-nigh wrecked railway systems of the country, and this campaign was aided and encouraged by every shade of radical in the country from "new freedom" pinks to communistic reds. The Congress was a Republican Congress, but there were plenty of Democrats, too, who stood forth in strong opposition to the plan. The scheme really didn't have a chance, and President Wilson, whether or not he was privately sympathetic to the proposal, enraged the brotherhood officials, who had been justifiably friendly toward him when, with Director General Hines, McAdoo's successor, he made counter proposals.

"We demand," said an "appeal to the public," issued August 4, 1919, under the signature of Warren S. Stone and other officials, "that the owners of capital, who represent only financial interests as distinguished from operating brains and energy, he retired from management, receiving government bonds with a fixed interest return for every honest dollar that they have invested in the railway industry. We ask that the railroads of the United States be vested in the public; that those actually engaged in conducting that industry, not from Wall Street, but from the railroad offices and yards and out on the railroad lines, shall take charge of this service for the public. These represent all the brains, skill and energy that is in the business."

The very phrasing of the demand would have done credit to the politician, Lenin, or the propagandist, Trotsky, in spite of its lack of grammatical correctness. It reads as well, and is as definitely a socialist demand, as though it had been lifted from a textbook of the Marxist school of political economy.

The officials of the railroad brotherhoods were uncompromisingly for the Plumb plan, and they were for no other. They were for nationalization of the railways, but they were, also, for the nationalization of industry generally—the railroads first, because they were, as the officials of the brotherhoods frankly said in their "appeal" of August 4, "the key industry of the nation." They were for socialism, and against capitalism, as definitely as the communists of Moscow and as clearly as the Socialist party of the United States had been in political campaign after political campaign since Debs was a youth.

"IF CONGRESS ADOPTS THE PLAN PROPOSED BY DIRECTOR GENERAL HINES AND PRESIDENT WILSON, WE WILL TIE THE RAILWAYS UP SO TIGHT THAT THEY WILL NEVER RUN AGAIN."

The quotation is from Bert M. Jewell, of the Railway Department of the American Federation of Labor, a member of the executive committee of the Plumb Plan League, as reproduced in the *New York Tribune* in its issue of August 10, 1919.

Of course, he and his colleagues never fulfilled this threat and were not then confronted with the test as to whether they could fulfill it, but it was, when uttered, a fair indication of the temper of the organized movement then on foot to sovietize industry in the United States, beginning with the "key industry," the railroads.

"It is plainly a venture into radical socialism that the brotherhood chiefs propose," the *New York Times* said of the plan; "more than that, it is a very long step toward the principles of Lenin and Trotsky and of soviet government." The plan, according to the *Times* view, was "so violently at war with all human experience and human reason," that it was the conclusion of that newspaper that the railway brotherhood chiefs entertained no serious hopes of its acceptance but, rather, were using the scheme as an instrument with which, if possible, to coerce Congress into granting wage increases to the amount of $800,000,000 payable out of the taxpayers' contributions to the national treasury.

Since President Wilson was himself perfectly willing thus to be coerced, and his counter-proposal to Congress virtually amounted to a granting of the wage demands at public expense, and in view of the belligerency of the brotherhood officials as indicated by the quotation from Mr. Jewell above noted, it would seem that the brotherhood chiefs were probably much more serious in their demands than the *Times* suspected. However this may be, the President's proposal was received with as much coldness on Capitol Hill, Washington, as had been the Plumb plan. Congress reminded the President that he already had been vested with sufficient authority to act in the emergency. I do not know what Mr. Wilson thought of this reminder; but, whatever he thought, it is to be noted that Director General Hines took one of the few firm stands against radicalized labor organizations in the Wilson administration, and the result was that neither was the Plumb plan "put over" nor did the railroad brotherhoods "tie the railroads up so tight that they will never run again."

The further history of this particular period is, however, of no great concern to the present narrative, and so I pass on from it to 1922—when the railroads had been returned again to private control, but when the Plumb plan for nationalization had not, by any means, been discarded by the railway brotherhood chiefs from their program for future action.

The hope of sovietization of the railroads had by no means been abandoned by the chiefs of the railroad brotherhoods in 1922. Far be it. The Plumb Plan League had been doing business at the same old stand, and its "campaigns of education" had received valiant support from every radical organization in the country.

It has been shown in an earlier chapter how the Moscow-controlled communist organization of America had determined upon a change of tactics, laying stress upon parliamentary political action and subordinating, somewhat, the program of violence which had been found so futile in 1919 and 1920 as a means of precipitating "working class revolution" in the United States. It should be said, however, that the program of violence was not and has not been abandoned. It was continued, and has continued, and will continue wherever and whenever it is possible to fan an industrial controversy into a flame of industrial warfare, however petty or sanguinary.

The railroad brotherhoods, dominated by radicals of one degree or another in official positions, had tried their hand at essentially coercive methods, too, without success. And they, too, had "come in on" a suggestion for a change of methods, and joining the socialists and "all radical and labor organizations in the country," to quote the Hillquit resolution, had now brought into being the Conference for Progressive Political Action. It should be said, also, in this instance, that adoption of a program for political action did not mean at all the abandonment of that earlier program of coercion operated, however unsuccessfully, upon the American public and the public's representatives in the Congress and in administrative executive positions. Coercion was continued, has been, and will be continued whenever and wherever there is the slightest hope of its getting somewhere, and so long as radical politicians remain the directing influences within well and extensively organized unions of the so-called "working class."

The Conference for Progressive Political Action, of socialist origin, dominated by socialists and depending principally for its existence upon the Socialist party and the railroad brotherhood, had been formed in February, 1922. During the months that followed, the "committee of fifteen," appointed to weld the various organizations and factions into a strong and homogenous unity for political action, set about its job of accomplishing this purpose.

The coal strike was on. Red influences were manifest in outbreaks of violence and the practice of "sabotage." Attorney General Daugherty in March gave warning that the government would be obliged to take stern measures if rioting and other forms of violence were not curbed. There developed instances that the warning was not idle talk on the part of the Attorney General. The "general amnesty" campaign was being continued, with the Attorney General an outstanding mark to shoot at, but his failure to be utterly "soft" in dealing with "class warfare" that put the government itself upon the defensive was the occasion for the hurling of missiles at him from every radical quarter, regardless of the redness or the pinkness of it.

Samuel Untermyer, the financing genius of Senator La Follette's People's Legislative Service, delivered himself of a broadside at the Attorney General and the Department of Justice at a meeting held in Washington under the auspices of the P. L. S. in May, the burden of the attack being that the Attorney General was "the connecting link between the administration and Big Business." Senator Borah introduced in the Senate in May his resolution calling for American recognition of the soviet regime in

Russia, which, of course, had no tendency to discourage the reds or to disconcert the pinks.

A month later there were put into circulation rumors that impeachment of the Attorney General was to be sought in the House. The railroad strike, the outstanding event of 1922, was then in the immediate offing, and it was not long afterward that the Attorney General revealed evidences of collusion existing between the promoters of the railroad strike and those of the coal strike.

The railroad strike began the 1st of July. From the very outset, indications of widespread bolshevist influence in the conduct of it were manifest from the prevalence of violence and the character of it, as well as from the evidence of "sabotage" on an extensive scale, revealed by investigations made for the Interstate Commerce Commission. The influence of the bolsheviki and the consequent riots, kidnappings, murders and sabotage, did not have the sanction of the chiefs of the railroad brotherhoods. The strike doubtless was beyond control of its leaders and most prominent sponsors. The explanation, if any, is for them to make; it is not needed from the present writer.

The outstanding fact that the American public was in grave need of the protection of the government was very quickly, emphatically and thoroughly demonstrated. This protection the government proceeded to give. The medium was the Federal Department of Justice and the courts. The agent was the Attorney General of the United States, Mr. Daugherty.

The public looked to the government for protection from a manifestation of civil warfare that might have wrecked the nation. It did not look in vain. It got what it looked for.

But in the soil of that protection there was planted the germ of what may very fittingly be called the conspiracy of 1922.

CHAPTER IX

"GET DAUGHERTY!"—WHY?

As has already been pointed out, the radicalism that now dominates in Mexico, bringing that country into a state of chaos and bolshevism not far removed from Soviet Russia, achieved its power by capturing control of the railway system of the country.

By attempted coercion and by a widespread propaganda, radical leadership in the railroad brotherhoods, and in other sections of the labor movement in the United States had sought to sovietize the railroads of this country by means of the Plumb plan. As heretofore shown, this contemplated capture of control of the "key industry" was intended as only the first step toward application of the same principles to all phases of industry in the United States.

Although I do not say that the decision of the communists to "come into the open" and engage in parliamentary political action, and the decision of the Socialist party to rally all radical and labor organizations for mass political action, and the decision of the chiefs of the railroad brotherhoods to bring about the railroad strike of 1922 were definitely related to one another, I do say that these decisions were reached within a few weeks of one another, in about the order named (in the summer months of 1921); and that if they are coincidences, they are very remarkable coincidences indeed. And although I do not say there was a definite agreement among these three general organizations, at the time of formulating these decisions, either for consolidation of effort in a political program for 1922 or for teamwork in support of the railroad strike of 1922, I do say that there was, indeed, remarkable teamwork among them both in politics and in the railroad strike.

Agreement or no agreement, understanding or no understanding, coincidence or no coincidence, it is almost self-evident hypocrisy for anyone to attempt to deny that the railroad brotherhoods had the whole-hearted support and active cooperation of the left wing communists and the right wing socialists, to say nothing of a galaxy of pinks and parlor bolsheviki, in precipitating and carrying out the railroad strike of 1922. And, as will be shown later, the respective and similar, if not in fact identical, political program—whether by agreement, understanding or coincidence—bore such intimate relationship in the Congressional elections of 1922 that to deny either the appearance or effect of cooperation and fraternity is to indulge in hypocritical quibbling.

When the Wilson administration had been succeeded by the Harding administration, one of the early accomplishments of the new administration was the return of the railways to their rightful owners under the provisions of the Transportation Act, which, also provided for a Railroad Labor Board for the adjustment of wages. The return of the railroads to their owners, of course, had been fought without stint by the railroad brotherhoods and by all shades of radicalism in the country, and the establishment of the Labor Board particularly enraged the chiefs of the railroad brotherhoods and Bert M. Jewell, head of the Railway Department of the American Federation of Labor.

"Immediately following the enactment (1921) of the Transportation Act," H. S. Jeffery, former chairman-counsel of the Philadelphia-Camden advisory boards of the Philadelphia branch of the Railway Department of the American Federation of Labor, wrote to Attorney General Daugherty, March 27, 1923, "Mr. Jewell sent for me at his office, then in Washington, and stated that it had been concluded not to go along with the law, but to stage a fight, and desired to know if I could line up all the men in Philadelphia. . . ."

"Later I had many talks with Jewell in Chicago, Columbus, Philadelphia, etc., also with William H. Johnston, president of the International Association of Machinists. Their whole plan was to force the board [Railroad Labor

Board] out of business and return to government operation
as during the war.

"About the middle of 1921 the strike call on July 1,
1922, was planned. I opposed the same, and the result was
that Jewell, Johnston, etc., made most clear to me that I
must support them 100 per cent or take the consequences.
I refused to support their insane policy. . . ."

"I could not begin to cite you all the facts that I am acquainted with, but do know that the shopmen strike of
July was a conspiracy against our government, and the
shopmen today do not know why they went on
strike." *

Jeffery took "the consequence," which he declared
Jewell and Johnston warned he would have to take. Perhaps the least of these "consequences" was his removal as
advisory board chairman-counsel and his deposition from
the labor organization of which he had for four years
been an official.

The railroad strike took place on July 1, 1922, as the
reader already is aware from reading the foregoing quotation from Mr. Jeffery. In an effort to make the strike
effective in every way and to prevent the transportation
of coal, food and other necessities, as well as the mails
entrusted to the United States government for distribution, the strikers, with the aid of particularly active communist elements and with the support and applause of the
whole radical movement of the country, sought every opportunity to damage and wreck the locomotives and roll-
ing stock of the railroads, to make defective the safety
appliances which the railroads, under the law, were obliged
to maintain, and completely to paralyze transportation by
practices of the most flagrantly criminal character.

"We will tie up every train, both freight and passenger;
every ferryboat and every railway shop, and not a wheel
will turn anywhere," was the boastful threat made and
circulated with official sanction from the brotherhood
chiefs who were the leaders in the strike and were the
official authority for the order which brought it about.
The threat was, in sound, at any rate, something of an
echo of the threat proclaimed by Bert M. Jewell in 1919

---

*See appendix "Jeffery letter."

when, as a member of the executive committee of the Plumb Plan League for nationalization of the railroads and as chief spokesman for the Railway Department of the American Federation of Labor, he said: "We will tie the railways up so tight that they will never run again."

The months of July and August were months of such paralysis in transportation and of such a widespread condition of violent industrial warfare in virtually every section of the country where railway tracks are laid that the situation was one closely bordering upon civil war. The patience of the government was great. It was so great, in fact, that popular restiveness and public demand for action of a vigorous and conclusive character became inescapably apparent to President Harding, and he went before Congress with a special message on the 18th of August, saying:

> We must reassert the doctrine that in this republic the first obligation and the first allegiance of every citizen, high or low, is to his government, and to hold that government to be the just and unchallenged sponsor for public welfare and the liberty, security and rights of all its citizens. No matter what clouds may gather, no matter what storms may ensue, no matter what hardships may attend or what sacrifices may be necessary, government by law must and will be sustained. Wherefore I am resolved to use all of the power of the government to maintain transportation and sustain the right of men to work.

Sympathetic strikes had been called by radical labor leaders responsive to influences from the most red revolutionary quarters, and others were in the making. The President told Congress:

> Deserted transcontinental trains in the desert regions of the Southwest have revealed the cruelty and contempt for law on the part of some railway employes, who have conspired to paralyze transportation, and lawlessness and violence in a hundred places have revealed the failure of the striking unions to hold their forces to law observance. . . . There is a state of lawlessness shocking to every conception of American law and order violating the cherished guarantees of American freedom. . . . It is fundamental to all freedom that all men have un-

questioned rights to lawful pursuits, to work and to live and choose their own lawful ways to happiness. In these strikes, these rights have been denied by assault and violence, by armed lawlessness. In many communities the municipal authorities have winked at these violations, until liberty is a mockery and the law a matter of community contempt. . . . . These conditions can not remain in free America. . . .

It is not my thought to ask Congress to deal with these fundamental problems at this time. No hasty action would contribute to the solution of the present critical situation. There is existing law by which to settle the prevailing disputes. There are statutes forbidding conspiracy to hinder interstate commerce. There are laws to assure the highest possible safety in railway service. It is my purpose to invoke these laws, civil and criminal, against all offenders alike.

In what manner was this promise of the President fulfilled? Naturally, here had arisen a situation which called for action, and what arm of the government acts in such an emergency?

So long as it can be made to survive the assaults of destructionists and detractors, the Federal Department of Justice, as I have said, is the bulwark of ordered civil government. Acting through the medium of the courts, it is for the Department of Justice to make the nation not merely safe from individual criminals, great and small, but safe from the chaos and wreckage of mob lawlessness as demonstrated in the railway strike of 1922.

President Harding went to his Attorney General in time of such a crisis as then confronted the country. The Attorney General was prepared for the emergency, not simply in his possession of an efficient organization adequately equipped and backed by the entire administrative department of the government, but by a knowledge of law excelled by few who have occupied the same position and by a personal courage surpassed by none.

On the 1st of September the government, through Attorney General Daugherty in his official capacity, acted in conformity to the promises President Harding had held forth to the people through his message to Congress. The action taken was deliberate, definite and determined. It was taken on behalf of a suffering American public, and in the interests of nobody else. It was taken in defense of a government the foundations of which were being attacked and their destruction threatened. The railway strike of 1922 had attained such proportions and such scope and such seriousness, that it was a matter entirely beyond and above either the railroads, the operators and owners of the railroads, the striking railroad workers, the officials who had called the strike or the men who had refused to strike or who had sought to fill the places of the men who had obeyed the strike order and who had turned their attention to practices of violence, sabotage, kidnapping and other forms of lawlessness characteristic of bolshevism in practice and mobocracy in action. The crisis was one to be met entirely independent of the interests of any of these elements. It was one to be dealt with solely as one of concern to the general public and of importance to the fulfillment of the chief function of the Federal Department of Justice—namely, the maintenance of order and the enforcement of law. Solely upon this principle, therefore, did the government act. Very definitely refusing to be joined by the railways or by any other interest than the public interest, and taking the step entirely as an officer of his government, the Attorney General acted for his government.

His case supported by evidence of no less than 17,000 instances of unlawful acts and upheld by affidavits and convincing circumstantial evidence of conspiracy against the government, Mr. Daugherty went, as Attorney General of the United States, himself personally before Judge Wilkerson in the federal court at Chicago and obtained a preliminary restraining order—a step preceding a temporary injunction and the subsequent court act of making the injunction permanent. The precedent was the Debs case of 1894. It was a court proceeding, not to enjoin the men from striking, not to compel them to return to work, not to deny the right of union organization or of collective bargaining or of any other lawful right recognized by the Constitution and by federal statute, but to enjoin the conspirators from further executing their conspiracy and to enjoin the law violators from the hindrance of the conduct of interstate commerce and the transportation of the United States mails by mob violence and lawlessness.

The preliminary restraining order was in itself a body blow at the strikers and their chiefs and a stern warning to the reds who were the leading spirits in violent manifestations of disorder and destruction. The effect was immediately discernable; enforcing officers throughout the country began to take their jobs seriously and to enforce the law; the lawless began to lose some of the courage and bravado they had shown; the strikers began to understand that the federal government meant business and had no intention of being long flouted, defied and trifled with; the transportation system began to function; the paralysis of passenger and freight traffic and of distribution of the mails began to be relieved.

And the Federal Department of Justice began at once to be the object of an exceptionally bitter assault from its natural foes. The reds, the pinks and the yellows now opened up on it with their heavy artillery.

Attorneys for the Railway Employes' Department of the American Federation of Labor *et al.* endeavored to make a show at contesting the legal step taken in behalf of the government and the public by the Attorney General. But the record of the proceedings is ample indication of their full consciousness of the futility of their cause before the law. They seemed to confine their defense to a systematic attack on the Attorney General. This was continued throughout his term and still continues. They never in court, much less out of court, discussed the facts or the law. That they sought to conceal by drawing him into a personal controversy. This they failed to do, for he made no answer to attacks but devoted his energies to the government's case and the law and facts involved. The government was loaded with evidence in support of its case and before the entering of the final court order the testimony of more than 700 witnesses had been heard and set down in a court record of nearly 4,000 pages. The witnesses were from fifty different railroads covering the entire country. Oral testimony and affidavits presented by the Attorney General showed that the cost of the strike, wholly aside from damages to property, losses incurred by business, loss by claims for damages, and from increased cost of doing business, had amounted to nearly $97,000,000. Practically all railway terminals, shops and roundhouses had been picketed, it was shown, and "the conduct and general demeanor of the pickets and strikers was aggressive, belligerent, violent and lawless."

The record in the case established such facts as the following:

Approximately a score of known deaths, due to violence and assault by strikers; some 1,500 instances of various kinds of assaults by strikers on employes of the railroads and on men seeking such employment; sixty-five cases of kidnapping, with accompanying brutal assaults; eight instances of victims of strikers or their sympathizers being tarred and feathered; fifty cases of arson and dynamiting, or attempted destruction by these means, of railroad bridges, for the purpose of wrecking freight, passenger and mail trains; 250 instances of bombing or burning, or attempted bombing or burning, of railroad property or property and homes of non-striking employes; fifty cases of train-wrecking or attempted train-wrecking by derailment; and innumerable instances of flagrant practices of sabotage in its various forms. One thousand mail trains required to be taken off and abandoned on account of the mobs.

The Attorney General had appointed six thousand deputy United States marshals all over the country upon the recommendations of courts and government officials prior to his application for the injunction to preserve property, protect lives and try to keep down disorder and interference with transportation. He spent over $2,000,-000, which Congress afterwards approved without a question.

In court the case for the strikers and conspirators was weak. It was so weak, in fact, that their own counsel confessed it to Judge Jacob M. Dickinson, special assistant to the Attorney General, handling the proceedings in the court at Chicago, on the final hearing. "Counsel for defendants told me on that day (May 2, 1923) that we already had sufficient evidence to win the case, and that, in view of this, their clients were unwilling to expend any more money." Judge Dickinson reported to the Attorney General the day the final hearing of evidence was held,

May 15, 1923. "I think it is perfectly manifest that they did not dare take the stand to deny the allegations of the bill, and subject themselves to cross-examinations and the exposure of their papers."

"The allegations of the bill are fully sustained," said Judge Dickinson further. "We have not, and could not expect to get any direct evidence of coming together and conspiring. The conspiracy must be inferred from proven facts showing concert of arrangement, purpose, and action."

With no case in court, but obliged nevertheless to make a show at contesting the determined steps taken by the government, through the Attorney General, without the risk of submitting the strikers' chiefs to cross-examination or their books and correspondence to the scrutiny of the court, the leading actors in the conspiracy sought to defeat the government by a system of threats and the practice of intimidation against the Attorney General and the Department of Justice.

As Attorney General of the United States, Mr. Daugherty symbolized the power of that arm of the government to circumvent not merely the conspiracy against the government indicated by the railroad strike of 1922, but other correlated and illegal movements and acts. "Get Daugherty!" therefore became the resonant slogan of the enemies of the government and of their pink defenders and yellow apologists.

The conspiracy of 1922 was but a prelude to the frame-up that was yet to come, and with which the most of the remainder of this book will have to do.

CHAPTER X

A PLOT THAT FAILED

HAD the United States Government not acted as it did and when it did in the crisis precipitated by the railway strike of 1922, the action necessarily taken by the Federal Department of Justice by duly legalized court procedure, it is not at all outside the realm of probability that the transportation system of the country would soon have been completely paralyzed and the country at the mercy of organizations dominated and directed by radical elements. Once legal authority over the means of distributing the necessities of life among the people of the country had been broken down or surrendered, those who break down that authority or those to whom that authority is surrendered have vested in themselves the power of dictatorship. Fortunately for the country, this authority, vested in the government, was not surrendered by those responsible for its maintenance—the President, primarily, and the Attorney General as the chief law-enforcing officer of the administration—nor was it broken down by the radical forces which strove so determinedly to break it down.

No sooner had the initial step been taken by Attorney General Daugherty to redeem the country from industrial paralysis and a "class war" the potential results of which it would be impossible to estimate, than the "Get Daugherty!" slogan became paramount among the reds, and almost at once it became the cry among the pinks and radicals of every shade.

The bill in equity, under which the government proceeded, was filed in the federal court at Chicago on September 1, 1922, and on that date the preliminary restraining order was issued by Judge James H. Wilkerson of the federal bench. It was but ten days later that Oscar E. Keller, a pink "progressive" representative in Congress

from Minnesota and a member of the National Council
of the People's Legislative Service, arose on the floor of
the house and "impeached" the Attorney General in a
resolution charging "malfeasance in office."

Already it has been shown that the People's Legislative
Service, of whose Executive Committee Senator La Follette was chairman, was one of the units affiliated with the
Socialist party and "all radical and labor organizations"
in the organization of the Conference for Progressive
Political Action. Already it has been shown that the People's Legislative Service was the link which connected the
sundry radical organizations of the country—red as well
as pink—with the legislative branch of the government.
And already it has been shown that the director of the
People's Legislative Service was the socialist, Basil M.
Manly, and that powerful influences in the Service were
the chiefs of the railroad brotherhoods, including William
H. Johnston, secretary-treasurer and member of the Executive Committee, who also was president of the International Association of Machinists and chairman of the
Conference for Progressive Political Action.

"Get Daugherty!"

Daugherty was given to understand that he would be
"got." Obviously the threat had a purpose, and the purpose was obvious. If Daugherty, who was not the kind
who could be persuaded from performance of a public
duty, and who, it had now become pretty well known, was
not given to making compromise with the foes of the
government he was serving—if Daugherty could be intimidated, if he could be made to fear for the safety of
his future political life, he might perhaps be dissuaded
from pressing the government's case. It was with this in
mind that the promoters of the railroad strike proceeded
to act. They may or may not have been then aware that
their case was hopeless in the federal courts and that the
government was almost certain to come through victori-
ous, but with their connections with the legislative branch
of the government, through the People's Legislative Service and its "bloc" in the House and Senate of the Congress, they were unquestionably of the opinion that they
could intimidate Daugherty and that they might be able

to "get" him by means of "impeachment" proceedings instituted in the House.

Now, in this they had the backing of every radical organization in the country, but particularly did they have the backing of the American Civil Liberties Union. It was only a week or so before the issuance of the temporary restraining order in the railway strike that special agents of the Federal Department of Justice had cooperated with state authorities in a raid on a secret and illegal gathering of communists held in a sequestered woods near Bridgeman, Michigan. This raid was productive of two barrels of documentary proof of communistic conspiracy against the government of the United States, not the most trifling of which proved of value to the government in meeting the issues presented by the court proceedings instituted to save the country from industrial paralysis and outlawry manifest in the railroad strike. Large amounts of this evidence have since been placed on record before a Senate committee whose chairman, Senator Borah, of Idaho, notwithstanding the sensational character of the documents, continues to favor a resolution calling for recognition of the Bolshevik Russian government and trade and diplomatic relations between the United States and the banditti who control and operate the soviet oligarchy.

In the raid at Bridgeman, a number of the communist conspirators, neglecting to make a getaway when warned of the presence of a federal government agent by William Z. Foster, who made the discovery, were arrested. Those arrested included Caleb Harrison, who, with Jacob H. Hartman, was one of the organizers of the Friends of Soviet Russia, heretofore referred to: William F. ("Big Bill") Dunne, of Butte, Montana, and New York City, and others who have figured in this narrative or will figure in it in the discussion of later events connected with it.

The American Civil Liberties Union was interested particularly in the "impeachment" of the Attorney General because of the Bridgeman raid, but it was interested, too, because of the government's interference in the railroad strike. The National Committee of the American Civil Liberties Union includes William Z. Foster, a participant in the secret gathering of communists near Bridgeman. William H. Johnston, as heretofore noted, is also a member of the committee, as also is Morris Hillquit. It is not here important to mention the names of the reds and pinks who constitute the imposing list of others who are members of the committee or hold executive official positions in the Union. But it is here appropriate to remind the reader that a considerable number of the personages dominant in the Civil Liberties Union also became leading factors in the subsequent operations of the Labor Defense Council, an organization of strictly communist origin but drawing to it for cooperative purposes various radical groups including some unions of the American Federation of Labor, the Socialist party and others.

Congressman Keller, a Minnesota radical, elected to Congress by the reds and pinks of his district, a Plumb plan advocate and the supporter of sundry socialistic pieces of proposed legislation, was the man picked to start the "Get Daugherty!" proceedings in the House. On the 11th of September, while the Attorney General was engaged in the important business of conducting the government's case, first to obtain a temporary injunction and then to obtain a final order of the court making the injunction permanent, Keller arose in the House and said:

"Mr. Speaker, I impeach Harry M. Daugherty, Attorney General of the United States, for high crimes and misdemeanors in office."

"When the gentleman rises to a question of this high privilege," said the Speaker, "he ought to present definite charges at the outset."

"The Chair means such charges as acts of the Attorney General?"

"Yes; definite charges."

"Very well," said Keller, "I will do so. First, Harry M. Daugherty, Attorney General of the United States, has used his high office to violate the Constitution of the United States in the following particulars: By abridging freedom of speech; by abridging freedom of the press; by abridging the right of the people peaceably to assemble."

And then followed a list of "high crimes and misdemeanors" which, stripped of the soapbox verbiage in which Keller enumerated them, were as follows:

Daugherty had conducted himself in a manner arbitrary, oppressive, unjust, and illegal.

He had used the funds of his office to prosecute "individuals and organizations for certain lawful acts," these acts being, of course, those attending the conspiracy behind the railroad strike and the attempted paralysis of the nation's transportation systems.

He had failed to prosecute other "individuals and organizations," notably "big business" and "malefactors of great wealth."

A resolution accompanying the charges thus voiced by Mr. Keller, in a speech typical of the radical soapbox orator, was referred to the House Committee on Judiciary. Five days later the committee held a meeting to hear such evidence as the accuser of the Attorney General had to offer. But he had none to offer.

Therefore the following remarkable colloquy:

"The committee should take the charges that I make, and they are true until they are proven not true," said Keller.

"Is it your contention," inquired Congressman Yates, of Illinois, in unfeigned surprise, "that this committee ought now to report this resolution favorably without any showing whatever by you?"

"I have made my charges," Keller protested, "and they are true until they are proven not true."

Had Representative Keller been familiar with the method of conducting trials in the bolshevik tribunals of Soviet Russia, which he may or may not have been, he could not have presumed more accurately to have introduced the method in the United States. He was reminded by the committee that in the United States the burden of proof is upon the accuser, and that the accused is presumed to be innocent until proven guilty. In Russia the process is precisely the opposite.

"I have made my charges," said Keller, "and they are true until they are proven not true!"

Please note the character of the charges—at the very outset a cry against the abridgement of "free speech," "free press" and "peaceable assembly." The interest of the American Civil Liberties Union in "getting Daugherty" is readily apparent. "The advocacy of murder, unaccompanied by any act, is within the legitimate scope of free speech," Roger N. Baldwin, director of the Union, has said. "All of them [the members of the organization] believe," Baldwin also said, "in the right of persons to advocate the overthrow of government by force and violence."

Which is precisely the kind of "free speech" and "free press" that was wanted by the radicals in the course of the railway strike—the kind of "free speech" and "free press" the Attorney General of the United States was committing "high crimes and misdemeanors" to abridge. It was the kind of "free speech" and "free press" to which William H. Johnston, president of the International Association of Machinists, chairman of the Conference for Progressive Political Action, and secretary-treasurer of the People's Legislative Service, subscribed and gave his sanction to as a member of the National Committee of the American Civil Liberties Union.

It was very soon revealed that Keller had no proofs in support of his charges, but that the whole scheme was to get before the committee some choice oratory from representatives of the striking railway workmen and others similarly interested in "free speech," "free press" and the right of "peaceable assembly."

Confronted with the demand of the committee for "proofs," Keller could do nothing but seek delay. The hearing was, therefore, postponed until a later date, and continued to be postponed from time to time because the accuser of the Attorney General was "not ready." In the meantime he continued to make denunciatory speeches in the House, for consumption by the press generally and the radical press particularly. To the October, 1922, issue of the *Locomotive Engineers' Journal,* on the eve of the Congressional elections, he contributed an article entitled "Why Daugherty Should Be Impeached," a diatribe of sensational but unsupported charges, chiefly to the effect that the Attorney General had illegally prosecuted and persecuted the "working class"; i.e., reds, rioters and industrial war conspirators—but had shown extreme partiality to "malefactors of great wealth."

Samuel Gompers, always loud in his protestations of "conservatism" and his want of sympathy for "radicalism," but always, nevertheless, playing into the hands of the reds in his great fear of losing power as the head of the

American Federation of Labor, issued a blast in the official organ of the American Federation of Labor, saying:

"It is the purpose of the American Federation of Labor to do everything possible to bring the impeachment proceedings to a successful conclusion. Labor will participate in the proceedings through its representatives, through its counsel, and through the presentation of testimony of witnesses."

Thus was revealed the hand of Gompers. The committee found it impossible to get Keller to produce proof of his charges, and it had almost as much difficulty in finding out who helped Keller prepare the charges. It did find out, eventually, that one Jackson Ralston, an attorney for the American Federation of Labor—the same Jackson Ralston of the group of pink lawyers employed to defend radicals in court and calling themselves the National Popular Government League, who had sought by similar means to "get" Attorney General A. Mitchell Palmer—had helped with the preparation of some of the charges. It learned also that Samuel Untermyer, the chairman of the Finance Committee of the People's Legislative Service, had helped with the preparation of some of them.

As time went on, however, Keller found himself deserted by Untermyer, and Ralston unwilling to assume any great responsibility in making good with the charges. In December, 1923, the committee finally got some "evidence," but it was principally on the side of the accused. Keller himself became disgusted and refused, even when served with a subpoena, to appear.

"If there had been no strike and the shopmen had continued at work and had not struck, you would have had no complaint to make to the Attorney General at present, would you?" Congressman Hersey at one of the hearings asked of Thomas Q. Stevenson, an attorney for the Brotherhood of Locomotive Firemen and Enginemen, who had been advertised as a 'star' witness for the 'prosecution.' "

"Probably not, sir," was Stevenson's reply, and the witness, displaying quite plainly his unwillingness to make the admission, did admit, nevertheless, that "impeachment" of the Attorney General appeared to be without very substantial basis.

The witnesses who did appear to present the case for

the "prosecution" plainly revealed the motive behind the charges, but they revealed nothing in the way of evidence to support them. All that was left for the committee to do, after a fiasco that would have been a colossal joke had it not been a preliminary to a more ambitious frame-up based upon similar motives, was to report to the House that "It does not appear that there is any ground to believe that Harry M. Daugherty, Attorney General of the United States, has been guilty of any high crimes or misdemeanor requiring the interposition of the impeachment powers of the House"—a report which the House adopted January 23, 1923, by a vote of 204 to 77, a small group of pink Democrats voting in the negative with the radicals, elected as Republicans or Democrats but wearing the colors of the People's Legislative Service. And all that was left for those who had made Keller their tool, and had sought this means to intimidate the Department of Justice and "get" its chief officer, was to babble "whitewash."

Denouncing the proceedings of the committee as a "whitewash," even before they had been completed but after Keller had abandoned them and gone south "for his health," the radical weekly newspaper, *Labor,* official organ of the railroad brotherhoods and the Conference for Progressive Political Action, said:

"Congressman Keller has already served notice on the Attorney General that unless the latter gets out of public life the impeachment fight will be renewed as soon as the new Congress convenes."

But Keller retired to an undoubtedly comforting and comfortable oblivion. The execution of this threat, intended to be conveyed by the big chiefs of the railroad brotherhoods through their official publication, was left to abler and more daring hands—hands more resourceful, and restrained even less, perhaps, by scruples.

"Have patience," was in effect the counsel of Burton K. Wheeler, of Butte, Montana, to the reds of his own State, "and leave it to me. I'll get Daugherty!"

CHAPTER XI

RED COMRADES WITH A PURPOSE

It has heretofore been emphasized that the determination of the reds and their pink dupes and sympathizers to "get Daugherty" was by no means a personal matter, but emphasis upon this point bears reiteration. To be sure, there was a certain element of hatred of the man, but this was due more to the fact that he symbolized the virility of the law-enforcing department of the federal government—the Department of Justice—than to any other cause. They were not so much interested in him as an individual, but they were tremendously interested in him as the directing head of a Department of Justice that was functioning so efficiently that a plot to bolshevize the key industry of the country—the transportation systems—by the intimidating processes of force, violence and destruction, was nipped in the bud. As the demoralization of the Department of Justice had been one of the main objectives from the outset, so it was after the injunction proceedings in the railroad strike of 1922 had been instituted, the only difference being that the natural enemies of the Department of Justice became all the more determined in their purposes.

Weeks before the filing of the government's bill in equity in the federal court at Chicago, September 1, 1922, the factors behind the railroad strike and the processes by which they operated were subjects of a widespread investigation by the Department of Justice; since, naturally, the government could not take so drastic a step without being sure of its ground. Seldom does the Department of Justice, when it is functioning efficiently, take a step when it is not sure of its position, and that is why the government so seldom loses cases it takes to court. The investigation of the railroad strike being under way during those weeks prior to the filing of the case in court, secretly conducted though it was, was not so profound a mystery that those concerned for the success of the conspiracy were not measurably cognizant of the fact. So that the attempts to intimidate the directing head of the Department of Justice did not begin with the Keller "impeachment" by any means. They began a long time before that, and during the summer of 1922 there were repeated "rumors" that Daugherty was to be "impeached." The "impeachment" of Daugherty was in contemplation many weeks before it was actually attempted, but until it finally came about threats of it were the means by which the intimidation of the Attorney General was sought.

Impeachments of federal officials must originate in the House of Representatives. They must be tried in the Senate. As Keller was the tool picked to institute such proceedings in the House, so was there a tool in prospect for an outstanding role in the Senate. I am not prepared to say how definitely the plan to "get Daugherty" had been worked out before the Congressional elections of 1922, and in the light of subsequent developments this is not of great importance. But the man who, in due season, essayed the role of tool for the red enemies of the Department of Justice and their pink accomplices and sympathizers; the man nominated for the Senate by the red and pink radicals who had captured the Democratic party organization in Montana in 1922; the man who had been the beneficent friend of reds in 1917 and 1918, and who had been their candidate for governor of Montana in 1920, became their hero and their champion in 1922, and was the man counted upon to "do his duty" when the "impeachment" should reach the Senate. This was Burton K. Wheeler, political comrade in 1922 as well as in 1920 of William F. ("Big Bill") Dunne and other reds almost, if not quite, as notorious as this avowed communist and official agent of the Moscow Internationale.

Of course, as is well known, the "impeachment" of Attorney General Daugherty never reached the Senate—which accounts for the desperate situation with which Wheeler was confronted after he became a Senator, pledged as he was to "get Daugherty" and counted upon to redeem the pledge. It accounts also for the desperate and daring program which he and his backers adopted to accomplish their purpose. The details of this program it is, of course, my intention to lay before the reader in succeeding chapters of this book, but most important to an understanding of the processes that operated for the carrying out of the program are the motives underlying it. These motives become conclusively evident, it seems to me, upon examination of the political career and political affiliations of the outstanding genius of that program, Senator Wheeler himself.

It is not important to go further back than the year 1917—a year in which Senator Wheeler was United States district attorney for the Montana district, a year in which he made so much money that he paid an income tax of $1,500 and thereby prompted a former attorney general of Montana, D. M. Kelly, to inquire somewhat curiously "how do you do it?"* Wheeler had been something of a protegé of Senator Thomas J. Walsh, and it was Walsh who had obtained the federal attorneyship for him. The manner in which Wheeler functioned as United States attorney for the Montana district during the years 1917 and 1918 is enlightening in that it affords the best explanation of the passionate allegiance bestowed upon him subsequently by the lawless reds of his state when he sought, with their support, the gratification of higher political ambitions.

"Big Bill" Dunne, a red by boast, preference and chief occupation long before he ever made the acquaintance of Wheeler, was booted out of Canada in 1916 because his chief occupation was antagonistic to Canadian interest in the outcome of the World War. This same "Big Bill" Dunne—none other than the "Big Bill" Dunne who is now one of the leading spirits of William Z. Foster's majority faction of the communist organization in America; none other than the "Big Bill" Dunne who was among the seventeen communists captured in the raid on their under-

---

*Extract from an open letter from Kelly to Wheeler, under date of October 1, 1918: "When I quit public office I did not have any income on which I had to pay $1,500 annual income tax. I did not have any five-story brick blocks, worth $100,000 in the business district of Butte. You confess that you have. How do you do it? Where do you get it?"

ground "convention" at Bridgeman, Michigan, in August, 1922,—this same "Big Bill" Dunne took up his abode and place of occupation in Seattle, Washington, upon decamping from Canada in 1916, but from Seattle he adjourned to Butte, Montana, by way of Helena, in 1917. His departure from Seattle was precipitate and necessary, for reasons similar to those which prompted his poste haste trip out of Canada.

To "Big Bill" Dunne, Butte was a haven, as it was to all other reds in 1917, and the great state of Montana was the same thing in six letters, h-e-a-v-e-n. The heavenliness of Montana, so far as "Big Bill" and his fellow reds were concerned, was due not exclusively but in a very large measure to the fact that the Montana unit of the Federal Department of Justice was not functioning for the benefit of the United States government, but rather for the protection of its avowed enemies and professional detractors. The head of that unit was United States District Attorney Burton K. Wheeler.

So flagrantly and frankly was Wheeler arrayed with the reds against the government whose interests he was paid to protect that his behavior was a state scandal, and had it not been for the presence in the state legislature of a considerable number of legislators owing their political preferment to radical constituencies the legislature unquestionably would have gone on record as demanding the resignation or removal of Wheeler from public office. As it was, thirty members of the legislature voted on February 25, 1918, for a resolution embodying such a demand, and the resolution was lost when three more than that number opposed the resolution, many of those opposed evidently taking the position that interference in a matter that should have been attended to by the executive branch of the United States government was not within the province of a state legislative body.

The State Council of Defense, however, took it upon itself to hail Wheeler and a group of his red admirers, including "Big Bill" Dunne, into a "court" of its own, and at the conclusion of a hearing lasting five days the membership of the State Council of Defense voted unanimously that Wheeler had been guilty of close affiliation with I.W.W. and other seditious elements and of refusal to prosecute them for acts of violence and other manifestations of lawlessness. The conclusions reached by the State Council of Defense prompted it to recommend to President Wilson the removal of Wheeler from office. A state meeting of County Councils of Defense, held later, with only three dissenting votes adopted resolutions similar to those voiced by the State Council, and a state gathering of Democrats, held at Helena, voiced its disapproval of Senator Walsh's continued approval of Wheeler.

It is small wonder, then, that Wheeler drew unto himself an admiring following in the radical movement of Montana, and that he was welcomed into the councils of it by such leaders as "Big Bill" Dunne.

Another notable red who joined Dunne in the reception of Wheeler into political comradeship was D. C. Dorman, a big chief in the councils of the Non-Partisan League of Montana. Dorman achieved the position of national manager of the Non-Partisan League, subsequently became a member of the National Council of La Follette's People's Legislative Service, and later we shall hear of him again as the secretary and treasurer of the Montana unit of the Conference for Progressive Political Action. "Dorman swore that he did not believe in the Constitution and was opposed to the flag of the United States; that the flag was nothing but a rag, or words to that effect, and that the government was no government at all and should be destroyed."*

Dorman had been a follower of the red flag of international socialism for years when he affiliated with Dunne and Wheeler in the radical politics of Montana. He participated in the political activities of the Socialist party in Minot, North Dakota, a dozen years ago, and once was the party's candidate for state senator in the Minot district. He too, like Dunne, was familiar with the interior decorations and routine of jailhouses, having spent some little time in one following participation in red riots at Minot.

Both Dunne and Dorman, as outstanding leaders of the Montana radicals, organized their forces behind Wheeler in 1920 to make him governor of the state. The

*Affidavit of Judge L. J. Palda, case of Ray McKaig vs. Frank Gooding, *New York Commercial*, Oct. 20, 1923.

state convention of the Non-Partisan League was held in Lyceum Hall, Great Falls, and it was none other than Dunne who took the floor of the convention and placed the name of Wheeler in nomination for the governorship. Wheeler, of course, accepted the nomination and he himself made a speech in which he is quoted by the *Great Falls Leader* as having said "I will run on the Republican ticket, the Democratic ticket, or any ticket this convention may pick." For the Non-Partisan League was following then, as it has since, the Townley system of "boring from within," and the radicals of the Montana organization were at that time in a fair way to capture the party machinery of the Democratic party of the state—a feat they accomplished two years later, to the utter disgust of Senator Myers who, seeing which way the political winds were blowing in his party, gave up the struggle for genuine Democratic representation of the state in the Senate of the United States and retired from politics, no longer able to stomach the advancing power the radicals in the party that had sent him to the Senate.

Wheeler was the candidate of the reds for governor of Montana in 1920. But the time was altogether too soon after the events of 1917 and 1918 which brought about his retirement from the office of United States district attorney under fire. He was defeated by 37,000 votes. The two years that followed, however, were made ample use of by the reds and the near reds that had sought to elect him. The "boring from within" system was worked to a finish in the Democratic party, and when 1922 with its Congressional elections rolled around the system had made sufficient strides to make the nomination of an avowed radical possible.

"Big Bill" Dunne had moved again, this time to New York. The Workers' party had been organized by the committee to camouflage their underground organization, of which Dunne was an important member. He blossomed forth as the Workers' party candidate for governor of New York. He had climbed considerably in the councils of the bolsheviki of America, and had been sent by them as a delegate to one of the Comintern Lovefeasts held in Moscow. He had attended the secret and illegal convention of the communists near Bridgeman, Michigan, in

August, 1922, made a speech there, and had been among the seventeen arrested.

Dunne was elated that his radical cohorts had been so successful in attaining such a powerful position in the party machinery of the Democratic party in Montana, and particularly was he elated over the nomination of his friend and comrade of the campaign of 1920, Burton K. Wheeler as the party's candidate for the Senate. He was perfectly familiar with the workings of Wheeler's mind, and like all the rest of the reds who acclaimed Wheeler's nomination, he felt certain that Wheeler's election would be an important stroke in behalf of "the cause" in the United States. Having been released on bond, following his arrest in Michigan, Dunne was on hand in Montana to do his share toward accomplishing the election of Wheeler. He was welcomed with open arms by his comrades in Montana. He was counted upon to deliver that hotbed of reds, Silver Bow County, for Wheeler, and this he declared he could and would do.

The paramount issues of the campaign of Wheeler for the Senate were "free speech" for seditionists and revolutionary agitators, the termination of "persecution" of red radicals by the Department of Justice, and the "Get Daugherty" slogan born of the Department's prosecution of the railroad strike injunction suit in the federal courts.

"I'll get Daugherty. I'll drive him from the Cabinet," Wheeler told the Montana radicals in speeches he delivered in his own behalf as a candidate for the Senate. Those may not have been his precise words, but those words express the substance of what he said, according to the sworn evidence of three witnesses whose affidavits are to be found among the appendices of this book.* These words constitute the essence of his pledge. They are the key, or rather they are among the several keys, to an understanding of the genuine motives behind his subsequent acts as a United States senator in this particular connection.

Wheeler's outstanding pledge was to the red radicals of his state, and it amounted to a pledge to the entire radical movement of the country, for there was plenty

---

*See Appendix B for the affidavits of Howard Squires, L. D. Glenn and F. P. Grieve.

of help from outside the state for his candidacy besides that afforded by "Big Bill" Dunne, the communists' candidate for governor of New York. It was a pledge that carried with it, if not a definite agreement, a very well grounded understanding, certainly, that in other ways he would, if elected to the Senate, serve the cause of those elements that had done the most for him in the furtherance of his political aspirations.

But if Wheeler was the candidate of the reds, how could he have been elected? Can it be that the majority of the voting population of Montana was of red persuasion in that year, 1922?

The answer to both of these questions is simple. A negative answer must be given to the second one. To the first the answer is this: but thirty per cent of the qualified voters of Montana elected Wheeler, and only thirty-four per cent of the voting population went to the polls. The reds and the pinks went to the polls in full force—they always do. Wheeler was elected by a noisy and radical minority, and by the passive and indifferent failure of a conservative majority to find its voice and let it be heard.

Except the inarticulate and inactive majority, conservative in thought and at heart true to their flag and country, Wheeler the detractor and destroyer, the champion of Red Russia and the political comrade of avowed apostles of bolshevism and followers of the red flag of international socialism, could not have been elected to the United States Senate.

But he was elected, along with a group of fellow reds and pinks of similar persuasion and of similar following, in the Congressional election of 1922, and the election of all of them may be traced without difficulty to the same causes.

CHAPTER XII

THE FRAME-UP GETS UNDER WAY

IN telling, in the first chapter of this book, about my trip to Mexico in the early part of 1922, and of my conversation with the communist Olson, alias Smith, alias Redfern, I said that Olson in his predictions concerning the Congressional elections of that year made particular mention of the state of Montana. I do not recall this, nor do I stress the details of events leading up to the election of Senator Wheeler, because of any desire specifically to attack Senator Wheeler. For Wheeler is no worse than his red or his pink allies. But Wheeler is the man to whom fell the star role in a drama of conspiracy which to the utter disgrace of the United States Senate, was later enacted for the purpose of breaking down the foremost bulwark of ordered government, the department of a government responsible for the suppression of lawlessness, the Federal Department of Justice.

Simultaneous with Wheeler's election to the Senate, La Follette was re-elected in Wisconsin on the Republican ticket, the Republican organization of Wisconsin having long been in the control of radicals, red and pink. That there might be no doubt whatever of La Follette's re-election, the Socialist party of the state indorsed him and took pains particularly not to put any candidates before the people who might prove embarrassing to La Follette. Frazier, of North Dakota, and Shipstead, of Minnesota, were elected to the Senate as avowed radicals. Dill, of Washington, and Ashurst, of Arizona, were elected as Democrats, but they were both pinks who received the benefit of radical support, red and pink. Brookhart, of Iowa, who was, with the possible exception of Wheeler, the nearest thing to a red who ever got a seat in the Senate, was elected as a Republican because the reds and pinks of the state had captured the party organization in Iowa. Norris, of Nebraska, like Ladd, of North Dakota, was already in. He was not up for re-election until two years later, when he was permitted to ride along in the Republican bandwagon notwithstanding endorsement of him by the radicals. Norris, of course, is no more a Republican than La Follette was or Brookhart is, or that Wheeler or Dill or Ashurst are Democrats. Norris is somewhat like Borah, though less subtle. One might better class him as a political anarchist than anything else. Both he and Borah are so "independent" they can't be hitched to any party, and can't be dragged into team work with any radical organization, although both of them incline to cooperate with the radicals rather than with anyone else —except just at election time when both can be depended upon to make use of Republican party organization for their own political success.

In the election of 1922 there were some others wearing the Republican or Democratic party label who were elected to the Senate with the frank approval and support of the conference for Progressive Political Action—the co-ordinated red and pink political organization which grew out of the action of the Socialist party on the Hillquit resolution heretofore discussed in detail. There must have been something pink about them or they could scarcely have counted on this radical support. These others were McKellar, of Tennessee; Kendrick, of Wyoming; Swanson, of Virginia; and Howell, of Nebraska.

As had been said, Wheeler was elected by thirty per cent of the qualified electorate of Montana. But only seventeen per cent went to the polls to elect Dill in Washington. Frazier was elected by thirty-five per cent; Brookhart, by twenty-nine per cent; twenty-eight per cent was all La Follette needed; and Howell required but thirty-two per cent.

The Wheeler campaign was typical of the campaigns waged in behalf of the other radicals who were elected to Congress in that 1922 election. Particular stress upon the "Get Daugherty" issue was evident wherever it was expedient to put that issue to the fore. The radical press and radical campaign orators urged the election of men to Congress who would impeach Daugherty. Benjamin C.

March, professional friend of the farmers and connected with the "labor" movement simply by the part he played in mobilizing gullible farmers when the Conference for Progressive Political Action was organized, was notably industrious in emphasizing the "importance" of electing men to Congress who were pledged to do their bit toward "getting Daugherty."

It ought, perhaps, to be noted at this point that one pro-Russian pink senator, Joseph I. France, Republican, was repudiated at the polls in the election of 1922, when Maryland expressed its preference for William Cable Bruce, a Democrat, who subsequently achieved note, as well as the bitter enmity of many of his party colleagues in the Senate, by maintaining a consistent opposition to the alliance into which the Democratic minority in the Senate was inveigled by the La Follette "radical bloc."

Immediately after the 1922 election, the radicals of both the new Senate and the new House began to mobilize for action in the sixty-eighth session of the Congress. Wheeler, the "Democrat," and Brookhart, the "Republican," at once were received into the fold of the People's Legislative Service, the radical rallying ground, by their comrades-in-service already in, Messrs. La Follette, Norris and Ladd. A love-feast of the red and pink elect was held in Washington under the auspices of the People's Legislative Service on December 3rd following the election, and that great apostle of uplift, Samuel Untermyer, of New York, whose love for the "common people" had become intensified by the vigorous methods of the Department of Justice in dealing with war profiteers, delivered an attack upon the Department of Justice and Attorney General Daugherty that was cheered to the echo. An "investigation" of the Department of Justice was urgently demanded by Mr. Untermyer, and Senator-elect Wheeler grinned with satisfaction the while Senator Brookhart, who had the day before taken the seat made vacant in the Senate by the resignation of Senator Kenyon, smiled with serene anticipation of the contemplated action called for by the chief financial prop of the People's Legislative Service, Mr. Untermyer.

It was the Sixty-seventh Congress that was then in session, however, and Senator Wheeler was not a member of it. His role at the time was largely one of getting ready for action when he should become a member of the Senate in the Sixty-eighth session. But the schooling to be had by him and Brookhart in the People's Legislative Service was kindergarten stuff to what they both were to have a few months later by first hand contact with the conduct of government as practiced by the geniuses of bolshevism themselves in Moscow, capital of Red Russia and headquarters of the world revolution for the overthrow of capitalism and capitalist government everywhere, including the United States of America.

Soon after the Congressional elections of 1922, while the government injunction suit in the railroad strike cases was pending and when the Department of Justice was being assailed by radicals in and out of Congress because of its suit and continued "persecution" of the red enemies of the nation the Borah resolution for the recognition of Soviet Russia by the United States was revived in the Senate; the "independence of the Philippines" movement received impetus from the radicals of the People's Legislative Service, assault upon the American government's "imperialist" policy of affording protection to the maintenance of orderly government in certain Latin-American portions of the western hemisphere was intensified by radicals of the same group. All of these "movements" were parallel and in strict harmony with the demands of the red radicals, as specifically set forth in the communist program and in theses from Moscow headquarters.

Senator Wheeler spent quite some time in Washington before the adjournment of the Sixty-seventh Congress, of which, as has been noted, he was not a member—being still only a Senator-elect. Senator Ladd, of North Dakota, was endeavoring to organize a group of American legislators and legislators-elect to visit Russia and obtain information first-hand about the way the reds were running their government. Whether Senator Ladd was taking the actual initiative in this move or whether he was simply pinch-hitting for Wheeler, I do not pretend to know. But the plan did not find the immediate response desired, and soon after the adjournment of the Sixty-seventh Congress, Senator Ladd announced the trip had been abandoned, and that Senator Wheeler alone would accept the hospi-

tality of the bolshevik overlords. So Senator Wheeler sailed
for Europe alone. Ditto, Brookhart. It was not so very
long, however, before Senator Ladd had found it possible
to organize his group for the visit to Russia.

The party included Senator King, of Utah. Senator
Walsh, of Montana, was invited to go, but declined. Why
Senator King was invited is something of a puzzle, unless
he was suspected of being "amenable to reason" because
he had opposed the Railroad Labor Board. I'm sure I
don't know. But it is certain the radicals lived to regret
the invitation, for Senator King learned a lot in Russia
which the others appear to have overlooked. He came
back charged with ammunition denunciatory of the soviet
regime, and frequently exploded some of it on the floor of
the United States Senate as a sort of antidote for the
singing of praises for that regime by Wheeler, Brookhart
and Ladd.

Wheeler was frankly a defender of the Russian government and its policies toward foreign governments before
he went—alone—to Moscow. His outpourings to the press
upon his return to the United States were even more
fervently pro-Russian than before he had had the advantage of first-hand investigation and entertainment at
the hands of the Moscow oligarchs. Senator Brookhart's
fondness for proposals to remake the American government along socialist lines seemed also to have been ac-
centuated by his trip abroad, but Brookhart's hobby, of
course, was government-controlled and federal-enforced
cooperatives "for the benefit of the farmers."

Soon after his return from Russia, Senator Wheeler
enlisted himself in the cause of strengthening the "radical
bloc" in the Sixty-eighth Congress, of which he was to
be a member, by going into Minnesota to campaign for
the election of Magnus Johnson, the Farmer-Labor candidate for the seat made vacant by the death of Senator
Knute Nelson. Wheeler had been elected to the Senate
as a Democrat, but he campaigned in Minnesota against
the Democratic candidate because he was not a radical
sympathizer, and for Magnus Johnson because Johnson
was. The left wing, or communist element, of the radical
movement had a strangle-hold upon the Farmer-Labor
party of Minnesota, just as it had a strangle-hold upon

the Farmer-Labor and Non-Partisan League outfits of North Dakota. Magnus Johnson was elected, but, as the reds and pinks now sadly relate it, Johnson proved to have nothing but a big voice, and was a terrific disappointment when he got into the Senate, which he did at the same time Wheeler did.

To know beyond any doubt whatever that the soviet government of Russia and the Communist (Third) Internationale are so inextricably woven together as to be identically the same thing; to know that the Comintern is the supreme authority recognized by the communists of the United States as well as everywhere else in the world; to know that all propaganda conducted directly by the communists themselves in this country and elsewhere is directed and in part financed by the Comintern; and to know that this propaganda is directed not only to the overthrow of capitalism and the existing order of government in the United States, but also to the destruction of the influence of the Christian religion, all it is necessary to do is to read the official communist publication and the authorized communist literature which is openly circulated in this country. For Senator Wheeler to have visited Russia and for him to have come into the intimate contact with the soviet authorities which he himself professes to have done, ignorance of these facts would have been impossible.

Yet, Mr. Wheeler, upon his return to the United States, directed the bulk of his attention to the job of spreading his praises of the bolshevik regime, of comparing the United States government unfavorably with it, and of making public denials that the bolsheviks were anti-Christian or that they were engaged in any sort of propaganda in the United States.

"That agitation in the United States against the recognition of the Russian Soviet government is based upon the vilest propaganda is charged by Senator Burton K. Wheeler, of Montana, in a letter to Alton B. Parker, of New York, president of the National Civic Federation," said a special dispatch from Washington to the *New York Times*, November 22, 1923.

Senator Wheeler had been making speeches and giving interviews in the support of the proposal for recognition

of Russia by the United States government, and Mr.
Parker wrote him a letter asking him to give serious consideration to certain phases of the Russian situation before committing himself to the policy of recognition.

"I am not in accord with your statement," Wheeler
said in his reply to Parker, "that in case of recognition,
the soviet consulates here would be 'nothing more than
centers for communistic propaganda, including the promotion of atheism,' I am absolutely convinced that the
Russian government, *as such* [italics mine], is not promot-
ing communism and revolution in the United States nor is
it carrying on a propaganda for atheism."

"By reason of the opportunities afforded me on my
visit to Russia to observe and study the church situation,
I feel that I am able to speak with some authority on
that subject; at least I feel that my opinions are based on
facts, and not on the *mendacious propaganda that fills the
capitalistic press* [again, italics mine], and which you so
smugly endorsed in your open letter."

Some of this "mendacious propaganda" which filled "the
capitalistic press" emanated from the United States Department of State, Charles Evans Hughes, Secretary, and
consisted of the explanations of the United States government, through the Secretary of State, of its reasons for
continued refusal to bestow recognition upon the soviet
government of Russia. The bolshevik chieftains took
official recognition of the "mendacious propaganda" by
calling upon the government of the United States for proof
of its position. Fortunately, the proof was readily at hand.

Continuing a consistent and vigorous prosecution of
plots against the American government by reds recogniz-
ing allegiance only to the generals of the world revolution
in Moscow, defying the never-ceasing efforts of reds and
pinks to intimidate them, and refusing under heavy pressure from reds, pinks and yellows to recommend the release from prisons of the more flagrant war-time seditionists, Attorney General Daugherty also had directed
investigations which made the proof against Moscow's lies
and Wheeler's defense of them available. Evidence to confirm the soundness of the American government's position
was laid before the Secretary of State in voluminous
quantities, including a full report of the Bridgeman (Michi-

gan) communist convention which had been so precipitately terminated by the raid by state officers and Department of Justice agents and the arrest of seventeen of the chief pro-soviet, anti-American conspirators.

The Sixty-eighth Congress convened in December, 1923, and the "radical bloc" began to function as per advance program immediately. An alliance with the Democratic minority was quickly brought about by Messrs. La Follette and Wheeler in cooperation with a misled Democratic leadership which saw in the alliance certain political advantages but failed to see that a petted snake grows bigger and bigger and gets not a whit tamer or less dangerous to the petter.

The "radical bloc" went to the support of the Democratic nominee for the Chairmanship of the Committee on Interstate Commerce in the Senate, and his election gave heart to the Democratic party organization. It made it easy for the radical program in some of its essential details, and there was no shortage of glee in the souls of La Follette, Wheeler, Brookhart, *et al*. The barrage of attack by the "radical bloc" and by Democrats seeing in it a way to success in the national election of 1924, impugning by wholesale the integrity of government officials—an attack studiously calculated by its red and pink instigators to destroy the faith of the American people in their government—so dazed those men in Congress, who might have been expected to meet the barrage with courage and with vigor, that nothing less than a panic among administration senators occurred.

The time was opportune for any daring scheme that might be concocted. The stage was set for the very sort of drama and intrigue that thereupon was created. No more prepared to go through with it than Keller had been with his impeachment proceedings in the House, but remembering well his pledge to the reds whose support had won him his place, Wheeler saw his great opportunity and experienced a feeling of courage in the belief that the radical coalition with the Democratic minority supplied a radical balance of power that would see him through to triumph in whatever step he might find himself obliged to take.

Wheeler introduced his resolution, attacking the Attor-

ney General and the Department of Justice and calling
for an "investigation," and the resolution went over with
a whoop and hurrah from the radical-Democrats alliance
and with a sickening sense of fear in the panicky hearts
of Republican Senators. It was terrible, this calamity! It
would break the administration! For the sake of the Republican party and the administration, the Attorney General ought to resign!

The Attorney General, not being the kind who runs
away and being clever enough to know the attack was not
a personal assault but an assault upon the administration,
upon the government itself, declined to quit under fire.
He was fully aware, even if nobody else was, that the
attack was a frame-up—not of himself, but of the administration—and that if it "got" him without a struggle,
it would only turn in another direction to "get" someone
else, and that the assault would be continued until every
official in the administration, from President down, would
find himself on the defensive.

The Senate passed the Wheeler resolution which, in
itself, provided an entirely illegal proceeding. It then
brushed rules and precedent aside by resolving to "elect"
the committee which should conduct the investigation.
With the Democratic minority allied with it and over-
whelmed with enthusiasm for the project, the "radical
bloc" succeeded in naming the committee. Brookhart, the
pro-soviet pink red, or red pink, from Iowa, was elected
Chairman, and with Wheeler, the Montana pink red, or
red pink, and Ashurst, the Arizona pink, on the committee, it was quite safely packed in favor of the
"prosecution."

The Department of Justice and its chief officer didn't
have a chance. They were foredoomed to take what came.
Wheeler had no more of a case than Keller had had, but
he had the committee packed and framed in his favor—
and that was a tolerably good beginning.

Gregory Zinoviev, chairman of the Executive Committee of the Comintern, announced through the columns of
Pravda that bolshevism had the right to "expect welcome
surprises from the American labor movement."

CHAPTER XIII

THE MEANS TO AN END

EUGENE V. DEBS, from his cell in the Atlanta Penitentiary, made the prediction, in 1920, when the Socialist party mission went to Russia, that "victory" for the proletarian cause in the United States might be expected in 1924. As noted in the previous chapter, Gregory Zinoviev in February, 1924, set forth in the *Pravda,* official organ of the Comintern, that bolshevism had the right to "expect welcome surprises from the American labor movement" in the year that had now come. Notwithstanding the factionalism and the jealousies and the difference of view as to methods of creating and maintaining a "united front" of the revolutionists, there was a "united front" so far as certain essential details were concerned. The "left wing" Reds—the communists—and the "right wing" reds—the socialists—were in complete accord, so far as the following demands were concerned:

Recognition of Soviet Russia by the United States, and the establishment of diplomatic and trade relations with Russia:

Adoption of the Plumb plan for the bolshevization of the transportation systems of the United States, as a preliminary step towards the extension of the same plan to all other industries of the country:

The greatest possible limitation of Congressional appropriations for the support of the American Army and Navy, that these defensive arms of the government might be weakened to as great an extent as possible:

Legislation providing for the independence of the Philippine Islands:

Withdrawal of all American soldiers from duty in insular territory where the United States exercised protective supervision:

111

A constitutional amendment taking from the Supreme Court the power to declare acts of Congress unconstitutional, and vesting in the Congress the power of veto over decisions of the Supreme Court:

Legislation to prevent the use of the injunction in connection with industrial disputes:

And some proceeding—impeachment or otherwise—to "get Daugherty."

The early sessions of the Sixty-eighth Congress, in which the La Follette radical bloc had become reinforced by the addition to it of Wheeler, Brookhart, Frazier, Shipstead and Dill, at once revealed that the radicals were in a position to maintain a balance of power, and the alliance between the radicals and the Democratic minority became apparent when it brought about the election of a Democratic chairman of the Senate Committee on Interstate Commerce. The election of Senator Smith of Georgia, as chairman of this committee was accomplished, however, only after a lengthy deadlock, and little was done by the Senate before the Christmas-New Year holiday recess.

The Borah resolution demanding the recognition of Russia and diplomatic and trade relations with the bolsheviki was an item in order at the beginning of the year 1924; Senator Borah was named chairman of a subcommittee of the Senate Committee on Foreign Relations to conduct public hearings on his resolution. Perhaps no effort in Borah's life has been greater than the one to bring about the recognition of Russia. The government had in its possession an abundance of records and reports showing the activities and the propaganda of the Russian reds intended to influence the recognition of the Soviet government. These documents also showed their methods and violent acts in Russia and in this country.

During the winter of 1923-24 an assistant attorney general had asserted that there was no evidence in the possession of the government of the above character. This assertion was seized upon with great glee by the reds and Russian sympathizers to dispel any opposition in this country to the recognition of the Soviet government.

To the surprise of those observing the movement, Attorney General Daugherty, on the 9th of January, 1924, issued the following statement:

> My attention has been directed to certain publicity supposed to have emanated from the Department of Justice in connection with the Communist propaganda in this country, and pertaining to that publicity already made public by the Department of State.
>
> I beg leave to call attention to the fact that some time ago, and before any publicity had been given out, I announced that the Department of Justice would give out no information in connection with this propaganda; that the Department of Justice would furnish the State Department, as it has done, all the information in its possession, and that publicity on the subject would be given out only by the State Department.
>
> Personally, I have given out nothing for publication since making this announcement, nor authorized anybody else to do so.
>
> I have only this to say further. Apart from the question of prosecutions or of technical requirements to meet the provisions of particular statutes, it should be clearly understood that the Department of Justice has abundant evidence to support the position of the Department of State with respect to Communist propaganda, directed from Moscow, in this country.

This statement was published in every newspaper in this country and extensively abroad. It created great consternation in the red ranks. At this time Senator Borah's activities against Attorney General Daugherty and his urgency upon the President to change Attorney Generals, became notoriously apparent.

Neither Attorney General Daugherty nor Secretary of State Hughes has ever explained why the Attorney General issued this statement. But it can be fairly presumed that Attorney General Daugherty would not have published the statement involving subject matter under the direction of the State Department without a specific request from the head of the Department. It is known, however, that this announcement by the Attorney General intensified the feeling of the reds and the pinks both in and out of office.

At the same time, the Teapot Dome investigation, originated by Senator La Follette, was under way with Senator Thomas J. Walsh, of Montana, as "prosecutor."

The chronology of the Senate's activities in these early weeks of the Sixty-eighth Congress is both interesting and significant. In sizing up these activities, the reader should have two things clearly in mind: First, the "demands" of the reds, both "left wing" and "right wing," as enumerated above; and, second, the radical "balance of power" and the alliance with the Democratic minority, accomplished through the help of misled and duped Democratic leadership which saw in the coalition political advantages that might be conducive to a return to power in the next national election.

The Senate on January 14th adopted the Borah resolution calling upon the State Department for copies of all reports, for six years past, on Russian affairs. On the same day, Senator La Follette introduced his bill for the granting of independence to the Philippine Islands. Although there had been a few outbursts, apropos of Teapot Dome, prior to then, it was on this day that the guns of slander and defamation were let loose in earnest—and it became almost a daily occurrence thereafter for such oratorical fire-brands as Walsh, of Montana; Heflin, Ashurst, Caraway, Robinson and others to join with the avowed radicals in the recital of rumors, falsehoods, insinuations, libels and slanders, under protection of senatorial immunity, in an effort to extract from the case of Teapot Dome support for a campaign intended to demonstrate that the entire Republican administration was rotten with crookedness and that the government was everything that the communists, socialists, pinks and yellows said it was.

Senator Ladd's resolution to investigate the regime of General Wood in the Philippines was introduced on the 17th of January. This supplied ample excuse for another fiery campaign in support of another red demand—independence for the Philippines.

The State Department, on January 21st, complied with the provisions of the Borah resolution, and supplied the Borah committee with a vast quantity of reports and documents, much of it of the most confidential character. Additional documents and reports were turned over to the committee by Secretary Hughes the next day. It should be noted in this connection that Secretary Hughes found it necessary, sometime later, to warn the Borah committee that certain of these reports must not under any circumstances be made public, for to do so would be "incompatible with the public interest."

By the 28th of January, the daily harangues in the Senate—almost wholly outside the record of the Teapot Dome committee's hearings—had developed such a state of panic among administration senators that only the feeblest sort of attempt was made by them in defense of the administration and of the government it represented. On that day—which was the same day on which President Coolidge announced steps would be taken in court to protect the government's interests both in Teapot Dome and in the Elk Hills reserves of California—Senator Walsh in the Senate demanded the resignation of Secretary of the Navy Denby, not because the Secretary had committed any crime, but because of what the Montana senator termed his "stupidity." The President's announcement was that he would nominate special counsel to represent the government, Attorney General Daugherty having recommended that such a step be taken. There are certain significant phases of the Teapot Dome case, which the reader is entitled to know, but to these I want to direct attention a little later, and shall not, therefore, go into that case further at this point.

A day later, January 29th, Senator Wheeler introduced his resolution calling upon President Coolidge to demand the resignation of Attorney General Daugherty. Senator Shipstead, on the 1st of February, delivered his initial broadside in the Senate against the Treasury Department, charging that the department, under Secretary Mellon, was engaged in a "conspiracy with big banking interests."

Ten days of oratory on the floor of the Senate, a source of intense rejoicing among the leaders of every radical group in the country—communist, socialist, "liberal"—followed, and then on the 11th of February there took place Senator Walsh's introduction of his formal resolution calling upon the President to demand the resignation of Secretary Denby. The panic among administration senators had been supplemented by voicelessness and impotence. The resolution was adopted with scarcely the sound of a struggle.

"We cannot impeach Denby," said Walsh. "There is no evidence upon which he can be impeached."

But—

"We can pass a resolution calling upon the President to compel Denby's resignation."

He could not be impeached, in other words, but he could be officially lynched, possibly, and the result would be the same.

"No official recognition can be given to the passage of the Senate resolution relative to their opinion concerning the members of the Cabinet or other officers under executive control," said President Coolidge in a Lincoln Day address.

"I do not propose," said the President, "to sacrifice any innocent man for my own welfare, nor do I propose to retain in office any unfit man for my own welfare. I shall try to maintain the functions of the government unimpaired, to act upon the evidence and the law as I find it, and to deal thoroughly and summarily with every kind of wrongdoing.

"In the meantime, such steps have been taken and are being taken as fully to protect the public interests."

Unfortunately for the future power and value of these forceful utterances, Secretary Denby—undoubtedly wearied of the impotence of Republican senators who should have been standing by their country and fighting for the preservation of the integrity of its administration —surrendered. He sent his resignation to the President on the 17th of February, and the President made the unfortunate mistake of accepting it.

In the meantime, Senator Wheeler had been endeavoring, through one liaison or another, to establish a connection between himself and one Gaston B. Means, indicted by Daugherty for bribery, at that time awaiting trial; but, at the time of this writing, convicted and serving time in the Atlanta penitentiary.* According to Means' own story of it, his wife wired him at Palm Beach, Florida, that

*For Means' detailed story of his connections with the Wheeler investigation of the Attorney General and the Department of Justice, and how these connections came about, see Appendix C.

Wheeler, "through a very close friend, had requested that
he [Means] see him [Wheeler] in connection with a contemplated 'investigation' of the Department of Justice."
Before the link between Wheeler and Means had been
welded, however, Wheeler introduced in the Senate, February 13th, his resolution providing for an investigation
of the Department of Justice. The resolution pended for
nearly a week before Wheeler took the floor of the Senate
(February 19th) and delivered a scathing arraignment of
Attorney General Daugherty, concluding his speech by
making the unprecedented proposal that a committee of
his own choosing be designated to conduct the investigation. He made known his choice of a committee with
the following names: Wheeler, of Montana; Brookhart, of
Iowa; Ashurst, of Arizona; Jones, of Washington, and
McLean of Connecticut. The idea was, of course, as was
quite obvious to anyone possessed of even average intelligence, to pack the committee for a certainty against
the Attorney General, the Department of Justice, the
administration and, in fact, against the government. For
the committee proposed by Wheeler was composed of
three pinks—of the "radical bloc"—to two Republicans,
such an alignment being possible because Brookhart had
been elected as a Republican and Wheeler and Ashurst
had been elected as Democrats. The proposal was little
short of a stroke of genius, in the minds of the misled
dupes within the Democratic minority, and for several
days these joined with the radicals in support of the
Wheeler resolution and of the personnel suggested by
Wheeler for the committee. There was almost a grave-
like silence among the distressed administration senators
on the Republican side of the Senate chamber—except
for Borah, who had been keeping the road hot between
the Capitol and the White House in his endeavor to con-
vince President Coolidge he should dismiss his Attorney
General, "for the sake of the party." And Borah, whose
love for the party is on a parity with La Follette's or
Norris's or Brookhart's, arose on the 23d of February
to deliver himself of a blast at Daugherty.

But Senator Bruce, the Maryland Democrat, who was
not unfamiliar with the aims and aspirations of the pro-
bolshevik pinks, having come out on the top side of a

campaign with one—Senator France—to get his seat in
the Senate, was one man on the Democratic side of the
chamber who detected the odor of a mouse and did not
hesitate to tell the Senate so. In a speech to the Senate
on February 29th, Senator Bruce expressed emphatic objection to Wheeler's naming the committee or to his
having his way as to how the committee should be chosen.
The Maryland Democratic senator revealed the reason for
his opposition by declaring it was because "everyone knows
that the author of the resolution [Senator Wheeler] is
closely affiliated with elements of our population [the
radical elements, of course!] which have particular reasons for objecting to Mr. Daugherty."

But Wheeler was destined to have his way. The alliance of the "radical bloc" with the Democratic minority,
combined with the pussyfooting impotence of the Republican opposition, made this inevitable. His resolution was
adopted March 1st. La Follette took a hand by making a
motion that the committee be elected, instead of appointed, as per rule, by the presiding officer of the Senate, and that the following constitute the committee:
Brookhart, chairman; Wheeler, Ashurst, Jones and
Moses, Senator Moses' name being substituted for that of
Senator McLean, originally suggested by Wheeler.

Upon the return to Washington from Palm Beach of
the aforesaid Gaston B. Means, whose fame is such now
that words or phrases intended to establish his identity
would be the quintessence of ultra-refined superfluity,
Means was brought "into conference" with Senator
Wheeler, and, to quote Means, "it was agreed that I was
to assist him in the investigation of the Attorney General and the Department of Justice in the way of furnish-
ing evidence, examination and coaching of witnesses, etc."

"Wheeler grew desperate in his efforts to find some
information on which he could base charges against the
administration and against the Department of Justice,"
swears Means, "saying that he was working with La Follette and had certain plans in view that made it imperative that he make good in connection with his public
statements as to the conditions in the Department of Justice, and that the Department of Justice be connected
with the alleged oil scandals."

Means was chary about his dealings with Wheeler. He was not so unscrupulous that his prospective role did not give him an attack of indecision. Although he had failed to get the ear of the Attorney General, himself, he sought to get it indirectly. What was going on in Wheeler's office, preliminary to the investigation, and his own assertions that "an effort was being made to frame Mr. Daugherty," were reported to the Alien Property Custodian, Col. Thomas Miller, and the information in turn was conveyed to Daugherty.

"Colonel Miller reported back," again quoting Means, "that Mr. Daugherty said that it would be impossible for anybody to successfully frame him up, and that he 'did not give a damn' about what was going on in Senator Wheeler's office. However, Colonel Miller, understanding more of the details of what was going on, requested that the efforts to secure this information not be dropped, but be reported to him, which I did, from day to day."

Attorney General Daugherty, for a mistaken position which he took with respect to the so-called investigation which Wheeler proposed should be made and which the Senate authorized to be made, is to be excused, no doubt, on the ground that the proceeding, as it developed, was entirely unprecedented. That any senator could make such a proposal as Wheeler's and succeed in carrying it out was too incomprehensible. So that, it is probable Attorney General Daugherty's was a natural mistake when he gave official recognition to the "investigation," even welcomed it; and, supposing it would be conducted in an ethical, as well as legal manner, engaged counsel to represent him before the committee. To give the action of the Senate, and subsequently, that of the Wheeler-Brookhart committee official recognition, by employing counsel to appear before it or by giving it any official attention whatever, was a blunder on the part of the Attorney General; but, as I say, undoubtedly an excusable blunder when it is remembered that so flagrant a defiance of ethical rules and law, and so palpable a repudiation of the processes prevailing in an orderly government as were exhibited by Wheeler and his predominating colleagues on the committee, never had been known in the annals of the United States.

Such a nefarious plot was impossible, thought Daugherty, and that is why he met Colonel Miller's transmission of information, supplied by Means, with impatience, and said that he "did not give a damn" about the goings on in Wheeler's office, preparatory to the start of the "investigation."

"Up until the time I took the stand in the investigation," says Means, "I understood that I should seek information as to what Senator Wheeler was going to do, and on the day before I took the stand received information that Mr. Daugherty said I could 'go to hell,' so far as he was concerned."

And that determined Means. He was severely ruffled by Daugherty, and he suffered no longer from indecision. His alliance with Wheeler was thus made secure. "Go to Hell!" He'd be damned if he would. He'd show Harry Daugherty the fruits of such rough talk!

And that accounts for the star witness against Daugherty, this arch-collaborator of Wheeler in the unscrupulous development of as conscienceless a frame-up against a man, a government and a people as it is possible to imagine in any country with the exception, perhaps, of Red Russia itself.

CHAPTER XIV

THE REIGN OF THE AMERICAN CHEKA

TESTIFYING before the Lusk Committee in New York, John A. Embry, who had been United States Consul at Omsk, Siberia, told of his experiences and of what these demonstrated to him following the ascendancy to power of the bolsheviki in Russia. At Belebei, about which Mr. Embry testified specifically, control was in the hands of liberated criminals, operating as the Central Executive Committee of that Soviet.

"Now, this executive committee," said Mr. Embry, "had under it several other bolshevik committees, or commissionaires. One of these committees was known as the Extraordinary Investigation Committee, which had the peculiar power of sentencing to death without trial."

"Now, another one of the committees," continued Mr. Embry, "was a kind of bolshevik court which attempted in some cases to give a trial; but, as we were informed by these judges, the Extraordinary Investigation Committee, which had no court and which had the power of executing people, never allowed this bolshevik court, which the bolsheviks themselves had established, to operate, and it was as if it were non-existent, and there was no justice to be had."

William Henry Chamberlin, writing in Moscow, under the date of March 10, 1924, for the *New York Nation,* Oswald Garrison Villard's pro-Russian "liberal" journal for pinks and parlor reds, detailed the trial of a bolshevik banker, Alexander Krasnoschokov, and his brother, Jacob, a Moscow building contractor, and four accused employees of the industrial bank of which the banker was president. The defendants were a long time incarcerated before they were brought to trial.

After a long interval, [wrote Chamberlin] the trial of the Krasnoschokov brothers and of the four accused bank employes opened on March 4th in the Supreme Court of the republic. (The republic referred to was the Far Eastern Republic.) The small courtroom was crowded with spectators. . . . On a raised dais at one end of the room sat the chief judge, Solz, a short, thick-set man with bushy iron-gray hair. He has a reputation for severity and belongs to the Central Control Committee of the Communist Party. He was flanked by the two assistant judges . . . .

To the left of the judges sat the prosecutor, Krilenko, a slight, wiry man, with tense face muscles and something of an air of a hunter ready to spring upon his prey. "He hates and despises everyone who is not a thoroughgoing communist," someone whispered, referring to the prosecutor.

In an indictment covering seventy-two pages, and which it took three hours to read, according to Mr. Chamberlin's story, the bank president was charged with almost every crime imaginable, including "broad living" and being enamoured of gypsies. "From a legalistic standpoint," said Mr. Chamberlin, "the indictment was a curious indictment."

The rumors that Krasnoschokov had somehow absconded with hundreds of thousands of dollars were exploded [wrote Mr. Chamberlin]. The dubious transactions with his brother's firm were shown to have involved no actual loss to the bank in the shape of nonpayment of obligations, although the prosecution claimed that the bank should have made a few thousand dollars more by charging higher interest rates—. . . . On the other hand, his administration of the bank, as was conceded by the prosecution, had been distinctly successful . . . .

The final duel between prosecution and defense centered largely about the issue whether violation of communist ethics should be considered legal offenses. "I do not defend my client as a communist," said Chlenov, Krasnoschokov's eloquent lawyer. "He did not always live up to communist standards of conduct. But you cannot try a - man in a civil court for ethical offenses. For that purpose you have a party code of discipline and party courts."

But Krilenko would not admit this distinction. "Our revolutionary justice erases the distinction between ethics and written law," he declared in a harsh, metallic voice. "Just because Krasnoschokov had such a distinguished revolutionary past, just because the party reposed so much confidence in him, his treason before the party and the soviet power is all the greater."

The prosecution won the case, of course. As Mr. Chamberlin put it, "Krasnoschokov must have known the party and its workings too well to have expected mercy after its powerful machinery of destruction had been set in motion against him."

But this was in Red Russia. The Wheeler-Brookhart committee was functioning in the United States of America. How was the chief officer of the Department of Justice of the United States to know, or why should he even suspect, that its procedure would be, as it turned out to be, so strikingly like the system in use in Russia under bolshevik rule? The conduct of the Wheeler-Brookhart committee of the United States Senate was so nearly an adaptation of the methods of the Extraordinary Investigation Committee of Belebei, described by Mr. Embry, and those of the Supreme Court of the Far Eastern Republic, revealed by Mr. Chamberlin, that the arch-concocters of the Senate committee's processes may well have learned the technique while they were being entertained and instructed as to the idealistic beauties of the bolshevik system by the soviet chiefs in Moscow.

The committee of the Senate which began on the 12th of March, 1924, its "investigation" of the Attorney General and the Department of Justice under his administrations, was a triumvirate of radicals, and the triumvirate remained in indisputable control throughout. The chairman was Brookhart, and the other two were Wheeler and Ashurst. It is true there were two other members of the committee—Senators Moses, of New Hampshire, and Jones, of Washington—but these members (and nobody realized this more than they after the proceeding got under way) might just as well have been totally non-existent.

The radical triumvirate were judges and jury in all instances, with one of them as "prosecutor," and they would brook no interference nor tolerate any counsel or

suggestion, however mild or courteous, that did not fit in
unqualifiedly with their program and their determination
to convict the Attorney General and the Department of
Justice and all of his and its works. From a legalistic
standpoint, to paraphrase Mr. Chamberlin's description of
the Krasnoschokov indictment, the proceeding was not
simply curious—it was a crime, and all the worse crime
by reason of the fact that it could be and was put into
effect in the capital of the nation and by the authority of
the Senate of the United States. Both as to method of
procedure and as to demeanor in his conduct of the case,
Wheeler may as well have borne the name of Krilenko.

At the outset of the first session of the committee, Paul
Howland, of counsel for the Attorney General, sought
to make a preliminary statement, in accordance with the
custom in similar instances. The futility of the Attorney
General's being represented by counsel before the committee became immediately apparent.

"I move that we proceed with the hearing without any
statement by counsel," said Wheeler, after some colloquy.
And Ashurst seconded the motion.

"I vote for the representatives of the Attorney General
to be heard," said Senator Jones.

"I vote no on the motion by the Senator from Montana," said Senator Moses.

"I vote aye," came from Ashurst, and Brookhart, not-
ing his own vote and Wheeler's in support of the motion,
said: "It is the decision of the committee that we will
not hear you for an opening statement."

And such invariably was the vote at every stage of the
proceedings for the weeks that followed whenever any
move whatever was attempted on the part of the Attorney General's counsel to make of the hearing a two-sided
rather than an endlessly one-sided inquisition.

"Now, Mr. Chairman," said Howland, "as a matter of
right I request this—not as a privilege, as was my first
request, but as a matter of right, that the representatives
of a coordinate branch of the government, now under
investigation by this Senate committee, be permitted to
plead to the resolution. I demand that as a matter of
right before this investigation is begun."

"The Attorney General," retorted Brookhart, "is not a

coordinate branch of the government; only the President is. We are not going to proceed like we were in a technical trial. This is a Senate investigation."

"If we are not to be permitted to make a statement, I submit the request that we may have the statement we would make printed as a part of your proceedings," said the other defense attorney, former Senator Chamberlain.

"You may submit the statement, and we will pass on it," was Brookhart's significant reply.

More colloquy, and two or three votes, with the line-up noted above, but at the conclusion of the day's proceedings the statement was read by Wheeler and passed by him as containing nothing calling for his "censorship."

But Senator Ashurst let counsel for the Attorney General know the point to which they would be allowed to go when Mr. Howland questioned the competence of the first witness, Roxie Stinson, to relate stories about and alleged statements of a dead man, Jess Smith.

"Let the matter be understood," said the Arizona senator. "Counsel for Attorney General Daugherty are rendering their client very poor service if they attempt to interpose here technical objections." And so forth.

"And they will certainly not get anywhere by trying to bulldoze somebody on this committee," was Wheeler's angry interposition.

"No; do not misunderstand me," said Howland. "I am not trying——"

"I do not misunderstand you," Wheeler retorted, proceeding with an angry arraignment of the Attorney General's lawyers.

Both Howland and Chamberlain, whose attitude had been of exceeding and studied dignity, were taken completely aback. Ashurst hurled hotly at them that the committee expected from them "a large amount of silence" and Wheeler reminded them they were present "by the courtesy of the committee."

The protests of Senators Moses and Jones were in vain, as were sundry and all of their subsequent protests against the strong arm methods of the triumvirate that prevailed from the start to the finish of the "investigation." Endeavoring, as they did, to meet insults and intimidations with soft words, these two Senators might just as well have remained silent. And striving, as they did, to do battle against fire and conscienceless intrigue by the practice of their profession according to law and the ethical rules they had learned in the law colleges and the courts, Messrs. Howland and Chamberlain might just as well have conserved their energies and taken a vacation, far, far away.

The term perjury, applied to the so-called testimony, is perhaps technically from a legal stand-point improperly used for the reason, that, as held by Judge Cochran, the committee had no jurisdiction or authority to make the investigation nor to administer an oath. And witnesses were advised by those working for the committee that these two elements especially being necessary to constitute perjury under the law and being absent, together with other elements to constitute perjury, they were immune from prosecution for that offense. This is the reason why the witnesses at the time were not prosecuted for perjury and certain other persons were not prosecuted for subordination of perjury.

"The testimony given before the Wheeler committee by Roxie Stinson, R. Momand, myself and the majority of the other witnesses," Gaston B. Means has since confessed, "was nothing but a tissue of lies put in the mouths of these witnesses by Senator Wheeler primarily to confound and discredit the Department of Justice and the administration. These witnesses and myself were persuaded to make these false statements by Senator Wheeler under threats of indictment in some cases and by promises of gain and aid in others."

That it was in truth a riot of perjury and a parade of criminals, convicts, ex-convicts and convicts-to-be that constituted the backbone of the "prosecution" in this flagrantly lawless proceeding before a red-inspired and a radical-controlled committee of the United States Senate, ought to have been obvious to any unprejudiced observer giving the case the test of analytical scrutiny; and that Wheeler, daring and cunning though he is, could have succeeded with it as he did is above and beyond the realm of understanding.

There were men, Americans, believers in law and order, optimists as to the welfare of the nation, lovers of the flag and born with the impulse to fight for the defense and preservation of their country at the slightest sign of peril—there were men like this who began to ask, after the Wheeler-Brookhart inquisition had proceeded but a short way: Where are the defenders of the American Constitution in the forum of the nation, the Congress of the United States? Where are the champions of law and order in the Senate? Have none but cowards been elected to sit in that body? Are there none there but the detractors and the defamers, and those who have been cowed into a state of frightened silence, driven to cover by the mobocracy which seems to have seized the power of control in the American Congress?

"The great Senate of the United States has fallen to a new level in these days," was the accurate conclusion reached by a former Congressman from Iowa, Albert W. Jefferis. "The Constitution used to be referred to and adhered to within its confines with just and honorable pride. It is so thought of no longer. The order of the day during this Wheeler, Walsh, Heflin and Robinson era is to belittle the House of Representatives, usurp its functions and powers, and dominate and dictate, if possible, the powers and functions of the executive department and the judiciary. The marvelous leadership of this Wheeler from Montana gives notice to the thinking people of the nation that there is work to be done by them if they are to preserve and protect the Constitution which has guided the nation so well through all its years of progress. . . . The overthrow of the Constitution was once tried by rebellion and war. That effort failed. Whether this latter method now being tried in the Senate shall be successful, the future only can tell."

Under the influence of reds and pinks, and with a radical-Democratic alliance, purposefully proposed by the radicals, blindly entered into by the Democrats, the controlling forces of the Senate had deliberately and quite frankly repudiated the Constitution, and were able to do so because the opposition was either buffaloed or scared to death.

"This is not the time to waste the time of the Senate talking about the Magna Charta and the Constitution," were the sneering words of Senator Robinson of Arkansas.

Lawlessness was in the very spirit of the Senate, and if explanation of how the Wheeler-Brookhart-Ashurst triumvirate succeeded with everything except murder is needed, it is to be found in that spirit and the impotency of Republican leadership to combat it and overthrow it.

CHAPTER XV

A TALE FROM THE TOMB

A GOOD many years ago there was an orphan boy in Washington Courthouse, Ohio, in whose welfare the Daugherty boys—Harry and Mal—interested themselves. His name was Jess W. Smith. It was the Daugherty boys who financed young Jess and set him up in the mercantile business. He was quite adept at the business, made a go of it in that small Ohio town, paid off his debts to Harry and Mal, made more money, accumulated a small fortune, and became attached to the Daugherty boys with a devotion almost dog-like in its intensity.

Smith became enamoured of a young woman bearing the name of Roxie Stinson. She was striking, as to looks, at that time, and had a way with her that was fascinating to young Jess beyond all resisting. He fell in love with her and she enjoyed to the uttermost her triumph of "landing" the prosperous young merchant. So Jess and Roxie were married.

Time passed, and it developed that the Jess Smith household was none too tranquil. Social evenings in it became fewer, fewer people accepted invitations to play at cards, and the common report was that Roxie's temper was incompatible with social contacts. Jess lamented that so many of his personal friends shied at his hospitality and blamed it on his wife's proclivity for insulting them by the use of an uncontrollable tongue. Anyway, they agreed to disagree, and there was a divorce, Mrs. Smith reclaiming her maiden name.

Jess went to live elsewhere. But he never recovered from his infatuation for his somewhat tempestuous wife, and evidently regretted the untying of the matrimonial knot. For Roxie there appeared to be no such regrets, for she had negotiated a settlement with Jess that kept the wolf at a very respectable distance from her door-step, and her freedom gave her the privilege, in addition, of "living her own life" in the way she wished to live it. She began to have other men friends, and the variety of them was a puzzle to Jess. To hear of it aroused Jess' jealousy beyond endurance. He went to see Roxie, and somehow or other made a most remarkable truce with her. Thereafter he became her most intimate friend, and his attentions and standing in the household became very much the same as they had been before the legal bonds of matrimony had been duly and judicially severed.

But Jess, if the almost unanimous conclusion of the citizenry of Washington Courthouse is worthy of belief, did not cut out all the rest of the men on Roxie's string, and he had to remain content with being the leading man and the one upon whose financial resources his ex-wife exercised a foremost lien. The arrangement was not exactly according to Hoyle in the eyes of Washington Courthouse; but, the world being more or less perverse, in some respects, Jess seemed to be the object of pity rather than contempt.

Jess Smith never flagged in his canine devotion to the Daugherty boys, nor did he ever relax to any notable extent in his attention to Roxie. To any and all advice to "put her out of his life" and stop her endless access to his money he turned a deaf ear. It was the one sub-ject, in fact, about which he could work up a real case of indignation against the Daugherty boys, whose protégé he had been and whose fondness for him, inexplicable as it may have seemed to many, was interminably enduring.

It must be remembered that Smith had been a sort of executive secretary to Mr. Daugherty throughout the en-tire campaign which was managed solely by Mr. Daugh-erty and which resulted in the nomination of Senator Harding for President and also during the campaign which resulted in the election of Harding and Coolidge.

These services of Smith to Mr. Daugherty were con-tinuous and the duties so numerous that Smith lived with him most of the time, as Mrs. Daugherty, long an invalid, was compelled to spend practically all of her time in hospitals.

When Mr. Daugherty came to Washington as the Attorney General in the cabinet of President Harding, he brought Jess along to serve as a sort of unofficial intermediary between the Attorney General's office and the pests and ax-grinders that invariably hover about that office, as they do every other office of a government official in the city of Washington. He had found Jess serviceable, in this capacity, during political campaigns, and Jess had a knack of knowing Mr. Daugherty's desires and of being able to perform the duties of a lackey without appearing to be a lackey and without being himself conscious that he was one. Also, here might be one way to get Jess "out from under" the ever-present proprietorship of Roxie. Jess was for bringing Roxie along to Washington, to be sure, but Mr. Daugherty has a very emphatic way of saying "No!" and the suggestion all but died a-borning on Jess Smith's lips.

So Jess came to Washington and left Roxie behind, much to that lady's chagrin. He never had any official capacity or connection at the Department of Justice, and performed the duty as buffer to the varied assortment of visitors with axes to be ground who considered Mr. Daugherty to be the real spokesman for President Harding; ran personal errands for Mr. Daugherty; was companionable when the Attorney General wanted company and kept his place when the Attorney General did not want company. He was, in Mr. Daugherty's opinion at any rate, loyal to his benefactor and friend. But he was by no means a confidant—for Mr. Daugherty knew him too well to let him in on any state or official secrets. For he was a notorious gossip, had a considerable feeling of his own importance, strutted his stuff as only a nine o'clock fellow in a midnight town like Washington, D. C., can do, and while it would scarcely be just to characterize him as a man deliberately careless with the truth, it cannot be denied that his imagination would have served him well had he been skilled in the field of literature. I can offer no testimony as to the honesty of Jess Smith. But if you ask people who knew him they will tell you most emphatically that they believe he was honest.

Asked about the position of Jess Smith at the Department of Justice, Mrs. Mabel Walker Willebrandt testified before the Extraordinary Investigation Committee—

the Wheeler-Brookhart-Ashurst committee of the senate
—that Jess was "a sort of glorified personal servant" to
the Attorney General. It would be more accurate to say,
perhaps, that he was a *self*-glorified personal servant.
And the most conspicuous outlet for his self-glorification
was, by the very nature of things, the feminine object of
his ever-burning infatuation—Roxie Stinson. Jess was the
sort of chap who, if he met some prominent man
while enacting his role as buffer for the Attorney General, delighted in feeding Roxie, to impress her with his
own importance, with the sort of talk that would give the
impression, perhaps without actually saying so, that the
man was a personal friend who called him "Jess, old
boy," and whom he called "Tom," "Dick," or "Harry."
And, in turn, Roxie was adept enough at the same game
of self-glorification to have no trouble at all in convincing
herself that she was herself on intimate social terms with
all the big men in the Harding administration, from the
President down.

Jess Smith's career came to an end in Washington on
the 30th of May, 1923. He died from a bullet wound,
self-inflicted. The suicide occurred in the apartments of
the Attorney General. The Attorney General was absent
at the time. Smith had been suffering from diabetes for
a long time, and for many months he had suffered anguish
from the effects of this disease and complications that
had developed in connection with it. His afflictions became
worse after an operation he underwent about a year before his death. That he was "losing his grip" on himself was apparent to the Attorney General and to all others who had a friendly interest in Smith, but none
suspected that he might end his own life. He did not
seem to be the type that commits suicide. But he did,
and the only honest explanation of it in the face of
known facts is that he preferred death to continued physical suffering.

The suicide left a will. That he should leave substantial shares of his little fortune to those who had been his
benefactors in early days and his most nearly kin-like
friends in his last days, was entirely natural. It was
not strange that he should appoint Mal Daugherty his
administrator inasmuch as a few months before Mal

Daugherty had closed out his store business for him in Washington Courthouse.

Two events were saddening to Roxie Stinson—Jess Smith's death was one, and the other was the revelation of the contents of Jess Smith's will. Of the two, the latter, in all fairness, may be said to have been the more tragic. That her hold upon Jess was not, as she had thought, strong enough to make her the sole beneficiary in his will, was a keen disappointment to Roxie. The Daughertys stood none too well with her to begin with, but now she held them strictly to account for being such an influence in the life of Jess Smith that he should leave them anything by his will, and not leave her everything. Her hatred of the Daughertys was, and is, undeniable. She was convinced in her own mind that, but for the Daughertys, she would have got what Jess Smith left at death in its entirety.

Roxie had letters from Jess Smith by the bale. He was a prolific correspondent. Letter-writing is one of the most notable accomplishments of gossips, and as a gossip Jess Smith was no exception to the rule. It is a truth well known to students of the mental processes of mankind that the letters of a gossip manifest one glaring characteristic. This is the characteristic of conveying ideas that may be subject to more than one interpretation. The gossip says something in a cryptic and knowing manner and leaves it to the other fellow to give it the significance that supplies the most kick.

A bright idea struck the mind of Roxie Stinson close to the spot wherein reposed the idea that, but for the Daugherty brothers, she would have had enough from the provisions of Jess Smith's will to have justified her wearing mourning for him the rest of her life. She had benefitted plentifully from Jess Smith during his lifetime because he suffered from an infatuation for her.

Al Fink, broker and promoter, was in Cleveland, Ohio, on the 18th of February, 1924, to start a campaign for the sale of securities of the Ideal Tire & Rubber Corporation. He found himself short of funds adequate to the campaign and was in something of a quandary as to what to do about it.

A bright idea came to Mr. Fink's rescue also. As he

confesses it now, in an affidavit * which is one of the
appendices of this book, he recalled having read in the
papers that an old sweetheart of his, Roxie Stinson, had
become an heiress by the will of one Jess Smith, and it
occurred to him that she might be good for a stake. He
got in touch with her by telephone, and induced her to
join him in Cleveland. I quote from Fink's affidavit:

> We went to the Hotel Hollenden, where we regis-
> tered as man and wife, under the fictitious name of A.L.
> French and wife of Pittsburgh, Pennsylvania," So upon
> going to Room 452, which was assigned to us, I im-
> mediately started to talk to her about my business prop-
> osition, when she interrupted and said, "I have a far
> bigger deal on right now and you ought to come in on
> it." I asked her what it was and she said she was being
> defrauded out of her portion of Jess Smith's estate by
> Harry Daugherty, and that she wanted revenge upon
> Daugherty because he refused to recognize her or to
> allow Jess Smith to have her in Washington during the
> time Daugherty was in office, and that she was prepared,
> if necessary, to invent stories and piece stories together
> that would incriminate Daughtery to such an extent that
> he would be forced to resign from office; also that she
> expected to sell her story for $150,000, which she felt
> she was entitled to, and she asked me if I would get
> some strong Democrat to purchase her story, which she
> concocted, and also pay her $150,000.*

As a further indication of her desire to exact more
money from the Jess Smith estate than was bequeathed
to her under the terms of the will, Roxie has since sued
Mal Daugherty, as the executor of the estate itself, for
an additional amount of more than eleven thousand dollars. Two courts have already heard this case and both
promptly decided against her.

The affidavit of Fink is a voluminous one, and is available in full as an appendix to this book if the reader
desires to read it, but many of the details may be passed
over here as not of great importance to the present narrative of more important events. It is sufficient to say
that Roxie's threats did not scare the Daughertys, who

*See Appendix D, Page 1.
*See appendix F for Henry O. Ellis' statement.

were not the kind to be frightened, and Roxie was informed politely but firmly that she could take her letters and her story and go to the devil. By a devious way, she went, instead, to Senator Burton K. Wheeler of Montana.

From the time of Fink's meeting with Roxie Stinson in Cleveland, a couple of weeks had elapsed when Henry Stern, a lawyer of Buffalo, New York, retained by Fink when he had run somewhat afoul the law at Rochester, New York, sent for Fink. Fink had apprised Stern of his adventure in Cleveland. Stern, it appears, among his other law business attachments, had become connected somehow with the Extraordinary Investigation Committee of the United States Senate. It is Fink's charge that Stern, holding over him the shadow of serious legal difficulties if he didn't, and of more favorable consequences if he did, induced him to make a trip with Stern to Washington.

It was through Fink, therefore, that Wheeler accomplished his connection with the woman who hated Attorney General Daugherty; and, fed by her hatred and her desire for money, went upon the witness stand in Washington to lay the groundwork for the colossal frame-up of perjury, insinuations, innuendoes, twisted truths and misinterpreted facts by which the Attorney General was to be driven from office, the Department of Justice demoralized, the integrity of the government impugned, and the reputations of public men crucified without stint and without conscience.

Wheeler took Fink and the lawyer, Stern, with him to Columbus, Ohio, to serve Roxie with a subpoena and induce her to come to Washington to tell her yarn. "After boarding the train and starting for Washington," says Fink's affidavit, "Wheeler spent several hours with her talking. The following morning Wheeler came back to the smoking compartment and said, 'At last I have gotten this girl to testify the way I want her to, and I had better get her right before the committee before she gets a change of heart.' He said, 'You and Stern go to the hotel and then come over to Room 410 Senate Office Building, and we will start the hearings at once.' The hearings started that morning."

Fink became alarmed over the possibility of trouble

with his wife, if the episode of the Cleveland hotel came out, and it is his story that Roxie, after her initial testimony, was kept off the stand for several days to allow time for Wheeler to "fix it" with Fink's wife. *

The testimony of Roxie Stinson was vast in quantity, but it will be remembered clearly, no doubt, by those who followed it, that virtually all of it rested upon her and Wheeler's interpretations of expressions in Jess Smith's gossipy letters and upon what she invariably referred to as information and events which the dead Jess Smith "told her about." Jess said this, and Jess told her that, she told the committee, but at no time did she testify to anything that she herself knew, and the tale in all its details and ramifications was a tale from the tomb—a dead man's tale, which the dead man could not be asked about—retold with all its twisted embellishments in the language of a vindictive woman who would hesitate at nothing.

On the witness stand she was often the clever actress, and particularly was this the case when asked about "The Little Green House on K Street." It was an arresting line, an attractive phrase, daubed with romance and painted with mystery. Conan Doyle could not have conceived a more fascinating scene for plots, intrigue and devilments to engage the attention of his great detective, Sherlock Holmes. Asked about the K Street house, Roxie was exceedingly demure.

"What, if anything, do you know with reference to the K Street house?" Wheeler asked her.

"I would rather not answer," she replied, assuming an attitude of shame and almost tearful distress that she should be obliged to go into matters so terrible as those associated with the "Little Green House on K Street."

For some little time, she "would rather not answer," but upon being duly pressed, she did answer.

The cue came from Wheeler as follows:

"You know that Mr. Smith and the Attorney General met at the K Street house on a number of occasions?"

---

*Very enlightening supplementary affidavits of Mrs. Fink, Fink's Secretary, Howard Edmonds, Gaston Lecollier and Arthur L. Brent are to be found in Appendix D.

"I don't mind saying that," was her reply. "I WAS TOLD SO BY MR. SMITH."

"Do you know the number of the house?" inquired Senator Moses.

"No. I never saw it in my life."

And the fact of the matter is, she had never even heard of it in her life—until she had come to Washington and had worked out, with Wheeler, Gaston Means and others, according to Means' affidavit, the details of the yarn she was to recite upon the witness stand.

The further fact of the matter is, "The Little Green House on K Street" was a melodramatic myth, so far as its relationship to the Attorney General and the Department of Justice was concerned. Daugherty was never in it in his life, and never saw it in his life either inside or outside.

At one stage of the proceedings, Senator Jones of Washington, had his attentions arrested and his curiosity aroused by the fact that Roxie, in the course of her testimony, was reading her replies from a typewritten memorandum. It seemed just a trifle out of the ordinary, in the mind of Senator Jones, and he was prompted to gratify his curiosity, if it were possible to do so.

"You are apparently reading from a typewritten memorandum?" the senator from Washington interposed.

"Yes, sir."

"When did you make that?"

"This was made by my companion here in Washington, from notes that I had made."

"Since you came down here?"

"The notes were made at my home, at the time."

"When were the notes made?"

"On the 23d of February."

"That is, the next day after you had been up to Cleveland?"

"No; I was in Cleveland—I returned on the 21st. . . . Then on Saturday is when I made my notes, through the advice of a friend; just a personal friend whom I had told about the Cleveland frame-up (Roxie's version of it) only. It was on that advice."

"Have you those notes now?"

"No, sir; I have not; unless—I have destroyed them—

you see, there was someone sent as a personal envoy from me to get my letters and general correspondence and everything from my home which I did not bring with me."

"You brought those notes down here with you?"

"I did not."

"You had them here, may I ask?" put in Senator Wheeler, in an effort to rescue her from a bit of thin ice.

"I understood you to say you had them typed by your friend here—by your companion here, when you came down here in response to the subpoena," said Jones.

"Yes, sir."

"Then of course you must have had the notes?"

"Yes. But in the meantime I did not bring those notes with me; they were sent for and brought to me."

"Were they destroyed?"

"I think I tore them up, after I elaborated these. I will look at the hotel—"

"I wish you would."

"These are absolutely—I would almost say word for word."

"I would like very much to see those notes," Senator Jones persisted.

"Are they important?"

"Yes."

"They are only just items—just as this is."

"I know. They are very important to my mind; and I wish you would look and see if you can find them."

"I shall look; but I doubt that."

"When did you make these notes?" asked Wheeler.

"Twenty-third day of February."

"Were the notes in pencil or ink?" asked Senator Moses.

"Pencil."

"Did anybody suggest that they be typewritten?"

"No; I just asked my companion here to do this for me, *because I can not read my own writing very well.*"

"As a matter of fact," put in Wheeler apprehensively, "you had never shown those notes to me, either?"

"No; nobody has seen them."

"You had never shown even the statement you had typewritten to me?" coached Wheeler.

"No, sir."

"Had anybody ever seen those notes before you had them typewritten?" Senator Moses enquired.

"No sir, I do not discuss——"

"Except your companion, of course? I suppose she saw them, or did you read them to her?"

"I read them off."

"She did not examine them herself?"

"I read them off. I read this off, and she wrote it from my reading. That was the first time I had ever dictated anything in my life."

The "companion" to whom she referred was Wheeler's sister, Mrs. Mitchell, in Wheeler's employ as a confidential stenographer. It is probably superfluous to say that the "notes" were never produced, and the curiosity of both Senators Jones and Moses concerning them was never adequately satisfied.

Roxie Stinson's recital of a highly fantastic tale from a dead man's grave constituted the groundwork for the entire case built up for the political assassination of Attorney General Daugherty and for the demoralization of the law-enforcing branch of the federal government. Its only corroboration came from the equally fantastic tales of Gaston B. Means, who was being kept out of jail by Wheeler and the Extraordinary Investigation Committee, and from an array of underworld characters, confidence game operators and discharged employes of the Department of Justice, coached for their parts by Means and Wheeler, and influenced to go through with them by threats of dire punishment in some instances and promises of financial or other rewards in others.

The rebellion of Al Fink against going through with his part of the plot, as detailed by himself under the oath of an affidavit, appears to have been a source of much embarrassment and annoyance to Wheeler, judging from the allegations of a corroborating affidavit made and sworn to by Florence Fink, Al's wife:

H. S. Edmonds, my husband's secretary advised me that he was in receipt of a telegram from Washington sent on a government "frank" and signed "Henry" telling him to bring me at once to Washington, that my husband was desperately in need of me.

Mr. Edmonds and I arrived in Washington Friday morning, and I was led to Senator Burton K. Wheeler's office, Room 440, Senate Office Building. Upon meeting him, he asked me to come into his private office. He appeared very much worried and said to me in substance, "Mrs. Fink, your husband is a very foolish man. He is holding up the committee hearings by threatening to refute Roxie Stinson's testimony. Now, I want you to be sensible and tell him that he has to allow her to continue to testify. He is going to be given a splendid appointment in Buffalo as Collector of Internal Revenue if he does what I want him to do. I am also going to make Mr. Stern a federal judge if we are able to make Daugherty resign. You should not be jealous over this woman, and you should prevent your husband from throwing away this opportunity. Mr. Stern tells me that unless you urge him to help us 'get' Daugherty, he will destroy the evidence that will exonerate your husband in the case in which he is representing him in Rochester. So you see, little girl, it is up to you to do this to save your husband."

By this time I was crying, and I finally promised Senator Wheeler that I would not desert my husband because of this episode with this woman.

Senator Wheeler then took my husband and me back into his office and continued to explain to us how valuable it would be to us if we would consent to join him in his 'frame-up' of Daugherty. As a further inducement he told me that he was raising a sum of money among the Democratic senators who were his friends for the purpose of playing the stock market as soon as he learned, as he would in advance, that Daugherty would resign; that he intended to reimburse Miss Stinson to the extent of twenty-five per cent of this fund to make up for the $150,000 that she had originally demanded for her story. Senator Wheeler said that he would send my husband to New York to place this money, and that he would receive a share of the profits for himself."

Whether or not Roxie Stinson, the materialistic medium of the Senate seance, whose voice was the voice of vengeance and greed for gain pretending to speak from the tomb of the dead, ever got the twenty-five per cent, or any other per cent, the writer of these pages does not profess to know, and ventures not to suspect. But Al Fink appears to be confident that he, for one, never got his, and it is common report that a number of the crooks and con men who took the witness stand to add zest, if not truth, to Roxie's yarn have been whistling in vain for theirs. If this be true, sad though it be for them, they are irretrievably out of luck, for somehow or other the scurvy trick of cheating cheaters is not of itself a crime under the laws of the United States.

CHAPTER XVI

THE BANK THAT COULDN'T BE WRECKED

"No rogue e'er felt the halter draw,
With good opinion of the law."

EVERY I. W. W., every communist, every bolshevik, every left-wing socialist, every rioter, every bootlegger, every bootlegger's source of supply and every profiteering war contractor, therefore, was at one with every pink, every right-wing red, every short-sighted Democrat and every yellow Republican in giving the appearance of unanimity to the assault upon the Federal Department of Justice and the demand for the resignation of the head of that department, Attorney General Daugherty.

The hearings of the Wheeler-Brookhart-Ashurst Extraordinary Investigation Committee were attended daily by a throng of disciples of sundry subversive movements, applauding every insult to the legal representatives of the Attorney General and every breath of defamatory gossip and self-convicted perjury, audibly admiring the grim and melodramatic poses of Senator Wheeler, hissing every witness with a good word for the government or the Attorney General, and booing every futile attempt of counsel for the accused to obtain a modicum of consideration for the legal rights of their client.

To insure forcible ejection from the confines of the committee room one had only to let himself be heard giving expression to comment adverse to the tactics of the committee or in deprecation of the testimony of the particular crook or gossip-monger who chanced at the time to be undergoing the leading and suggestive examination by the Krilenko-like "prosecutor," Wheeler.

The timidity and impotence of intimidated and panic-stricken administration senators and congressmen lent zest to the operations of the triumvirate on the committee, pep to their satellite cheer-leaders, and daring to the underworld characters upon whom they chiefly depended. Through them they made the record of their case a daily front page news source for the radical, the yellow and the "framed" press of the country. Never was so much pressure brought to bear upon a President for the accomplishment of an end than that which was brought to bear upon President Coolidge. From the foes of the administration, and particularly from those foes who were conscious of the real motives behind the operations of the committee, there were sent messages to the White House and messages to dupes who would see to their transmission to the ears of the President, conveying the alternative of the Attorney General's resignation or of untoward consequences to the administration, even to the President himself. To supplement these, there was a procession of frightened Republican politicians, both in the Senate and out of it, seeking the ear of the President to urge upon him the political necessity of asking for the resignation of his Attorney General. They went singly and in delegations, and they pleaded individually and in chorus.

The courage of the President was of high order. His stubbornness was exasperating. It appeared that he was immovable. But the time came when he could stand up under the pressure no longer—and he yielded.

The Extraordinary Investigation Committee sent to the Attorney General a demand upon him for a wholesale production of the confidential files of the Department of Justice and its secret service division, the Bureau of Investigation. The Attorney General was confident he knew the purpose of this demand. He was convinced that it was sought for no reason except to supply ammunition for the cause of red radicalism and to reveal to the leaders of various subversive movements just what the government knew about their intrigues against the government. He refused, therefore, to comply with the demand, apprising President Coolidge of his conviction that to do so would be "incompatible with the public interest."

The President had yielded. He found it impossible to withstand the pressure of argument within his party and of intimidation from without. He made of this incident the opportunity to request the resignation of Daugherty. The request was complied with. Both the request and the compliance with it were mistakes—but both, doubtless, excusable, since no man can be right always.

So they "got" Daugherty in this way, and the reds of Moscow and Montana and the pink bollweevils of American politics triumphed. And in their triumph, they proceeded to do precisely what Daugherty, and the scant few with courage sufficient to confess their agreement with him and his position, said they would do. They did not let up on the Department of Justice—and have not let up on it yet—since it was the primary objective, and not any individual directing head of it. But in addition they expanded the assault upon the administration and government in other directions.

They had "got" Denby without a struggle. They had now "got" Daugherty after an arduous and bitter battle. So next in order was the job of "getting" whoever might in any sense be vulnerable. Senator McKellar of Tennessee, elected with the endorsement and support of the radical Conference for Progressive Political Action, training his guns upon the Department of the Treasury, charged that Secretary Mellon was holding his office illegally, and demanded his resignation from the Cabinet.

The Teapot Dome investigation committee began emulating the tactics of the Wheeler-Brookhart-Ashurst committee by issuing subpoenas for witnesses of the same character, calling Al Jennings, ex-train robber, to the stand to recite an impossible yarn about "intrigues" behind the nomination and election of President Harding and to give publicity to other so-called "evidence" having no more pertinence to the Teapot Dome inquiry than Hans Christian Andersen's fairy tales have to a presidential election in Honduras. Al Jennings' tale also came from the tomb, the dead man in this case being Jake Hamon of Oklahoma, who had come to his death by a gun in the hands of a woman. It was planned that the slayer of Hamon be brought to Washington from California to testify, also, but it appears she didn't know or suspect anything of a sufficiently scandalous import, and the project was abandoned.

Senator Dill, the radical Democrat from Washington,

elected with the endorsement and support of the Conference for Progressive Political Action, delivered a broadside against the assistant Secretary of the Navy, Theodore Roosevelt, and introduced a resolution demanding his resignation.

With the Senate galleries packed with the same crowd that was making the sessions of the Extraordinary Investigation Committee such a success as a combination melodrama and burlesque show, the Heflin-Caraway-Robinson-Stanley-Norris group of senatorial scandalmongers made the atmosphere in the Senate chamber blue and putrid with their daily amplifications of and speculations upon what passed for evidence before the Extraordinary Investigation Committee and other investigation committees of Congress, defaming and libeling, under the cloak of senatorial immunity, every official of the government whose name came into mind, from President Coolidge down to the lowliest. Heflin was the Democratic senator from Alabama, who, belaboring the Department of Justice for its reputed shortcomings and alleged failure to prosecute criminals, neglected to explain the hook or crook by which he, some years previously, had escaped prosecution for an unjustified and deadly assault upon a negro. Heflin had broken into print, in this connection, by drawing a gun, shooting and seriously wounding a negro passenger on a trolley car in Washington, shooting also a white pedestrian, causing a panic among the passengers and endangering the lives of men, women and children who were riding in the car at the time of the assault. Caraway was the Arkansas senator upon whom similar notoriety had fallen by reason of a brutal and inexcusable assault upon a disabled veteran of the World War, the weapon used in this instance being an umbrella. And Robinson, the fire-eating Democratic minority leader, is recalled by the membership of a golf club near the capital of the nation for another physical assault, the victim being a member of the club who was not playing his game fast enough to suit the pace of the over-energetic dignitary of the United States Senate who was trailing him.

The radical press of the country, supplied with "news" by the Federated Press, a propaganda association controlled by a combination of communists and radicals of less lurid hue, and the yellow press, to say nothing of misled newspapers whose editors were too dull to comprehend the frame-up against their own reputations for truth and fairness, printed columns, pages, sections, extras and supplements of incredible scandal and palpable perjury and falsehood, subversive to the orderly processes of the courts and the government's executive departments. The "news" from Washington, deleted or colored according to requirements necessary to give it the most sensational character and at the same time give it a semblance of credibility, was sent to the newspapers and news associations by a horde of correspondents, some of them deluded, some of them in conscious sympathy with radicalism and others drawing pay from sources with special interest in the success of the campaign of calumny, demoralization and destruction, and what these correspondents were fed upon was intended to and did have a tendency to break down the faith of the American people in their government. Most of these correspondents, except perhaps the deliberately corrupted ones, have since experienced a consciousness of their part in the frame-up of their own employers, and if they were frank about it or unafraid of the loss of their jobs they would now admit the fact, as something more than a corporal's guard already has done.

As the sessions of the Extraordinary Investigation Committee proceeded, one of the pet bits of "evidence" put into the record was the testimony of some bootlegger or head of a ring of bootleggers who told the committee —which gave him a vacation from the confines of the penitentiary, if it gave him nothing more—that for a certain sum of money paid some collector who had to split the bribe with Jess Smith or Daugherty or both of them, or somebody else, he would get a pardon if already convicted or have the indictment quashed against him if he had not yet been tried. Charles Vicente, of Baltimore, Maryland, for instance, according to one fragment of this line of evidence introduced by Wheeler, was to pay $50,000 to Elias H. Mortimer as graft in the event of Vicente's release from the Atlanta penitentiary before the expiration of his term. But in this case, as in the case of every other alleged graft contract negotiated by some crook claiming "influence" and the ability to bribe Smith or Daugherty, the one who was to pay the money or did pay it—if he did—went to jail just the same, was convicted just the same, or stayed in the penitentiary just the same if he had already been convicted. In every single, solitary instance, in which it was alleged money was solicited or offered, paid or bargained for, the crook or ring of crooks that paid it or agreed to pay it was tried and convicted, went to prison and stayed there. And in every instance, the crook or ring of crooks was in prison, at liberty on bond pending appeal from conviction, or awaiting trial when Attorney General Daugherty resigned— unless the crook or ring of them had already served the sentence of the court and obtained freedom by the orderly processes of the law and justice.

In the Glass Casket case, let it be remembered, the defendants claimed to have paid money to Gaston B. Means and his co-conspirators on the theory that Means *et al.*, could bribe the Attorney General, Chief Justice Taft of the Supreme Court and William J. Burns, to prevent their prosecution. And let it be remembered further that, under Mr. Daugherty's direction, Means and his pals were indicted in connection with this very thing, and after Means had, through Wheeler *et al.*, obtained postponement after postponement of the case that he might continue to serve as both witness and coach for Wheeler, Means and his associates who had professed their ability to purchase "influence" with the head of the Department of Justice were convicted, and Means now reposes within the restraining walls of the Atlanta penitentiary—convicted in two cases instituted and directed by Mr. Daugherty as Attorney General.

One of the most notable of the crooks obtaining a vacation from a federal prison, through the obliging graces of Senators Wheeler and Brookhart, that he might appear before the Extraordinary Investigation Committee and reel off a yarn suitable to the needs of the committee in bolstering the tale from the tomb recited by Roxie Stinson, was one George Remus of Cincinnati, Ohio. Remus was taken before the committee and testified that he paid a bribe of $30,000 to Jess Smith at Indianapolis,

Indiana, while Smith was there with the Attorney General in connection with the dismissal in federal court of the government's coal strike cases. As shown by the record in those cases (Docket No. 1652) the date upon which Remus, according to his testimony before the committee, paid the $30,000 to Jess Smith was June 28, 1923. So if Remus did pay the money, he paid it to Jess Smith's ghost, for JESS SMITH DIED ON THE 30TH OF MAY, 1923, and the grass had begun to grow upon his grave at Washington Courthouse, Ohio. And if the ghost of Jess Smith accepted the $30,000 which Remus testified was paid to influence the Attorney General against sending him to prison, Remus was the victim of a ghastly joke, for it was under the direction of the Attorney General that this distinguished Cincinnati "king of bootleggers" was prosecuted, tried, convicted and sent to the federal prison at Atlanta to serve the full term of years meted out to him by an unsympathetic federal judge.

Remus, like Means, has subsequently repudiated his testimony in its entirety, and swears in an affidavit to be found among the appendices of this book* that Henry Stern, the lawyer for the committee heretofore mentioned, came to him at the Atlanta penitentiary as an emissary from Wheeler; and, with promises that the committee would help him get out of prison, induced him to go before the committee and perjure himself in the interests of the "prosecution" against the Department of Justice.

Another choice bit of "evidence" which supplied the newslead for many columns, topped by flaring headlines in the public prints, was the recital by Means of how a Jap gave him $100,000 in $1,000 bills which had to be divided with Jess Smith and the Attorney General to bring an end to prospective prosecution in the Standard Aircraft case, evidence which Means has since confessed was a fabrication out of whole cloth. But it was perjury on the very face of it, for there was no such case either of record or in prospect in the Department of Justice or of the Bureau of Investigation of that department, and the case had not reached the Department of Justice, if ever it has

---

*See Appendix E for affidavit of Remus, and other affidavits corroborative of his statements therein contained.

reached there, up to the hour of the resignation of Harry M. Daugherty as Attorney General.

And some of the best evidence of the incorruptibility of the Daugherty regime in the Department of Justice is to be found in the facts connected with the Dempsey-Carpentier motion picture deal, about which a sensation was sprung during the early stages of the Extraordinary Investigation Committee's operations. For an examination of the records shows that Daugherty caused the prosecution in twenty-five different states of people engaged in the illegal transportation of these pictures, and that the Attorney General was responsible for two indictments of Tex Rickard, the promoter of the Dempsey-Carpentier fight.

An important adjunct of the Extraordinary Investigation Committee of the Senate was a "detective" organization with a staff of forty "operatives." The director of this organization, and its financial angel was Frank A. Vanderlip, who acquired such distinction as a gossip and scandal-monger by his circulation of slanderous reports about President Harding and the President's sale of his newspaper, *The Marion Star*. Vanderlip was such a success as a purveyor of scandal that he was sued for libel by the purchasers of *The Marion Star*, and he was so unsuccessful in meeting the allegations of libel made against him that he paid heavy damages which made it possible for the owners of the *Star* to finance their newspaper liberally and make of it a notable financial success.

It was among Vanderlip's boasts that he and his staff of sleuths were rounding up witnesses for the defamation mill operated as a Senate committee by Wheeler, Brookhart and Ashurst and that he was giving every aid possible to Wheeler in his plans for driving Attorney General Daugherty from office. The "secret service" financed by Vanderlip was exceedingly energetic, particularly in practices of intimidation aimed at government officials and at witnesses who might show an inclination to say something creditable to the Department of Justice. How many of the "operatives" employed in the service of the Extraordinary Investigation Committee were professional crooks I have never gone to the trouble of finding out. One of them that I know of, however, who had such a penchant for sleuthing that he had been convicted in Chicago for impersonating a federal prohibition officer, was James S. Sanders. He appears to have followed his service in the cause of clean government and law enforcement, as an "investigator" for Vanderlip and Wheeler, with practices requiring the enforcement of law against himself. He was convicted of larceny in New York City June 17, 1925, and was sentenced in federal court to serve a term of three years in the same penitentiary that now includes the persons of Gaston B. Means and George Remus—the United States penitentiary at Atlanta, Georgia.

The Wheeler-Brookhart-Ashurst Extraordinary Investigation Committee had been in session several weeks quite satisfactorily to the minds of the "investigators." Their strangle hold on any attempt to deny the perjury they were grinding out by the wholesale had been eminently successful; when an untoward accident happened. The same Al Fink who had produced Roxie Stinson for the committee underwent a change of heart. Fink had been under subpoena of the committee for several months, but Wheeler had not called him.

As I said before, Fink had a change of heart, as he tells it; the lying attacks made on Attorney General Daugherty were too much for any decent citizen to stand. Fink knew all this, from first hand knowledge, but more than that he also knew that in a measure he was responsible, he had furnished the committee with its greatest fabricator.

And so, one bright day in May while Brookhart and Ashurst and their personal lobby of spectators were seated revelling in their scandal mongering, a portly man pushed forward to the witness stand and demanded in a forceful manner:

"I've been under subpoena by this committee for some months. I want to be heard. I want to tell the committee that Roxie Stinson's story is a pure lie. And that Frank Vanderlip tried to get me for $1,000 to agree to tell a 'framed-up' story on President Coolidge."

Ashurst found his voice first.

"Throw him out!" he shouted.

"Police!" bellowed Brookhart.

"If you don't throw him out at once, I'll do so myself," screeched Ashurst.

And so Fink was hustled to the door and out into the cool corridor.*

And Fink was never called or allowed to tell his story to the committee, although it will be found in the appendix of this book, which only goes to prove that some Senate committees acknowledge evidence as truth only when it agrees with their own plans and opinions.

The climax of the audacious lengths to which the men in control of the investigation committee were willing to go, however, revealed itself in the lawless raid which Brookhart and Wheeler attempted to make upon the Midland National Bank, Washington Courthouse, Ohio, of which Mal Daugherty, brother of the deposed Attorney General, was president. I call it a lawless raid that was attempted, because that, in plain words, was the finding of the federal court—Judge A. M. Cochran rendering a decision at Cincinnati on June 1, 1924, a decision which thwarted the attempt and sent the Messrs. Wheeler and Brookhart back to Washington empty-handed, minus the person of the president of the bank, minus the private papers and books of the bank, and their entire proceeding and the action of the Senate in authorizing it thoroughly and emphatically repudiated before the law.

The fact that it was the purpose of the Extraordinary Investigation Committee of the Senate, through Wheeler and Brookhart, to visit the bank, appropriate such of its books, papers and records of accounts as they might think desirable for their purposes, and to take Mal Daugherty with them under subpoena to answer questions about the confidential business of the bank, was advertised with a flare and blare of senatorial trumpets that made the proposed action a topic of conversation wherever two or more inhabitants of the little city of Washington Courthouse met. It may or may not have crossed the minds of Messrs. Wheeler and Brookhart that such a proceeding might cause the depositors of the bank to be seized with panic and precipitate a run upon the institution that would wreck it and blast the financial standing of the president

---

*As reported by the Associated Press on May 31, 1924, and printed in the *Washington Post* of June 1, 1924.

and the stockholders. However this may be, the solid faith of the community in the Daugherty brothers and the unshakable stability of the bank was fully demonstrated. There was but one depositor who was so touched with apprehension for the safety of his money as to visit the cashier's window to withdraw his account, and this solitary man of wavering faith has since endeavored in vain to re-deposit his money and reopen business dealings with Mal Daugherty's bank. But Mal Daugherty is so proud of the manner in which every other depositor stood the test of faith in his and his brother Harry's integrity that he has steadfastly refused to have business dealings with the one exceptional skeptic.

"What the Senate is engaged in doing," said the court, in enjoining the Messrs. Wheeler and Brookhart from in any manner interfering with the bank or its contents or its president, "is not investigating the Attorney General's office; it is investigating the former Attorney General. What it has done is to put him on trial before it. In so doing it is exercising the judicial function. This it has no power to do. It has not been conferred expressly. Its existence is negatived by the provisions of the federal Constitution in relation to impeachment proceedings, in view of which there is no possible ground for claiming that it exists by fair implication. As I view the matter, the Senate, in its action, has usurped judicial power, and encroached on the prerogative of the House of Representatives."

That decision of the court was a heavy-charged bomb that blew the whole proceeding of the Wheeler-Brookhart-Ashurst triumvirate and all its works into smithereens and scattered them to the seven seas. The committee never made a report or found a verdict, and it never will. Life in the Coolidge administration was restored, administration senators began to find their voices, the electorate sent delegates to the national convention in Cleveland who would tolerate no compromise with pinks, and give no ear to the voices of jaundiced pussy-footers, and the Republican party won its victory in 1924 because, and only because, there were enough courageous ones left to lead the way into a battle to a finish with the reds and pinks who had determined upon acquiring power and, that power once achieved, the actual overthrow of constitutional, republican government in the United States.

Perhaps the public does not remember that after the enforced resignation of Attorney General Daugherty, with the pack of red and pink wolves at his heels, fighting his election, he was elected a delegate at large from Ohio to the Republican National Convention at Cleveland by almost 100,000 majority.

CHAPTER XVII

FOES OR DEFENDERS OF LAWLESSNESS?

THE Wheeler resolution in the Senate, creating the committee upon which I think I have quite appropriately bestowed the title, "Extraordinary Investigation Committee," provided for an investigation "concerning the alleged failure of Harry M. Daugherty, Attorney General of the United States, to prosecute properly violators of the Sherman anti-trust act and the Clayton act against monopolies and unlawful restraint of trade; the alleged neglect and failure of Harry M. Daugherty, Attorney General of the United States, to arrest and prosecute Albert B. Fall, Harry F. Sinclair, H. L. Doheny, C. R. Forbes and their conspirators in defrauding the government, etc." No evidence ever went into the investigation, however, that the Attorney General neglected or failed to proscute any of the personages above named, for the very good reason that events moved too rapidly even for the astute and facile Wheeler.

Before the investigation could get under way, Attorney General Daugherty had advised the President of the United States that he ought to engage special counsel to represent the government's interests in the oil cases which appeared to be of very considerable importance. This advice was adhered to by the President, and the charges of failure and neglect on the part of the Attorney General in connection with the oil cases fell at once as flat as a rubber doormat. Also, before the investigation got under way, and a long time before it did, too, the case of Forbes was being investigated, and in the most expeditious fashion possible, Daugherty went to Chicago in connection with the grand jury proceedings, Forbes was indicted by direction of Daugherty, tried and convicted.

The inclusion in the Wheeler resolution, however, of

the charge of failure to arrest and prosecute Fall, Sinclair and Doheny was enough to set off the oratorical fowling pieces of Walsh, Wheeler, Brookhart, Heflin, Carraway, Robinson *et al.* in the chamber of the Senate. There the allegation was enlarged upon, and the Attorney General accused of complicity with Fall through the medium of his official capacity. Two emphatic refutations of the charge, however, are of record in the federal court at Cheyenne, Wyoming, where Messrs. Roberts and Pomerene, special counsel employed by the government, prosecuted the oil cases.

The first of these in Paragraph 24 of the bill of complaint which the government's attorneys filed before the court, reads:

> The said Albert B. Fall, acting as aforesaid, although a question was raised as to the legality of such a lease, steadfastly refused to take the opinion of the Solicitor of the Department of the Interior of the United States or of the Attorney General of the United States concerning the legality of the same.

And the other is a paragraph from the opinion of Federal Judge Kennedy of Cheyenne, delivered in support of his decision holding the Teapot Dome lease to be legal and valid, reading as follows:

> As to the charge that Secretary Fall refused to seek the advice of the Solicitor of his own department or the Attorney General of the United States, only one suggestion need be made. While the Secretary of the Interior is criticized in the bill for engineering the entire plan, the evidence shows—that when legal advice was thought necessary in regard to the legality of the proposed lease then under advisement, such advice was sought and received from the legal staff in the Navy Department. Under these circumstances, the criticism could scarcely reach further than an alleged error in judgment in the choice of lawyers.

The evidence of the falsity and absurdity of the charge of neglect and failure properly to prosecute violators of the Sherman and Clayton acts, and in fact the general charge of failure and neglect to prosecute violators of the law or to represent the interests of the government in cases at law generally, was of almost overwhelming volume when the so-called Wheeler-Brookhart-Ashurst committee set about the performance of its illegal and usurping functions. This evidence was of record in the Department of Justice and in the courts of the land everywhere there was a federal district and a federal district attorney. A summary of it may be perused by the reader of this book by turning to the appendices.*

It may be true that the Department of Justice, under Attorney General Daugherty, did not function 100 per cent, and that it only functioned 99 per cent or thereabouts. But if this is true, it is not entirely outside the range of possibility that the one per cent failure to function reacted to the benefit of certain of the Attorney General's most ardent detractors, as two or three instances pointed out in this chapter would seem to indicate.

One of these detractors, the leading one in fact, has been prosecuted, and will be further prosecuted. The credit for it has been rather persistently given to Daugherty. But this credit is entirely undeserved, since Daugherty had no more to do with it than Luke McLuke or the Sultan of Sulu. I have no doubt he would have taken and would now take some invigorating interest in officially participating in this particular prosecution, but the matter was and is entirely out of his hands, and rests now in the hands of Attorney General Sargent after having left the hands of Attorney General Stone upon Mr. Stone's elevation to the Supreme Court. The defendant to whom I now refer is the "prosecutor" of the Extraordinary Investigation Committee, United States Senator Burton K. Wheeler of Montana.

The criminal case against Senator Wheeler originated in the Post Office Department, and not in the Department of Justice. I went to Montana in March, 1924, to look into some matters pertaining to Senator Wheeler, at the instance of a newspaper. At that time I did not know Attorney General Daugherty and did not meet him until months after he had resigned. What I went there to find out principally was the radical connections of

*See appendix A for summary of activities of the Department of Justice, during the incumbency of Attorney General Daugherty.

Wheeler and to reach some conclusions concerning the real motives behind his enthusiasm for the destruction of Mr. Daugherty and the defamation of the Department of Justice. My sole purpose was to get material from which was written a series of articles exposing Wheeler's affiliation with the reds and the motives behind the movement to "get" Daugherty and discredit the Department of Justice. I had no sooner arrived there than I discovered the fact that Gordon Campbell, a Seattle oil operator, and Wheeler were then being investigated in connection with fraudulent operations for which Campbell was, in due time, prosecuted and convicted. The investigation was being conducted by inspectors from the Post Office Department. It is a well-known fact, of course, that the Post Office Department has its own secret service, and that this service—under the direction of the chief post office inspector—operates as a unit entirely independent of the Department of Justice. It investigates and prepares its cases before they even reach the Department of Justice or a federal district attorney.

It was natural that, upon learning of the investigation being made by the post office inspectors, I should have some curiosity about it, and I tried hard enough to obtain enlightenment from the inspectors at work on the case. They wouldn't tell me what I wanted to know, so I determined to find out for myself—which is something of a custom among men who have had experience as reporters for newspapers. Well, I did find out—not only what the post office inspectors knew, but a lot more; that is to say, information, supported by a number of witnesses from whom I obtained affidavits to the effect that Senator Wheeler had contracted to receive $10,000 from Gordon Campbell to use his influence as a United States senator to obtain from the General Land Office validation of a number of dummy permits for oil lands in Montana, the validity of these permits being necessary to the successful operation of the oil syndicate Campbell had organized.

I went to the federal district attorney, John L. Slattery, at Great Falls, Montana, with the evidence I had obtained. By this time the evidence of the post office inspectors had been laid before the district attorney, and when the infor-

mation I had obtained was placed before him he was convinced there was a strong case against Wheeler on a
charge of misuse of his senatorial office. The evidence
was placed before a grand jury, the witnesses I had discovered were heard, and the result of it was that Wheeler
was indicted. The indictment was obtained after Attorney General Daugherty's enforced resignation from the
Attorney Generalship, and the entire preparation of the
case for trial took place, not under the Daugherty regime,
but under that of Attorney General Harlan F. Stone, now
a justice of the United States Supreme Court.

At once the oratorical guns of the United States Senate
were directed at the Federal Department of Justice, not
because it neglected or failed to prosecute alleged violators
of the federal statutes, but because it did proceed to the
business of prosecuting one who chanced to be a member
of that self-righteous and super-sensitive body, The Senate. Wheeler and his allies arose on the floor of the
Senate and denounced the due process of the Montana
court as a "frame-up," and accused the already deposed
Attorney General of being the instigator of it. Wheeler
at first "demanded" an immediate trial, but later thought
better of it, and instead called for an "investigation" by
a committee of the Senate. As for his trial, which was
not held until a year had passed following the return of
the indictment, he sought delay after delay upon one pre-
text and another, and then had the audacity to blame these
delays upon the Department of Justice and the administration of that department by Attorney General Stone.

There was a time in the history of the United States
Senate when senate dignity forbade an indicted senator
from participating in the deliberation of that body until
he had been cleared of any criminal charges against him.
But not so under the rules as now laid down by the reds,
the pinks and the yellows. Wheeler instead of being an
outcast was treated as the hero of the Senate.

The "investigation" which he demanded in the Senate
was held with expeditious haste. Senator Borah was made
chairman of the committee, and in addition to this ex-
cellent choice of chairman, from Wheeler's point of view,
the committee was efficiently packed to adminster a
thorough coat of whitewash to the accused Montana

senator. In the conduct of this so-called "investigation," the tactics were a complete reversal of those operating in the proceedings of the Wheeler-Brookhart-Ashurst Extraordinary Investigation Committee. In the latter proceedings, defense of the accused was absolutely and unqualifiedly taboo. On the other hand, in the proceedings of the Borah committee, to "investigate" the charges against Wheeler, borrowing one of the expressive phrases of Octavius Roy Cohen, defense was the one thing "there wasn't nothin' else but." There was no "prosecutor" on the Borah committee, and any and all efforts to get before the committee evidence unfavorable to Wheeler met with insults and indignant rebuffs. As the Wheeler-Brookhart-Ashurst committee was out to "get" Daugherty, and would brook no interference with that purpose, so the Borah committee was out to whitewash Wheeler, and there was nothing in the world that could stop it.

The report of the committee, prepared by Senator Borah, "exonerating" Wheeler, was something of a joke on the chairman, however, since it found the accused senator innocent of violating a statute which had long since been repealed and under which he had not been indicted at all. The senator from Idaho, with a reputation as a great lawyer, was not a little chagrined later upon discovering that Wheeler had been indicted under a statute, the existence of which he (Borah) appeared to have been in entire ignorance.

It was astonishing with what enthusiasm Senators Borah, Walsh of Montana, Brookhart, Dill, Norris, La Follette, Shipstead, Ladd, Heflin, Carraway, Robinson and others went to the defense of an indicted man, simply because he was a member of their own crowd of presumably sacrosanct champions of their denunciations of the Department of Justice for alleged laxity in the investigation, indictment and prosecution of alleged violators of the federal statutes.

If the Department of Justice is to be assailed for any laxity in the investigation of individuals suspected of violating the federal statutes, there might be some justice in a charge of failure to investigate Senator Walsh of Montana for one, and Senator Dill of Washington, for another. Had Senator Walsh and Senator Dill been regular members of the Republican party, in good standing, supporters of the Coolidge administration and defenders of the Department of Justice and Attorney General Daugherty, I have no doubt the Extraordinary Investigation Committee of the Senate would have found a way to "expose" the failure of the Department of Justice to prosecute both of them.

Walsh was elected to the Senate in Montana in 1918 by a scant majority of 4,200 votes over Dr. O. M. Landstrom. Following the election it was discovered that probably he was elected by votes supposed to have been sent in by mail from absent voters. Three counties in Montana—Silver Bow, Cascade and Deer Lodge counties —returned something like 7,000 of these mailed votes. All three counties are Democratic strongholds, with a particular leaning toward extreme radicalism. The 7,000 votes are alleged to have been more mailed votes than ever were polled in these counties either before or since the election of 1918. This election at which Walsh was elected has always been under a cloud.

"An Associated Press dispatch from Helena, Montana," said the Spokane, Washington, *Spokesman-Review*, October 17, 1924, "last night reported that A. W. Dolphin, Spokane attorney, had submitted to the federal land office a petition for the cancellation of a special use water permit granted to the Beaverhead Ranch Company in 1912. The petition was received for filing by Frank L. Reece, receiver and recorder, and forwarded to Washington, D. C.

"Details of the Dolphin petition, which charges Senator T. J. Walsh of Montana with violation of a federal statute, were first given in the *Spokesman-Review* on Tuesday. Dolphin declared the permit was worth $140,000 and obtained with the intervention of Senator Walsh while a stockholder of the concern."

"The Associated Press dispatch from Helena adds:

" 'Large tracts were purchased by the company in Beaverhead County, according to county records here, and irrigated with water obtained fom the Beaverhead National Forest preserve under the terms of the special permit. Within the last eight years most of the land was sold to individuals in small tracts, with contracts for sufficient water for irrigation.' "

The Dolphin petition alleged correspondence between Walsh and Franklin K. Lane, while the latter was Secretary of the Interior in the Wilson administration, in the interests of the Beaverhead Ranch. Senator Walsh has announced that he has no recollection of having had such correspondence, but that his conscience is clear even if he did. He claims to have disposed of his holdings in the Beaverhead Ranch in 1915—to his daughter—and that the stock subsequently was disposed of to the president of the company.

Senator Walsh first came to the Senate in 1913, following ratification by the state legislature of his election in 1912. He was then holding, and until some time in 1915 held, $20,000 worth of the stock in the Beaverhead Ranch Company. He was one of the incorporators of the company. Associated with him in the organization of the company was J. E. Morse, who claimed the water rights to Boots Lake Reservoir. The Department of the Interior decided the claim was invalid. Walsh, serving in the Senate, demanded of the department that Morse be given a decision on the water rights. There is adequately authenticated evidence that Walsh had correspondence with Secretary Lane and the then Assistant Secretary, now Senator Jones, of New Mexico, and that as a consequence the Morse application for the water rights was reinstated. The land—7,000 acres—controlled by the Beaverhead Ranch Company was worth, prior to that, probably $1.00 an acre. The value thereafter is said to have gone up to $100 or more an acre.

Of course, the Federal Department of Justice is not to be held accountable for any failures or neglect in connection with Senator Walsh's election in 1918, since that matter is not within the province of federal officers charged with the enforcement of law. And as for the Beaverhead Ranch case, I make no charges whatever that the Montana senator violated any law or intended to violate any law. All I do, in this connection, is to venture the plausible suggestion that Senator Walsh, had he been a Republican and a supporter of the Coolidge administration, and more particularly a defender of the Attorney Generals who have served in that administration, instead of an assailant of them, the foes of the administration and

𝔘𝔫𝔦𝔱𝔢𝔡 𝔖𝔱𝔞𝔱𝔢𝔰 𝔖𝔢𝔫𝔞𝔱𝔢, *B-2*

COMMITTEE ON MINES AND MINING.

DEP'T. OF THE INTERIOR
RECEIVED
☆ SEP 18 1914 ☆
To Asst.Atty-Genl.
SEC'Y'S OFF.- MAILS & FILES.

Septmeber 16, 1914.

INTERIOR DEP'T.
RECEIVED
SEP'18 1914
OFFICE OF
THE SECRETARY.

Hon. Franklin K. Lane,
    Secretary of the Interior,
        Washington, D. C.
Dear Mr. Secretary:

    I am enclosing herewith a communication from the Secretary and
Treasurer of the Beaverhead Ranch Company, Mr H. H Pigott, of Helena,
Montana, together with a copy of a letter the President of the same company has addressed to the Acting District Forester at Missoula, Montana,
both of which explain themselves.

    Will you kindly furnish me with the status of the matter as it ap-
pears in your office, and if possible advise me how the appeal stands and
when the company may expect a decision, with the return of the enclosures.

    With assurances of my esteem, I have the honor to remain,

                    Very truly yours,

                    J H Walsh

This is the letter Senator Thomas J. Walsh could "not remember."

record as hardly to require discussion. A rule to show
cause referring to land in range 7, can not support a judgment of cancellation of rights in range 11 at least twenty-
four miles away. A charge of abandonment (failure to re-
pair).in 1902 will not sustain proceedings against a filing
or entry not made till 1906.   The charge was an impossible
one, and all proceedings under it are without validity.
When the Commissioner was thus informed of the errors on face
of the record, he should of his own motion have set aside the
cancellation and reinstated the reservoir filing. The application is accordingly reinstated.

Since this application was filed this Department
and the Department of Agriculture, November 14, 1914, adopted
joint regulations to govern procedure in applications for right
of way upon unsurveyed national forest lands (43 L. D., 448).
The Commissioner's decision herein is vacated and papers are
remanded to the General Land Office for further proceedings
under said regulations.

(Signed) A. A. Jones.
First Assistant Secretary.

Final page of decision in favor of Senator Walsh made by the now U. S. Senator
A. A. Jones of New Mexico.

The record of Senator C. C. Dill, of Washington, on file in the Department of the Interior at Washington. Section 113 of the Penal Code prohibits a senator from appearing for a client before a government department and fixes the penalty at fine and imprisonment.

Serial	Date when Mr. Dill first appeared in record	Power of atty. when executed	Claimant	County Washington	Amount	Status
Spokane 012559	Letter to Dill June 21, 1922	Filed Jan. 24, 1923 Nov. 6, 1922	Clara C. Burlingame, heir Amos M. Burlingame	Whitman	$100	Settled April 16, 1923
Spokane 012581	....	Filed Dec. 1, 1922	George Courchaine and Mrs. Alice Hutton heirs of Daniel Courchaine	Spokane	....	Pending
Walla Walla 08334	Letter to Dill Aug. 23, 1922	Nov. 28, 1921 Nov. 29, 1922 Received Jan. 4, 1923	Homer Hull heir of Harvey J. Hull Heirs of Harvey J. Hull	Whitman	....	Denied May 14, 1923
Walla Walla 08336	Letter to Dill Aug. 23, 1922	Oct. 24, 1922 Filed Jan. 4, 1923	Heirs of Josial Lee	Whitman	$150	Settled Nov. 6, 1923
Walla Walla 08338	Letter to Dill Aug. 23, 1922	Nov. 28, 1922 Filed Jan. 4, 1923	Mrs. Patrick O'Neill legal representative of Patrick O'Neill	Whitman	$200	Settled April 16, 1923
Walla Walla 08340	Letter to Dill Aug. 23, 1922	Oct. 7, 1922 Filed Jan. 4, 1923	Susan A. Baldwin Widow of Ephraim Baldwin	Whitman	$100	Settled April 18, 1923

of the Department of Justice would, in all likelihood, have shirked no scruples in charging the Department of Justice with laxity and neglect in its failure at least to investigate the senator.

Senator Norris, the Nebraska radical wearing the mantle of a Republican with pink decorations, was the author of Senate Resolution 175, in the Sixty-eighth Congress, directing the Secretary of the Interior to furnish a list of the names and records of ex-members of Congress and ex-members of presidential cabinets who had appeared before that department in opposition to the government and in the interests of clients. Inadvertently, it appears, the Secretary of the Interior included in his list the name of Senator Dill of Washington. Dill was a member of the Senate, not an ex-member. Norris did not send the Dill record back to the Department of the Interior, and there is no record that he presented it to his committee, and thereafter was rather notably silent on the questions covered by his resolution. Perhaps Mr. Norris will now explain.

Dill was elected to the Senate in November, 1922, as a Democrat, was known as a radical, and had the endorsement and support of the Conference for Progressive Political Action. The records of the Public Land Office show his appearance there in no less than six cases following his election to the Senate. He was not investigated, indicted or prosecuted. Had he been a Republican, supporting the Coolidge administration and defending the management of affairs in the Department of Justice, it is not at all improbable that the Wheeler-Brookhart-Ashurst committee would have leaped at the chance to charge the Department with "neglect or failure to prosecute" the senator from Washington. It does not seem likely, at this writing, that there will be any investigation or prosecution of Senator Dill, in whose case the statute of limitations if a crime has been committed, will have run in December, 1925. So I offer, purely as speculation upon my own part, the suggestion that the reason for this "failure and neglect" is due in all likelihood to a realization that Senator Dill's behavior was the result of his ignorance both as a lawyer and a statesman, rather than any felonious intent on his part to violate a federal statute. This further suggestion, however, may be added with some justice: If it was ignorance, then Senator Dill is out of place in the United States Senate, and is particularly out of place there as a critic and maligner of executive departments of the federal government.

CHAPTER XVIII

WHAT IS SAUCE FOR THE GOOSE

It may seem strange, but is none the less true, that when reds, pinks, yellows or professional reformers and purifiers of whatever shade run afoul the statutes, the first thing they do is strike an attitude of injured innocence, emit yowls about "persecution" and wail about the injustices of courts and the malevolence of prosecutors. It is what every socialist plotter, every I. W. W. rioter, every communist conspirator has done whenever the strong arm of the law has reached out, grabbed him, and hailed him before a legally constituted tribunal in whose presence his guilt or innocence may be determined by orderly procedure and according to the law and the evidence covering his case. One would gather from the line of argument they hand out and the character of reasoning they manifest, that they are people of a very distinct and sacred class to whom special privileges and advantages should be accorded not only by the enforcers of law but by the laws themselves.

The attitude of Senator Burton K. Wheeler of Montana, is simply a conspicuous case in point. With no feeling of consideration whatever in his own heart for the well known fact that an invalid wife, since deceased, of Attorney General Daugherty was suffering far more from the attacks upon her husband than did the Attorney General himself, Wheeler left no stone unturned and no avenue unentered in his determined endeavor to defame and besmirch Daugherty. But about the first words of complaint from Wheeler's lips, when the news was broadcast that he himself has been indicted on a criminal charge, were words of passionate recollection that for him to be charged with crime made his wife and children the innocent sufferers.

When Wheeler was indicted in the District of Columbia some months later, along with Edwin S. Booth, former solicitor of the General Land Office, and the recently convicted oil promoter, Gordon Campbell, on a charge of conspiracy to defraud the government out of millions of dollars worth of land acquired by fraudulent dummy permits, the howl about "persecution" was revived with even greater vigor than before. The indictment was obtained, after several careful investigations had been made at the direction of Attorney General Stone to make sure that there should be no ground upon which to rest a charge of "persecution."

Senator Thomas J. Walsh, counsel for Wheeler, made a spectacular fight on the floor of the United States Senate and in sessions of the Senate Committee on Judiciary to prevent the confirmation of President Coolidge's nomination of Attorney General Stone for a place on the Supreme Bench. The fight was waged around the charge that Attorney General Stone had caused the indictment of Wheeler in the District of Columbia, "many miles from his own home," and that this amounted to "persecution." Walsh sounded the rallying cry for a concerted restoration of life to the war upon the Federal Department of Justice that had been waging throughout the administrations of that Department by Palmer and Daugherty, and carried on without interruption after the resignation of Daugherty and the installation of Stone as his successor. That Albert B. Fall, Harry F. Sinclair and Edward L. Doheny had been indicted in the District of Columbia, "many miles from their homes," was nothing to touch the sympathetic heart and passionate soul of Senator Walsh, but that his protégé, Wheeler, defender of reds, advocate and apologist for Red Russia and "cleanser" of the infamous energies for law enforcement in the Department of Justice, should be so indicted was "persecution" of the most indefensible character, in the opinion of Senator Walsh. But Walsh's "prosecution" of Attorney General Stone before the Senate Committee on Judiciary and his speeches on the floor of the Senate were mere incidents in as brazen a campaign of intimidation against Stone and the Department in the interests of an indicted man as may well be imagined. The efforts of Walsh and Wheeler, and others allied in sympathy with them in the enterprise of preventing a trial of the conspiracy case against Wheeler in the District of Columbia were many, varied, energetic, and in a number of instances barely short of vulnerability on the ground that they were in contempt of court and of a tendency to obstruct the orderly processes of justice.

The fight upon Stone was a failure. There was not that support for it in the Senate that there had been for the fight on Daugherty, because administration senators had ceased to be quite so panic-stricken and quite so easily intimidated. So Stone's nomination for the Supreme Court appointment was confirmed. The war on the Department did not cease, however, by any means, and ever since the appointment of Attorney General Sargent as Mr. Stone's successor, it has been continued. Sargent has been maligned by Wheeler and his cohorts, and pressure of many sorts have been brought to bear in an effort to defeat the intention of the law-enforcing branch of the government to bring the case against Wheeler to a logical conclusion—either his conviction on the conspiracy charge against him, or an acquittal, as the case may be.

After the many delays of his case at Great Falls, Montana—delays for which Wheeler himself was responsible—the same came to trial. Perhaps the most material witness the government had had died. Wheeler's acquittal in the trial in Montana is accounted for because the indictment in that case failed to allege facts and acts necessary to justify a conviction, which are, however, fully covered in the Washington indictment. A verdict of not guilty was returned by the jury. Thereupon the newspapers carried a story playing up the supposed "fact," supplied to the correspondents by the Wheeler defense, that a verdict of "not guilty" was unanimously reached on the first ballot after the jury had deliberated only a few minutes. But this was not a fact at all. For the truth is, the jury deliberated upon the case for more than two hours, and the first ballot taken showed four of the jurors not voting for the acquittal of Wheeler.

Since the termination of that trial, there has been organized what is called the Wheeler Defense Committee. This committee is like all similar committees, such as the

Labor Defense Council, the General Defense Committee, the American Civil Liberties Union and the most recently organized of all these committees, known as the International Labor Defense Council. The last named, like the Labor Defense Council, was initiated by the communists, and it has taken over the machinery of the old Labor Defense Council. The Wheeler Defense Committee, like the rest of these committees, is an organization for propaganda, pure and simple, and the particular object of assault, as is the case with the others, is the law-enforcing department of the federal government.

The chairman of the Wheeler Defense Committee is Norman Hapgood, a noted radical, muckraker, professional uplifter and propagandist for Soviet Russia. Hapgood was named as minister to Denmark in the Wilson administration and resigned under fire—said fire reported as being charges of undue pro-Russian activity while representing the United States in Denmark. As this is written, Hapgood is in Europe writing special articles for consumption in the United States, telling how terrible it will be for this country if we do not recognize Soviet Russia and establish diplomatic relations with the bolsheviki, said recognition and relations being among the foremost hopes and desires of Senator Borah and the American pinks and of the communists in Russia and in the United States as well.

The vice chairman and chief publicity expert of the Wheeler Defense Committee is Basil Manly, director of the People's Legislative Service, one of the organizers and executive committeemen of the Conference for Progressive Political Action and a socialist writer and propagandist of many years standing.

Among the members of the so-called National Committee of this particular "defense committee" are Francis Fisher Kane, who took a hand in the attempts to "get" Attorney General A. Mitchell Palmer and Mr. Palmer's successor in office, Attorney General Daugherty; Donald R. Richberg and Edward Keating, both ardent participants in the long war upon Daugherty; Sidney Hillman, of the extremely radical Amalgamated Clothing Workers; William H. Johnston, head of the International Association of Machinists, an outstanding leader in the railway strikes of 1922, and chairman of the National Conference for

Progressive Political Action; Norman Thomas, well known New York socialist and red flag waver; Roger N. Baldwin, war "slacker" who did his bit in jail, director of the American Civil Liberties Union, and one of the most prominent agitators against the "persecution" of reds and defenders of reds, and a long list of other pro-soviet advocates, pinks and parlor bolsheviki.

The committee is engaged in the extensive circulation of propaganda in pamphlet and letter form, denouncing and defaming the Department of Justice and its present directing officials, and it is striving with might and main either to prevent the prosecution of the case against Wheeler, Booth and Campbell ever reaching the stage of trial in court before a jury, or to create an atmosphere of prejudice against the Department of Justice and in favor of the accused that it may operate to Wheeler's advantage and to the government's disadvantage when the case does come up for trial.

In justice to some of the individuals whose names appear upon the list of members of the National Committee of the Wheeler Defense Committee, it should be said that they have repudiated the committee, allege that the use of their names was without authority, and declare they do not subscribe either to the funds or the purposes of the committee.

The Labor Defense Council, which also engages in propaganda against enforcement of the law against reds and defenders or supporters of reds, was organized by specific direction of the communists through action taken by the Central Executive Committee of the Worker's Party. Among its members also were Roger N. Baldwin, of the Wheeler committee; John Haynes Holmes, also of the Wheeler committee; Francis Fisher Kane, of the Wheeler committee; Norman Thomas, of the Wheeler Committee; Eugene V. Debs, chairman of the National Executive Committee of the Socialist party in its support of Wheeler for Vice-President in 1924, together with such noted communists as "Big Bill" Dunne, who nominated Wheeler for governor of Montana in 1920 and campaigned for him for the Senate in 1922; William Z. Foster, C. E. Ruthenberg and Earl H. Browder.

Most of these individuals, particularly those of the

deeper hues of red and pink, are associates and co-workers for about every committee that is ever organized under the camouflage of defending somebody against the heartless persecutions of the Federal Department of Justice or of the law-enforcing officers of the country, states, as well as federal, but actually engaged in aiding and abetting radical causes and subversive movements of all kinds—movements that usually are of red origin or red suggestion, but which are more effective through pink execution.

Senator Walsh of Montana, Senator Borah of Idaho, and the sundry other leading lights of the Senate who rushed to the front for Wheeler when he was indicted, and charged "persecution" and "frame-up" when due process of law, with all its advantages to the accused, had been accorded Wheeler, were on the other side when lynch law was substituted for due process in the "indictment" and "prosecution" of the Attorney General of the United States. These gentlemen are not members of the Wheeler Defense Committee or any of these other defense committees, but they have feelings of partiality toward them. If actions speak as well as words, these distinguished senators were advocates of and participants in the practice of lynch law, when the Attorney General was on the defensive. But for Wheeler, even due process is too much for them, and they join him and encourage him and his red, pink and yellow admirers to fight on, and on, and on for the vindication of lawlessness enacted with senatorial approval, and for the conviction of the legally authorized law-enforcing branch of the American government—the Federal Department of Justice.

CHAPTER XIX

WHAT ARE YOU GOING TO DO?

OF COURSE, no attempt has been made by the writer of these pages to cover the entire story of the intrigues and purposes underlying the radical and pink alliances of the United States following the World War. The wealth of fact presented in this book is, after all, little more than a fragment of the truths to be found in the archives of the United States government. Many of these unrevealed facts are of a highly confidential character; others, although no longer secret, remain carefully obscured among the documents in the possession of the Borah subcommittee of the Senate Committee on Foreign Relations of the Sixty-eighth Congress.

Who represents Moscow, secretly but officially, in Washington?

Who represents the prospective concessionaires of the United States, unofficially and clandestinely, in Moscow?

Who in the United States are so interested in commercial concessions in Soviet Russia that they are putting up their share of the money that finances the persistent and unwavering propaganda to bring about American recognition of the bolsheviki and trade treaties with Moscow?

These are questions now under investigation. But, aside from the answers to them, much remains to be told, involving, however, purposes and personages subservient to war profiteering and the Wallingfords of international finance rather than those herein exposed. The story of these equally traitorous allies of the post-war assaults upon the American government is deserving of a volume unto itself.

Secretary of State Frank B. Kellogg has very forcefully and truly said that the American government and the principles of the republican Constitution of the United States are being "assaulted" by "propagandists who advocate the overthrow of the government and the substitution of class tyranny" and by a "considerable body of our citizens who, in the name of liberty and reform, are impatient of the constitutional restrictions and by insidious approaches and attacks would destroy these guarantees of personal liberty."

"I doubt if you are aware," to quote Mr. Kellogg further, "of the amount of destructive revolutionary propaganda which is being secretly [and he might have added, openly] distributed in this country by foreign influence. . . . There cannot rest on anyone a higher and more sacred duty than honestly and efficiently to serve his country and to preserve its ideals and institutions."

The same red hordes and the same pink phalanxes that were behind the attempts to destroy Attorney General Mitchell Palmer and Attorney General Daugherty, and that put the pressure of their combined weight behind the plot to demoralize the Federal Department of Justice and besmirch the entire administration of the federal government, were the same hordes and phalanxes that strove, in the election of 1924, to make La Follette President and Wheeler Vice-President, or, at least, to place them in a reinforced position of governmental control through deadlocking that election.

The men and women who have blossomed forth as members of the Wheeler Defense Committee, who occupy positions of influence in the Labor Defense Council, the American Civil Liberties Union, the Peoples' Legislative Service, the Congress for Progressive Political Action, the Plumb Plan League, the League for Industrial Democracy, and the almost innumerable other organizations of radicals, revolutionists, defenders of violence, promoters of class warfare and agitators for American recognition of socialist dictatorship in Russia and American acceptance of socialism in the conduct of government in this country—these are the elements who nominated La Follette and Wheeler for the presidency and vice-presidency, and succeeded in mobilizing for them 5,000,000 votes in the 1924 election.

It is not important to go into the presidential campaign of 1924 in any detail, for it is fresh in public memory.

But it is important to point out the hypocrisy of one particular gesture which was made in behalf of the candidates who sought to obtain power as a result of their campaign of political assassination and defamation. This was the gesture of La Follette, by which he "repudiated" the communists on the ground that they were apostles of the overthrow of government by force and violence.

It has already been explained that, notwithstanding the differences that exist among elements of the revolutionary radical movement, the common objective is the destruction of republican government in the United States and the substitution therefore of socialist "democracy." It has been explained that the "Left Wing" revolutionists are primarily bent upon precipitation of violent revolution, but that they are supporters of any and all subversive movements which tend to demoralize government, weaken it, and make it easier for the accomplishment of the revolution they have in mind. It has been explained that the "Right Wing" revolutionists profess to abhor bloodshed and overthrow of government by violence, but that they are defenders of and apologists for "Left Wing" political principles, and are bent upon the accomplishment of the overthrow of republican government and capitalism with a fervor that is not a jot cooler than the hot ardor of the "Left Wing" reds who criticize their milder tactics.

The "Right Wing" revolutionists in the United States were unqualifiedly solid in their support of the La Follette-Wheeler ticket in the campaign of 1924. Up to the moment of La Follette's so-called "repudiation" of the communists, they too were a solid unit in support of the plan for a "united political front" for the nomination of La Follette and Wheeler. Following the "repudiation," there was nothing left for the communists to do but go through the motions of retaliation, but it is not an unreasonable presumption that this, also, was a mere gesture, and that their desire for the election of La Follette and Wheeler was not a whit lessened. The communist support, of course, was not because of any love for La Follette, who was, in fact, always an object of contempt in the minds of the very red radicals. But for Wheeler they had a genuine and justified affection, and he was their man at all times, whether La Follette was or not.

In the pre-convention campaign, the communists were whooping it up strong for La Follette. The question, "Are we for La Follette?" was answered by C. E. Ruthenberg, executive secretary of the Workers' (Communist) Party, as follows:

"Should that come about [La Follette's nomination by a Farmer-Labor party], as it seems very likely, then we will unquestionably support La Follette in the election campaigns along with the masses of workers and farmers who are behind the Farmer-Labor party movement."

The Liberator, a monthly radical journal, the name of which has been changed now to the *Workers' Monthly,* and which is the official organ of the communist organization, had among its editors in the fall of 1923 Eugene V. Debs, who became national chairman of the Socialist party in the campaign for La Follette and Wheeler, and other red radicals, of both the "Left Wing" and the "Right Wing" of the revolutionary movement. In the September, 1923, issue of that journal, John Pepper, alias Pogany, alias Lang, sent to the United States by the Comintern of Moscow, and coming direct from Hungary where he had helped put Bela Kun into power, wrote of what he termed "the La Follette revolution":

It will be a revolution of the well-to-do farmers, small business men and workers; it will come through rebellion within the old parties, third parties and farmer-labor parties.

After the victory of the La Follette revolution there will begin the independent role of the workers and farmers and there will then begin the period of the fourth American revolution—the period of the proletarian revolution.

So that, although the communists were not deluded into the belief that the "La Follette revolution" was to be their revolution, they were confident that it was a necessary preliminary to whatever hopes they were justified in having for the accomplishment of their "proletarian revolution."

The La Follette and Wheeler campaign was waged on a platform paralleling in a number of important respects the platform of the communist program, as has already been pointed out. And the red revolutionists hoped for and worked for the success of the La Follette-Wheeler campaign because they saw in it, precisely what there was in it, the preliminary skirmishes of a revolution to overthrow American capitalism, bolshevize American industry and do away with the republican form of government provided for in the American Constitution.

The communists may have been "repudiated" by La Follette but they were never "repudiated" by Wheeler, and the communist press, as well as all other sections of the radical and so-called "liberal" press, continues to bestow praises upon him and hurl epithets at the federal government for its "persecution" of their hero who now is striving so energetically to escape the law by posing as a martyr before it.

There is no let-up in the clamor of the reds and the pinks for the recognition of Soviet Russia by the United States and the establishment of diplomatic and trade relations between the countries. The communists have been working for it, above everything else, from the time the proposal was first made officially in the U. S. Senate by the Borah resolution. Senator Borah has been indefatigable in his loyalty to this resolution, and in the next session of the Senate he is almost certain to renew the demand and the agitation for its passage by the Senate. The Idaho senator has the solid support of every communist, every socialist, every disciple of Senator La Follette and every follower of Senator Wheeler. The demand for American recognition and friendship to bolster up the losing game of the red dictators of Soviet Russia has not diminished an iota, and this notwithstanding the fact that every other nation in the world that has granted such recognition has either been gobbled up by the forces of red radicalism or has survived to regret the hour the bloody hands of the Moscow oligarchs were clasped.

The government of Mexico has become so infested with bolshevism and so subservient to the desires and program of Soviet Russia, that the United States government has been obliged to administer, in words of strong import, a warning to President Calles which that distinguished radical resented and replied to in arrogant tones. The whole of Latin America is being overrun with bolshevik agitators, crying aloud against the United States and using every means to stir up trouble between this country and the countries to the south which, but for the United States, would a long time ago have been gobbled up by European imperialists. One of the effects of this red agitation in Central and South America is a very noticeable falling off in the trade of American exporters with the importers of Latin American republics.

England, becoming too intimate with Red Russia, has been forced to back up on its policy of intimacy, and the British government is being constantly bedeviled at home with "general strikes" and violence, while in the colonies the bolsheviks have kept constantly at work sowing the seeds of revolution. France and Poland have had their fill of soviet influence. Japan is awakening to the error of her recognition of Russia and to the peril of getting the worst of it in the intrigues of the Far East, and the chaos and revolution and seeds of international war now fertilizing in China present problems to the civilized world that may prove the test of the very stability of civilization itself.

In the pages of this book there has been told something of the ramifications of red radicalism, much of the affiliations the American pink radicals have had with it, and the underground history of the conspiracy to demoralize and destroy the law-enforcing arm of the American government.

It was said at the outset, that as a menace to the country red radicalism is less potent than pink radicalism. And this is true. The United States government, under its Constitution, is peculiarly fortified against red radicalism. But when pink radicalism gets the reins, and exercises its power, as it did in the days of the Sixty-eighth Congress, when La Follette and Wheeler and Brookhart seized control and transformed the United States Senate into a lawless ally of every subversive movement in the country, the fortifications against actual revolution face the peril of destruction; and mob law and lynch law look up with hope and gloating eagerness to the reign that leads to revolution and the end of government by law and order and justice.

The deaths of Senators La Follette and Ladd should not be noted by their foes as events tending to signify the end of the radicalism these two senators personified. To say that either of them was in himself vital to the success or progress of such a movement is to misjudge the cohesiveness of the elements that supported the third party campaign of 1924. Who should know this better, who should be a better judge of this than Senator Borah?

"I think Senator La Follette's death was a great loss to the country," said the Idaho Senator on July 4, 1925, at Spokane, Washington, when interviewed by the *Spokane Daily Chronicle*. "But I disagree with those who seem to think his death will have any particular bearing on a third party movement. He was a very forceful figure in political parties. If they are political parties, they do not rise or fall in this country because of one man. The third party movement depends entirely upon economic conditions as they develop in this country."

The opinion expressed by Borah is well-grounded. He would have been preferable as the radical standard bearer in 1924, had he and not La Follette commanded the strategic nuclei of political organization, and if he can "serve the cause" to better advantage by retaining the Republican mantle upon his renegade shoulders, it is not fantastic prophecy to predict his ascendency to the throne and crown which are La Follette's legacy to the pinks and reds of the country.

The pinks play the game of the reds at every stage, yet professing to be uplifters of the most idealistic sort. Not long ago Senator Thomas J. Walsh was in Wisconsin to make a speech. He stirred a crowd of Wisconsin radicals to great enthusiasm by his denunciations of the government, by his repetition of the oft-heard cry of corruption and rottenness in the conduct of the government. Are these things true? Does Walsh utter the truth? If he does, the red radicals are perfectly right in their revolt against government, and they are perfectly justified in organizing for the purpose of overturning the government and setting up one of their own, and it is the thinnest kind of hypocrisy for pink politicians to remain aloof from open and outspoken alliance with the most radical of the communist organizations in the country. The pinks and the reds are at one in the charges they make against the existing government, and if these charges are true the pinks and the reds should get together unequivocally and put an end to this wickedness at one fell swoop.

But the charges are not true. The rantings of men like Walsh, Borah, La Follette, Wheeler, and that great line-up of lesser luminaries whose names appear in the cast of characters of this book, are but the maunderings of inferior men with super-yearnings for the political power that is possible to them only with the help of the red fringe in politics. But these men and their rantings and charges are dangerous to ordered government, for without them and their following the more extremely radical elements are but a puny minority all dressed up, but with no place to go. It is history, that over the bodies of men like La Follette, Borah, Wheeler and Walsh, whose tongues stir mobs and kindle hatreds, the Dantons, the Robespierres, the Lenins and the Zinovievs ride rough-shod to power.

Bolshevism is a mental disorder. It is as far wrong on the one side as autocracy is on the other. So tyranny and bolshevism are kindred diseases. The pendulum swing towards bolshevism inevitably meets tyranny. They are twin brothers, so much alike that, with France in the eighteenth century and Russia in the twentieth as ex-amples, they are indistinguishable. A hundred and fifty years ago the people of the United States were beset by tyranny; they answered it by the Boston Tea Party. If I am not mistaken they will meet tyranny's twin brother —bolshevism—in kindred fashion.

If it is the desire of the American people to repudiate bolshevism, render impotent the subversive and destruc-tive elements which seek to substitute socialism for re-publicanism, and if it is their desire that government shall continue to function according to law and the Constitu-tion, it is within their power to fulfill that desire entirely and emphatically. But it can't be done sitting calmly, or even disgustedly, at home on election day. The United States government ceases to be government by the peo-ple when the people do not exercise their right of suffrage. The kind of government—red, pink or red-white-and-blue —we shall have in this country henceforth is a matter entirely up to those who are qualified to vote and who do so.

What'll you do? It's up to you. You can vote red radicalism in or out—or do nothing. It's your country.

APPENDIX

APPENDIX A

It is now well known to almost everyone that the charge made by Senator Wheeler that the Department of Justice was not functioning, was just a common falsehood. But for the benefit of those who are not enlightened a short resume is herewith given.

This is taken from a speech made by Attorney General Daugherty at Columbus, Ohio, on the event of his home-coming, after President Coolidge had asked for and received his resignation. Ohio's principal citizens gave Mr. Daugherty a testimonial dinner on his return to his native state and the following extract is taken from his address:

On the 27th day of March, 1924, the day upon which President Coolidge was forced, through misrepresentation, to request my resignation as Attorney General of the United States, the Department of Justice was functioning more efficiently than at any time in the history of the Government. It was, in fact, the greatest and most successful law office in the world. One of its most important branches was the War Transactions Section, having jurisdiction of war fraud cases. This department had to do with the extraordinary volume of business growing out of the war contracts. The wisdom of its creation by the Attorney General is fully proven by the remarkable results obtained, and which are matters of official record.

Constant and unjustifiable criticism has been heaped upon the Department of Justice and upon the Attorney General by those who anticipated and deserved action against them in war fraud cases, anti-trust cases, prohibition cases, postal fraud cases, and radical cases. But notwithstanding all this, the Department was shock-proof and driving along with most successful results in all its various branches.

President Coolidge well knew this, and so expressed himself frequently. Many of those who struck the hardest blows against the Government, the Department of Justice, and the Attorney General, officially and personally, were deceived and misled into doing so, but they cannot be altogether excused, because the reports of the Department were available and dependable and showed conclusively the wonderful accomplishments of the Department since its organization and especially during the past three years.

In justice to the clean and capable men and women to whom credit is due for the almost incomprehensible results accomplished by the Department of Justice, and because you are entitled to know the facts, you will permit me, I am sure, to give you in concrete form and as briefly as possible some idea of what the Department has done in the past three years as compared with the three years just preceding.

In making this comparison I assure you it is with no disposition to criticise my predecessor or his assistants.

In the years 1918, 1919 and 1920, the period just preceding the present administration, there had been 100,913 criminal cases disposed of.

In the years 1921, 1922 and 1923, covering the period of my administration of the Department of Justice, there were disposed of 168,606 such cases.

There was collected by the government in the years 1918, 1919 and 1920 in such cases the total sum of $14,297,548.00; where as in the three years of 1921, 1922 and 1923, there was collected in cases of this class $32,556,467.00.

The increase of civil business disposed of by the Department during the comparative periods was even greater in proportion than the criminal business to which I have referred.

The number of anti-trust cases tried and disposed of in the past three years was greater by 33 1/3 per cent than the number disposed of in the three years just preceding.

Fines collected by the government in this class of cases within the past three years were more than twice as much as the total amount in the three years preceding.

Until the present administration was installed, not a single person had ever been sent to prison for violation of the anti-trust laws. In the trial of cases arising out of the violation of the anti-trust laws, the Department of Justice urged the courts to impose prison sentences as well as heavier fines upon those convicted. The courts held that in order to stop such violations prison sentences should be imposed, and during the past three years many violators were given prison sentences. Some of them happened to be millionaires. They were not sent to prison because they were millionaires. That was just an incident. I will say, however, that a prison is an uncomfortable place for millionaire offenders to take the rest cure, and they have many ways of representing to the public that the Attorney General is not a fit or proper man for the job.

During the war and thereafter there was much cry and criticism against men and concerns who had transacted business with the government in war time. But not until 1921, when the Harding administration was installed, was anything done to investigate war-time transactions or to recover moneys fraudulently obtained from the government.

It takes many months after a change of administration to re-organize properly the Department of Justice, to establish its definite policies, and to select the men and instruct them in the practical work of carrying out such policies.

The law business of the Department of Justice, as far as suits and claims are concerned, originates in and comes to the Department of Justice from the several other governmental departments. This is true in the case of claims and disputes growing out of war transaction and contracts. The war ended in 1918, yet up to the time the new administration was installed in 1921, the Department of Justice had not instituted a single suit or made any collection in so-called war transactions. Congress had made no appropriation to pay the extra expense of the Department in investigating claims of this character and instituting suits on such as were found necessary. In May,

1922, upon the request of the Attorney General, Congress appropriated $500,000.00 for this purpose. Thereafter the work progressed as fast as it could be done thoroughly, and on February 5, 1924, there were pending 117 suits involving $62,343,741.00.

Nineteen claims were pending with receivers or trustees in bankruptcy involving $2,686,418.00. Ten claims had been reduced to judgments amounting to $48,308.00. Eighty-two claims were disposed of, and collections of over six millions in cash paid into the government treasury. Three hundred claims, involving a total of $41,000,000.00 were under investigation. The Department of Justice, therefore, has had before it in excess of $100,000,000.00 of war claims in dispute. On the first of March, 1924, there were settlements in process of consummation amounting to $4,480,000.00, which will shortly make the total amount received to date over $9,000,000.00, with an expense to the government of $1,000,000.00, and all the work of organization and preliminary legal study and investigation completed.

I might here add that a settlement practically agreed upon before I left the Department was accepted day before yesterday under which the government is to receive $1,000,000 cash.

In addition, there were pending in the court of claims in December, 1923, 2,200 cases, involving $1,783,830,467.72, and of these cases 1,514 arose out of the World War.

About thirty days before I resigned as Attorney General of the United States, claims against the government aggregating more than $350,000,000, and which were involved in 28 cases arising out of claims by German ship owners whose vessels were seized during the war, were won in the Court of Claims by the Department of Justice acting in behalf of the government. The court dismissed all of the bills in these twenty-eight cases outright, which means that this enormous amount was saved to the government.

In the period of a year and a half ending December, 1923, 387 cases growing out of the World War were handled by the Department of Justice in the Court of Claims alone. In these cases the total amount claimed against the government was $13,052,974.00. The total amount of judgments obtained, against the government in these cases, was $3,061,476.00, of which amount the government had always admitted a liability of $1,250,-000.00.

Cases of this class take no priority over other cases in the courts, and considering the congested condition of court dockets throughout the country, no additional number of men could have tried any greater number of cases than were tried in the past three years.

Looking back over the four years during which the National Prohibition Act has been in force, one is amazed at the volume of business which the federal courts have handled during that period. More than 115,000 criminal cases arising under the prohibition act have already been terminated. Of this great number of cases, eighty per cent, or 92,411, have resulted in convictions and have brought to the government in fines, $15,726,593.

The volume of litigation arising under the prohibition act has increased so rapidly and enforcement has been speeded up so effectively that a glance at the number of cases commenced, terminated and convictions obtained is very interesting and at the same time gives conclusive answer to the critics whose criticism is not in good faith.

Fiscal Year Ending June 30	Cases Commenced	Cases Terminated	Convictions
1920 (6 mos.)	7,291	5,095	4,315
1921	29,114	21,962	17,962
1922	34,984	28,743	22,749
1923	49,021	42,730	34,067

Under my administration of the Department of Justice a policy was adopted, under Section 22 of the National Prohibition Act, to employ the use of the injunction to close up, as nuisances, thousands of breweries and saloons throughout the country.

EXHIBIT A 1.

NIAGARA LIFE INSURANCE COMPANY
1630 Land Title Building
Philadelphia, Pennsylvania

March 27, 1923.

To the Department of Justice,
  Washington, D. C.
Gentlemen:

I have read in the North American, Philadelphia, an account that on May 2 you will proceed to secure permanent injunction against the railways employees department and affiliated organizations.

For four years the writer was chairman-counsel of the Philadelphia-Camden advisory boards, local branch of said railway department, and resigned my post due to my non-belief in the program and policy on the part of B. M. Jewell and associates.

Immediately following the enactment of the transportation act, Mr. Jewell sent for me at his offices, then in Washington, and stated that it had been concluded not to go along with the law, but to stage a fight, and desired to know if I could line up all the men in Philadelphia.

I told Mr. Jewell I would not have any part in any such program, and my only advice to him and his associates was to subscribe to the law. I quoted them former Mayor Mitchell of New York who stated that if a law was bad, the best way to rid one of that law was to enforce it.

Jewell and his associates then concluded to follow the law, but made most clear that their plan would be to do away with the Labor Board, and force government ownership. The latter also I did not believe in.

Later I had many talks with Jewell in Chicago, Columbus, Philadelphia, etc., also with Wm. H. Johnson, president of the International Association of Machinists. Their whole plan was to force the Board out of business and return to government operation as during the war.

About the middle of 1921 the strike called on July 1, 1922, was planned. I opposed the same, and the result was that Jewell, Johnson, Good, etc., made most clear to me that I must support them 100 per cent or take the consequences. I refused to support their insane policy.

In August and September, 1921, N. P. Good, president of System Federation No. 90, with offices at Pittsburgh, called upon me at my office in Philadelphia a number of times, to inform me that he had had many talks with Jewell, Johnson, etc., and that they demanded to know my position, and refusal on my part to support them in any steps taken, be what they may, would result in the entire labor board movement so far as they could command it, to bury me, and before they finished I could count myself finished financially and otherwise.

I had at that time the financing of a bank, and this they stated they would wreck, and anything and everything else I was interested in or connected with directly or indirectly.

But I declined to support their sordid and un-American program, making my position known to the railroad men of this section, numbering about 10,000, and the result was a split. In October, 1921, when the Pennsylvania shopmen voted on the matter of strike, which strike was called July 1, 1922, about thirty-five per cent voted to strike. The union rules required a two-thirds vote to carry the strike, and failing to secure such, orders were given to get the required vote anyway; therefore, Alfred E. Hart and W. P. Weller, officers of System Federation No. 90, together with Thomas Kelley, Lodge 87, machinists, Thomas Egan, Lodge 517, sheet metal workers, Harry A. Martin, Lodge 753, electrical workers, Dennis Carroll, Lodge 815, carmen, forged the names of members to ballots, thereby securing in that manner the required two-thirds vote.

When the strike took place, hundreds of the men refused on my advice to strike. I will here say that I resigned my post March 1, 1922, or four months prior to the strike. Jewell, Johnson, Good, etc., had in the meantime sent an army of their strong-arm men to this city to follow me, spread falsehoods, and destroy my standing, credit, etc.

They circulated the statement that I was in the secret employ of the Pennsylvania Railroad and had already received $30,000. However, would advise that I fought my own battles, had to finance them myself, forcing me to sell my house and fairly everything else, and ran into debt considerably.

I could not begin to cite you all the facts that I am acquainted with, but do know that the shopmen strike of July 1 was a conspiracy against our government, and the shopmen today do not know why they went on strike.

I shall be glad to render any service I can to my government in its efforts to secure the desired injunction. Had I joined with Jewell, Johnson, Good, etc., I am satisfied, thoroughly so, that the entire force of the shopmen on the Pennsylvania Railroad system would have gone on strike, which railroad is the largest and most important in the United States * * *

I can be reached at 1630 Land Title Building, Spruce 2873, or at 3349 Market street, second floor.

Cordially yours,

H. S. JEFFERY.

APPENDIX B

But for the following documents Senator Wheeler might have convinced a portion of the gullible American public that his fight on Attorney General Daugherty was an honest or sincere effort to cleanse the government. The following affidavits prevent any such interpretation by even the most unsophisticated. Wheeler pledged the radicals two years before "his investigation" that he would "get Daugherty" because Mr. Daugherty had performed a legal act not to the liking of the reds and radicals; namely the railroad injunction. This injunction has since been upheld by the United States Supreme Court as necessary in performance of his duty as Attorney General of the United States. So they "got Daugherty" for doing his duty.

STATE OF MONTANA,
COUNTY OF WHEATLAND, SS.:

AFFIDAVIT

Howard Squires, being first duly sworn, deposes and says, that he is a citizen of the United States and past the age of twenty-one years; that he is a resident of Harlowton, Montana, where he has continuously resided for the past seven years; that during all said period of time, he has been and now is the editor and publisher of The Harlowton Times; that affiant was in Harlowton when Mr. B. K. Wheeler, now United States Senator from Montana, made one or more campaign speeches in his campaign for the nomination and election to the office of United States Senator during the year 1922, and affiant heard the said B. K. Wheeler, in his talk to a group of people here consisting chiefly of union laboring men say that if he was elected to the Senate of the United States from the State of Montana, as he believed he would be, he intended to fight Attorney General Daugherty on account of the part he took in the injunction against union railroad men, or words to that effect; that affiant would not be certain of the exact language used by the said B. K. Wheeler in his political speech, but affiant is positive that a part of his said speech was a direct attack upon the said Attorney General and the part he had taken in the injunction cases.

HOWARD SQUIRES.

Subscribed and sworn to before me this 11th day of March, 1924.

L. D. GLENN.

Notary Public for the State of Montana, residing at Harlowton, Montana. My commission expires Sept. 26th, 1925.

(Notarial Seal.)

STATE OF MONTANA,
COUNTY OF WHEATLAND, SS.:

AFFIDAVIT

L. D. Glenn, being first duly sworn deposes and says, that he is a native born citizen of the United States and past the age of twenty-one years; that he has resided in Harlowton, Montana, continuously since September, 1907, and during said period of time has been and is now engaged in the practice of law; that he has been personally acquainted with Mr. B. K. Wheeler, of Butte, Montana, for more than ten years last past; that he knew the said B. K. Wheeler, now United States Senator from Montana, during the time he was making his campaign for the nomination and election to the United States Senate in 1922, and heard the said B. K. Wheeler make two or more political speeches in Harlowton, and heard the said B. K. Wheeler in his talk to a number of people, consisting principally of union laboring men, make the remark that if he was elected as the Senator from Montana to the United States Senate, as he believed he would be, one of the first things he would do would be to force Attorney General Daugherty from the President's cabinet, or words to that effect; that the said B. K. Wheeler also

at the same place and in the same talk made reference
to the injunction cases which Mr. Daughtery had started
against labor unions, and it was not difficult to infer
the purpose of the speaker in making these statements.

Further affiant sayeth not.

L. D. GLENN.

Subscribed and sworn to before me, this 11th day of
March, 1924.

W. A. LYNN,

Notary Public for the State of Montana, residing at
Harlowton, Montana. My commission expires March 21,
'25.

(Notarial Seal.)

STATE OF MONTANA,
COUNTY OF WHEATLAND, SS.:

AFFIDAVIT

F. P. Grieve, being first duly sworn, deposes and says;
that he is a citizen of the United States and past the
age of twenty-one years; that he is a resident of Harlowton, Montana, where he has continuously resided since
the 20th day of February, 1921, and during which period of time he has been and now is the duly elected,
qualified and acting County Treasurer of Wheatland
County, Montana; that for many years prior to taking
the office of County Treasurer, affiant resided at Judith
Gap, in said county; that affiant was in Harlowton, Montana, when one B. K. Wheeler, now one of the United
States Senators from Montana, made one or more political
speeches here in his campaign for the nomination and
election to the office he now holds, in the year 1922;
that affiant has met the said B. K. Wheeler and heard
him in one or more of his political talks in Harlowton, Montana, make a statement to the effect that if
he was elected to the Senate of the United States
from the state of Montana, as he believed he would be,
one of the first things he would do when he got down
there would be to force Attorney General Daugherty
from the President's cabinet; that the said B. K. Wheeler,
in the same speech at Harlowton, in the presence of a
number of people, among which were many union labor-

ing people, he made reference to the injunction cases that Attorney General Daugherty had started against labor unions previously, and that it was not difficult to infer the purpose of the speaker in making these statements. Further affiant sayeth not.

F. P. GRIEVE.

Subscribed and sworn to before me this 11th day of March, 1924.

L. D. GLENN,

Notary Public for the State of Montana, residing at Harlowton, Montana. My commission expires Sept. 26th, 1925.

(Notarial Seal.)

APPENDIX C

Herewith are presented Gaston B. Means' affidavit and the correspondence which led up to it. It was Means' gossip about Mr. Daugherty which was printed as true by the newspapers of the country. If this sworn statement is not worthy of belief, then his testimony was not worthy of belief. Means first made this statement in August, 1924. A radical news association, the next day spread a report that Means had repudiated his repudiation. Means repudiated his repudiated repudiation and just before entering the Atlanta federal prison, where he is at the date of this writing, having been indicted and convicted by Attorney General Daugherty for bribery; Means made a new affidavit a part of which is herewith printed. If Means' testimony before the Wheeler committee was untrue, as it was, then there was no foundation for any of the rumors of suspicion against the Department of Justice.

The reader may take his choice. However, this one thing he must bear in mind; Means was indicted by Attorney General Daugherty and awaiting trial at the time he testified against Mr. Daugherty. Also that Senator Wheeler gave him a friendly subpoena from the Wheeler committee and that this subpoena superceded the authority of the court in which he was to be tried and that as long as Means was willing to tell stories about the Department of Justice; Wheeler kept him from going to trial on the charges on which he was later convicted.

This affidavit must be taken with more credence than his testimony, because; in testifying as he did he kept from going to trial and to prison. Would such a state of facts prompt a man of Means' character to lie? The reader can draw his own conclusion.

> 136 N. Union Street,
> Concord, North Carolina,
> Feb. 19th, 1925.

Hon. Harry M. Daugherty,
     Columbus, Ohio.

Dear Sir:

The reason for this letter is my request for a personal interview with you, and my sincere desire to speak to you of many matters, of which, I feel sure, you have no knowledge and of which I cannot adequately write.

It is with no hope nor expectancy that you either will or can help me in my present predicament, that I ask you for an interview, and this I earnestly beg you to understand and believe, or else the whole spirit and aim of this letter may have failed.

In the first place, I feel that by my testimony before the Brookhart-Wheeler Committee, I did you a great injustice, and am willing and anxious, in any way you think proper, to make amends for what I did, as far as possible.

My wife and others close and dear to me, immediately after I testified before the Brookhart-Wheeler Committee, and who knew the facts, urged me to correct publicly, at once, the injustice done you. There were circumstances then of which I will tell you, that made such a thing impossible, although I attempted three times to correct my error and failed, through no fault of my own, which you will agree is true when you know the facts, if you will give me an opportunity to lay them before you. The subject of the true facts at this time, leads me to express the opinion that you yourself, and certainly the public at large do not know the real purpose of some of the members of the Brookhart-Wheeler Committee.

On account of the stigma cast upon my little boy by my ingratitude and repudiation of you, and because

I want to clear my name as far as possible for the sake of his future, I desire to do what I can in atonement. In my possession are authentic and unquestionable documents to verify every statement I will make to you.

Hoping and trusting that you will advise me when and where I can, most convenient to yourself, see you, I am,

Yours respectfully,
(Signed) GASTON B. MEANS.

Columbus, Ohio,
March 7, 1925.

Mr. Gaston B. Means,
  136 N. Union St.,
    Concord, N. C.
Dear Sir:

Upon my return from an absence of more than a month I find your letter of the 19th ult., in which you request a conference with me.

As you know I have constantly refused, for good reasons to me at least, to have a personal interview with you since the date when, at the instance of Mr. Crim and Mr. Burns, I re-employed you as an agent of the government to perform services in one particular matter only. You have brought all this trouble upon yourself, I think, but I have no disposition to lecture you or to advise you. After conferring with my attorneys I have decided that if you desire to have a conference with me, as stated in your letter, I will consent to meet you in the presence of my attorneys and possibly a representative of the government. I have no promises to make to you, of course, but I am willing to hear what you have to say and to see what you have to present. I would have no objection to the presence of your attorney, or some friend at the conference, for I have no desire to take advantage of you in any respect. I expect to be in Columbus only two or three days, but your letter will be forwarded to me and if the suggestions herein are agreeable, I will fix the time and place for a meeting under the circumstances above indicated.

Very truly yours,
(Signed) H. M. DAUGHERTY.

---

136 N. Union Street,
  Concord, North Carolina,
    March 9, 1925.

Hon. H. M. Daugherty,
  150 East Broad Street,
    Columbus, Ohio.
Dear Sir:
  Your letter of the 7th inst., was received this morning, and the suggestions and conditions you mentioned for the conference are satisfactory to me, and the opportunity you give me for a personal interview is appreciated.
  If agreeable to you, and if Mr. W. J. Burns is willing, I should like to request that he be present at the conference.

                    Yours respectfully,
                        (Signed) GASTON B. MEANS.

AFFIDAVIT

  Gaston B. Means being first duly sworn on oath deposes and says that * * *
  While at Palm Beach, Florida, my wife advised me that Mr. Stansbury of the Hearst International or Universal service had phoned her that Senator Wheeler of Montana was anxious to see me in connection with an investigation to be made of the Department of Justice and Mr. H. M. Daugherty, the attorney general. Upon receipt of this advice from my wife I mentioned the fact to Mr. McLean that I had received such a request to meet Senator Wheeler, but that I had never met and did not know who Senator Wheeler was and that there was such a Senator from Montana by the name of Wheeler. In other words—seeking information from Mr. McLean because I had never heard of Senator Wheeler. Mr. McLean told me that what I was telling him was very interesting and that he would get in touch with Mr. Daugherty who at that time was in some other locality in Florida. I then told Mr. McLean that I had been very anxious to see Mr. Daugherty since my indictments and prior to my indictments, because the indictments were unjustifiable and unwarranted and I wanted to explain to him the situation and facts that I felt sure he had no knowledge of.
  As I understood it at the time Mr. McLean did get in touch with Mr. Daugherty over the telephone. At any rate a plan was perfected by which I was to keep in touch with Mr. Daugherty who was about to return

from Florida to Washington through Mr. Tom Miller, the Alien Property Custodian.

On my return to Washington I immediately got in touch with Mr. Tom Miller and advised him of the situation and I know that Mr. Miller did make an effort at my very first conference with him to get in communication with Mr. Daugherty, because he talked to Miss Carroll, Mr. Daugherty's secretary, over the telephone in my presence from his office, in reference to a future appointment with Mr. Daugherty. Colonel Miller advised me by all means to see Senator Wheeler and find out the motives, causes, reasons, etc., for the attack he (Senator Wheeler), was about to make on the Department of Justice and Mr. Daughterty.

I then got in touch with Mr. Stansbury and over the phone a date and hour were set for me to call on Senator Wheeler at his office in the Senate Office Building, * * *

At my first meeting with Senator Wheeler I stated to him that I had called at his request but hardly knew just exactly what he wanted to see me about, and this first visit as I remember it, must have been around February 11th, or 12th, or 13th, 1924, and the conference took place in his private office in the Senate Office Building. In substance he stated that he had had many callers at his office who had filed complaints against the Department of Justice and the Attorney-General Mr. H. M. Daugherty, and that these complainants had invariably stated to him that Mr. H. M. Daugherty had caused my indictments and that I was familiar with many facts concerning the Department of Justice and could give him details and accurate information and that I was very bitter against Mr. Daugherty and that they believed that if he would get in communication through some friend with me that I would be disposed to give him confirmatory information concerning rumors, etc. He stated that these complainants further added that unless he got in communication with me through some friend that I would not be very apt to call to see him and that he (Senator Wheeler), had then set out to find some friend of mine and had finally landed on Mr. Stansbury.

I promptly asked Senator Wheeler the names of some of the complainants and he was not frank in giving me on this first visit the names of the complainants. I then asked him to give me the nature of the complaints and he was not frank in this, but requested me to call again. I immediately, on leaving his office, reported this visit to Senator Wheeler to Colonel Miller.

From the day of my first visit to Senator Wheeler up until the day that I took the stand before the Brookhart-Wheeler Committee I held conferences with Senator Wheeler either at his office or at his home, both in the day-time and at night, or communicated with him over the telephone every day or every night. My visits to him were numerous and many. Also in the meantime I had met Senator Brookhart. All of these visits I reported to Colonel Miller and kept him posted and advised and I know at the time he was trying to convey information to Mr. Daugherty of the situation as it existed at the Capitol at that time and not until two or three days before I took the stand did I ever intend to take the stand and until Colonel Miller delivered this final message from Mr. Daugherty, namely: that Senator Wheeler and Means both can go to Hell and the Committee, because there was nothing against him that could hurt him, etc. But I knew what Mr. Daugherty did not know, namely: that Senator Wheeler had entered into a conspiracy to wreck the life of an innocent man (Mr. Daugherty) * * * I realized all along the situation was too big for me, and at my first diplomatic opportunity I got in touch with Mr. W. J. Burns and reference to this first contact with Mr. Burns after having met Senator Wheeler, will be gone into in further detail later and in chronological order.

After my first several conferences with Senator Wheeler he began to grow more confidential and enumerated numerous alleged charges that amounted to absolutely nothing against the Department of Justice and which he admitted amounted to nothing that he had learned from disgruntled or discharged employees of the Department of Justice. He cited only one piece of evidence that could by any possible chance have any merit to it, and that piece of evidence was in connection with the moving pictures of the Carpentier-Dempsey fight, and when Senator Wheeler discussed this with me he said he was really afraid to bring it out because the law was absurd and as a matter of fact the American people, that is, the majority of the American people, were not opposed to sports of any kind, including boxing, if conducted properly and that to lay any stress on this point would hurt him politically. He further stated that he had kicked up a whole lot of furore and had absolutely no evidence upon which to back his innuendoes and insinuations.

All the time in these various conferences with him he was asking me whether there was any chance of him dealing confidentially with Mr. Daugherty. My invariable reply was that I had tried to see officials of the Department of Justice and Mr. Daugherty prior to my indictments and since my indictments to explain the injustice of them, but that I was never able to get such a conference. I did not understand then nor do I know positively now that I understand, why he wanted to have, if possible, a confidential conference with Mr. Daugherty, but at any rate among our early conferences he told me that (and I am positive about this), certain of his political enemies in Montana, (and this was before the hearings of the Brookhart-Wheeler Committee had begun and even before the resolution had passed in the Senate to make the investigation of the Department of Justice), were attempting to cause him some trouble in connection with oil lands in Montana, and the basis of this trouble lay in the fact that he had talked to some wealthy oil capitalist about financing some oil project that he had on hand with some friends in Montana. He further asked me whether I could learn or ascertain whether the Department of Justice had interested themselves in any way in connection with this trouble that his political enemies were trying to cause him in Montana, and he told me that he knew that I was the collector for Mr. W. J. Burns, Mr. Daugherty and Mr. Jess Smith. I told him repeatedly that this was absolutely untrue and that if he really believed or anybody believed that I had ever collected a dollar and given it either to Mr. Burns, Mr. Daugherty or Mr. Jess Smith they were fools.

Soon after this I enumerated to him absolutely truthfully every dollar that I had collected and the details in connection therewith and just what had become of the money, and at his request later in my own handwriting I wrote out in detail what I had stated to him verbally, and I am positive that somewhere among my papers I have a carbon copy of this original statement to him. And in addition I told him that I would gladly give him my records, documents, and files confirmatory of my statements, and he said to me then that he would not like to have such records except in an official way for

fear that the government might see fit to issue a subpoena duces tecum or some other kind of official documents for them.

He thereupon in my presence on February 21, 1924,
dictated to his sister, Mrs. Mitchell, in his private office,
the following

"UNITED STATES SENATE,
Committee on Indian Affairs.
Washington, D. C.
February 21,1924.

Mr. G. N. Means,
  903-16th Street, N.W.,
  Washington, D. C.
Dear Sir:

You have in your possession certain documents, pa-
pers, records, diaries, et cetera, pertaining to the reso-
lution which I have introduced demanding an investiga-
tion of the Department of Justice.

I request that you immediately turn those documents,
papers, records and diaries over to me for my use in
this investigation.

Respectfully,

B. K. WHEELER.

BKW-M"

(NOTE: This was the occasion when I first met Mrs.
Mitchell, who is Senator Wheeler's sister, and he advised
me that I could deal with her confidentially at any
time when he was not present at his office. He also
instructed her that she should allow me to enter his
private office through the door in the main hall, which
did not bear his name, as is customary with all the
offices of the senators.)

After this letter was dictated my recollection is that
I went down to the Senate restaurant to get a pack
of cigarettes while Mrs. Mitchell was transcribing her
notes, and when I returned it had not been signed by
Senator Wheeler and that Mrs. Mitchell actually signed
it. However, I am not positive about this—at least I
remember distinctly it had not been signed and there
was a delay in getting the signature.

After receiving the letter I thereupon delivered to him
in part, and later, all of the records, files, data, diaries,
etc., that I had, which enumerated truthfully and ac-

curately all my dealings and which he admitted confirmed the verbal and written statement I had given him pertaining to any alleged receiving of any money for Mr. W. J. Burns, Mr. H. M. Daugherty or Mr. Jess Smith. In fact after he got through with the papers he said he was "in a hell of a situation" and that his only hope in carrying out the plan as devised by himself, * * * was to begin at once to frame up a situation.

Prior to the passage of the resolution in the Senate creating the Brookhart-Wheeler Committee, Senator Wheeler was very much disturbed as to whether the resolution would pass and the wording and the preparation of this resolution apparently was very difficult on the part of his private secretary Mr. Hayes, because it was drafted and redrafted in my presence a number of times, and in addition Senator Wheeler had the names of several senators that he thought and believed would oppose the resolution, * * *

After the passage of the Senate Resolution authorizing the investigation of the Department of Justice and Mr. Daugherty, Senator Wheeler became extremely nervous as to the possibilities of being able to make good his charges against the Department of Justice and Mr. Daugherty, and he began again to show a disposition and by his request, if possible, to have a confidential talk with Mr. Daugherty. We devised a plan with this idea in view upon my suggestion that he could possibly see Mr. Daugherty by coming in contact with Mr. E. B. McLean. Therefore he first told me that he and Senator Walsh had had several confidential conferences with Mr. Wilton Lambert, Mr. E. B. McLean's attorney, and for me to see Mr. McLean and urge him to meet Senator Wheeler in a confidential conference, but not to tell Mr. McLean that the purpose of the conference was for a confidential meeting between Mr. Daugherty and himself (Senator Wheeler).

Acting upon this I called upon Mr. McLean at his home, "Friendship," three times, possibly more, and urged him to see Senator Wheeler without his attorney. Mr. McLean told me that he could not do this and would not do it without first consulting his attorney, Mr. Wilton Lambert, but that I was right in my knowledge of the fact that Senator Walsh, Senator Wheeler and Mr. Lambert had had one or two confidential conferences since his arrival in Washington from Florida.

Senator Wheeler further stated that he did not want anybody except himself and Mr. McLean present at the conference.

The final conclusion of this matter was that Mr. McLean point blank refused to see Senator Wheeler and as I assumed on the advice of his attorney. Mr. McLean knows these are the facts because in his presence he heard me on one occasion talk to Senator Wheeler at Senator Wheeler's home in regard to this matter.

From the date of the passage of the resolution until the day that I actually took the stand Senator Wheeler was apprehensive as to whether I would carry out the plan for him that he had devised for the framing-up of Mr. Daugherty, and every day he would cite me the name of some person who had told him that my whole object in the matter was to lead him into a trap, and among those he mentioned who insisted upon him not putting any dependence in what I would say for him on the stand he quoted Senator Walsh of Montana.

Now until Senator Wheeler heard of Roxey Stinson his idea was to use me as his first witness and the reason for this was because any other of the alleged evidence that he had, originated with people of such apparent prejudice that he realized the newspapers would not carry the story like he hoped to be able to get it over.

Some few days prior to the actual beginning of the hearings before the Brookhart-Wheeler Committee Senator Wheeler phoned me to come to his office immediately in connection with a very important matter. I met him in his private office and he asked me whether I knew of a woman named Roxey Stinson. I told him that I did, that she was a former wife of Mr. Jess Smith and I had heard of her through Mr. Jess Smith. He told me that he had been advised that Roxey Stinson had a number of letters from Mr. Jess Smith and that he understood these letters were compromising to both Mr. Smith, Mr. Daugherty and their close friends. He asked me further whether I believed she had any such letters. I told him I believed she had some letters from Jess Smith from what Jess Smith had told me on one or two occasions, but I did not believe that she had any letters which were compromising in any way and which would be of any real value in establishing any charges against the Attorney-General Mr. Daugherty. He went on to say that he had heard that she was quite a striking and handsome woman.

After this interview with me concerning Roxey Stinson I left his office and he later phoned me that same day asking me whether it was possible for me to go to Columbus, Ohio, with him, as he had decided to go there to at least have a talk with Roxey Stinson and possibly bring her on to Washington, D. C. He did go to Columbus, Ohio, and on his return he phoned me that he had Roxey Stinson with him and we discussed over the phone what arrangements could be made for her accommodations while in Washington, and it was later decided that she should go to the Hotel Washington.

Prior to her appearance on the stand Senator Wheeler was convinced from his statements to me, except for the fact that the situation smacked of a social scandal there was nothing to any evidence she had, but that it would be of enormous interest to a certain element of the public because of the social scandal, and that to bring out any material, essential matter Miss Stinson would have to be coached. Her testimony is a matter of record and by going over it line at a time and word for word I can explain Senator Wheeler's premeditated motive in his question and the premeditated and prepared answer that he expected. This feature in this statement I will not go into unless requested because the analysis of her testimony here would make this statement too voluminous.

I will refer to one striking feature of her testimony when she alleges that she saw Jess Smith with seventy-five $1,000 bills or notes. This statement was absolutely a creation of Senator Wheeler's mind to corroborate the statement he was asking me to make about having collected supposedly from a Jap in the Bellevue Hotel in Washington, D. C., one hundred $1,000 bills and given them to Jess Smith. Senator Wheeler could never make Miss Stinson on the stand say that she saw Jess Smith with the $75,000 bills soon after January or February, 1922, although he tried to coach her on this point, but for some reason he could not get the idea clear in her mind that under no circumstances must she have seen Jess Smith with the $75,000 bills prior to January or February, 1922, and except on a date shortly thereafter.

It was after February 21, 1924, on which date I turned over to Senator Wheeler my diaries, records and papers and after I had prepared for him my written statement covering all matters that he had asked me about and after

February 29, 1924, when the resolution was passed in the United States Senate creating the Brookhart-Wheeler Committee that Senator Wheeler began, so far as I know, his conspiracy to destroy the Department of Justice, to destroy Attorney-General Mr. Daugherty, * * * and the details of this I will take up step at a time and endeavor to show exactly what took place and his method of procedure.

Now when I discovered that Senator Wheeler was actually entering into a conspiracy to drive Mr. H. M. Daugherty and others from their Cabinet positions, and to absolutely discredit the government, if possible, I was more persistent than before in my efforts that Mr. Tom Miller, Alien Property Custodian, get in touch with Mr. Daugherty and ascertain whether he was interested in learning the facts, and Colonel Miller in the days intervening between February 29 and March 14, 1924, in my presence phoned Miss Carroll, Mr. H. M. Daugherty's secretary, on quite a few occasions in an effort to make an appointment with him.

Soon, or as I remember it, immediately after the resolution creating the Brookhart-Wheeler Committee had passed, on one Sunday Senator Wheeler phoned me at my home to come to his home (I had been there on a number of occasions before), where he introduced me to Mr. Frank Vanderlip and a man (whose name I did not catch), whom he said was Mr. Vanderlip's secretary, also Mr. William Flynn, former head of the Bureau of Investigations of the Department of Justice was at Senator Wheeler's house, and later I met Mr. Pinchot, a brother of the Governor of Pennsylvania. In addition I was introduced, not in the presence of the others, to a man whose name I have forgotten but who was designated to me as the creator and organizer of the Farmer-Labor Movement and Party.

It was just around this time—on the night of this very Sunday, that Senator Wheeler for the first time told me that if they could not find anything on the Department of Justice and Mr. Daugherty and the Administration, and so far they had not been able to find anything, then framed evidence would have to be produced, that they had gone too far in their insinuations and innuendoes as to graft and corruption, otherwise he and his associates would be ruined; that he had believed that proper overtures long before this would have been made to him by some close friend or friends of Mr. Daugherty which would lead to an adjustment of his and Mr. Daugherty's differences.

At Senator Wheeler's house on this Sunday I talked privately to Mr. Vanderlip in Senator Wheeler's dining room and Mr. Vanderlip advised me that he had been making some very extensive investigations concerning corruption that he knew existed in every department of the government from President Harding down, and that any and all statements that he might make concerning such corruption were based on facts that came to him after the most careful investigation through experienced investigators.

Mr. Vanderlip further stated that he had, or was just about to open an office in Washington which would be headquarters to investigation in a most thorough way all the activities of the different departments of the government where he already knew corruption existed, for the purpose of obtaining evidence that would lead to indictments of high officials. He further stated that Mr. William Flynn would be employed as head of his bureau of investigation; that he was interested in employing other experienced investigators and asked me whether I would consider a proposition. He then made careful inquiry as to whether I knew anything relative to President Harding's private life that was improper, and in part as to his relations with any women, etc.

He also said that he understood that Mr. E. B. McLean had locked up in his safe at the office of "The Washington Post" quite a few papers pertaining to some private, confidential financial transactions in which President Harding was involved, and these papers would show to a certain extent at least that Mr. McLean was acting as a kind of confidential trustee in the interest of Mrs. Harding, and that he would like to be put in touch, or have Senator Wheeler put in touch, with anybody close to Mr. McLean who might have some knowledge of the foregoing mentioned supposed facts, and asked me whether I knew any such person.

I advised him that I knew Mr. William Duckstein, one of Mr. McLean's secretaries, quite well and this fact he immediately mentioned to Senator Wheeler by leaving the dining room and walking to the living room and so informed him, and when he returned he requested of me that I bring Mr. Duckstein to Senator Wheeler. Later, at the urgent and persistent request of Senator Wheeler I was finally able to get Mr. Duckstein to call to see Senator Wheeler at Senator Wheeler's house.

After Mr. Pinchot had left, Senator Wheeler handed me for the first time a long series of typewritten questions with the answers below each question and asked me what I thought about those questions for me to answer as a jolt to the Department of Justice, Mr. Daugherty, former government officials and the members of other departments of the government, etc. I read over the questions and the answers also and I saw at once that he prepared his questions primarily from my diaries and records that I handed him some days prior and which he later returned to me in part. He then told me that the whole object and purpose of the investigation would be solely for political purposes and he believed that if an investigation was handled properly he could become the Democratic nominee for President, and if not, for Vice-President certainly, and that if he could get the nomination he would be supported by the Democratic wing of the Republican party, and that if matters did not shape themselves around along these lines then a new party would have to be created. He also said that when he first started the agitation against Mr. Daugherty and the Department of Justice he had an entirely different motive in view in starting the agitation, but that when such a man as Vanderlip and the Pinchots were willing to back him financially he believed that the time had come to lead the movement along the lines he indicated in the statement I had just heard Mr. Pinchot make, and that La Follette had an enormous following; that in reality he himself was a La Follette man and that he was advising with La Follette in connection with everything that was being done. Then he went into a detailed account of the type of man La Follette was, etc., and explained the political situation as concerned possible candidates before the Democratic convention, namely: McAdoo, Smith and the influence of the Catholic and non-Catholic vote, etc., as well as the political situation that would confront the Republican convention.

It was after this meeting where Senator Wheeler first made his ideas so plain to me, that I began to know Senator Brookhart, although I had already met him on quite some few occasions only for a short interval of time. Senator Brookhart apparently was absolutely sincere in his denunciation of the wealthy and as he termed them "capitalists of the country." Any man, so I sized it up, in Senator Brookhart's opinion who had any real money was a thief and a scoundrel right on the start. Senator Brookhart agreed with Senator Wheeler's aggressive attitude and to use Senator Brookhart's own expression, "You have to fight fire with fire and use the same methods that the other crowd uses to awaken the people to the true situation of conditions as they actually exist." Therefore, to the actual extent of Senator Brookhart's knowledge of the length to which Senator Wheeler was going I have no definite information except his constant approval of all of Senator Wheeler's plans. Senator Brookhart would end most of our conferences with the expression, "The American people are willing to believe anything and everything against the government, and the thicker we can put it on the better."

Besides Senator Wheeler said La Follette and Senator Brookhart's agitation against the Democratic party or the Republican party in power and the constant consultations between La Follette, Wheeler and Brookhart, also Senator Walsh of Montana, was more active than merely interested.

I had met and known Senator Walsh to some extent through his son-in-law, Mr. Emmet Gudger, of North Carolina, who was a college mate of mine at the University of North Carolina, and later became pay-master, holding an officer's rank on the "Mayflower" during the Wilson administration, and this position threw Gudger into close contact with President Wilson. So Senator Walsh, through Mr. W. C. Phillips, a former operator of the Bureau of Investigation during the Wilson administration, sent for me through Phillips to come to his home for a conference with him, which I did, and Phillips went there with me. Senator Walsh, after he took me into his parlor, letting Mr. Phillips sit in the reception hall, recounted the fact that he knew that his son-in-law Emmet Gudger and myself had been quite good friends and that Gudger had been able to be of some service to me when I was a secret service operator for the German Government prior to our entrance into the war and that because of this connection he wanted to ask me a few questions in an endeavor to gain some unimportant information in regard to whether I knew a Mr. Edward H. Bohner, who was the bodyguard of President Coolidge when he was Vice-President and an investigator with the Bureau of Investigation under Mr. W. J. Burns.

I told Senator Walsh that I did know Mr. Bohner and

had known him when he was an investigator for the W. J. Burns International Detective Agency before he came with the Government. Senator Walsh then asked me just what type of man Mr. Bohner was and other general questions concerning whether he was a single man or a married man and whether I knew how many trips he made with President Coolidge when he was Vice-President, etc., and whether I was on friendly terms with Mr. Bohner. All of these questions I answered.

Senator Walsh then asked me whether I had ever heard that Mr. Bohner had stated that he knew that President Coolidge when Vice-President, had full knowledge of the Fall-Doheney-Sinclair oil transactions and that he (Mr. Bohner), gained this information in connection with some telegrams or correspondence that he had seen while with Mr. Coolidge on trips when Mr. Coolidge was speculating on the oil stocks in which the Doheney-Sinclair crowd were interested.

I told Senator Walsh that I had never heard Mr. Bohner make any such statement * * * but the question was to be able to make Mr. Bohner live up to the statement and tell * * * what he knew in connection with such stock transactions on the part of Vice-President Coolidge. Senator Walsh said that of course he knew that a man like Mr. Bohner would not want to lose his position with the government and that he could not be blamed for this, but that he thought that if the matter was investigated a little further that some way might be found out of the situation that would warrant Mr. Bohner in telling the truth, even if he did lose his position, and Senator Walsh virtually ended the conference by saying that the matter was delicate and of such an important nature that he would like to ascertain more facts and take it up further with me when he would send for me again.

Senator Walsh never did take this matter up further with me, but Senator Wheeler did * * *

Because of confidential relations existing between Senator Walsh and myself, through his son-in-law, Mr. Emmet Gudger, as an intermediary, Senator Walsh was in a position to talk to me in a confidential way, and besides discussing the immediate business at hand he also went into some detail in regard to the activities and whereabouts of Emmet Gudger and his wife (who was Senator Walsh's daughter), and their family life, etc. Also Senator Walsh advised me that he understood the Department of Justice, through Mr. Daugherty and Mr. W. J. Burns,

had caused an investigation to be commenced in the late
Fall of 1921, or early Spring of 1922, in reference to oil
matters and that I had conducted a feature of this investigation and had come in contact with a Mr. Cole.

(Note: Evidently Senator Walsh had gotten this information through Mr. Wheeler, who had seen my reports
on my investigation of Mr. Cole.)

Senator Walsh wanted to know whether during my
investigation I had gained any information in regard to
some investments that he had made in oil matters. To
this I replied, "No." He then asked me as to whether I
knew whether the Department of Justice in making an
under-cover investigation in regard to oil matters had obtained any information in regard to his own investments
and interests in oil matters. To this I replied it was possible that the Department had made such investigations,
but that I had no knowledge of such activities on the
part of the Department of Justice, and he then asked me
whether there was any way of finding out whether the
Department of Justice had or was then conducting an
investigation as to any interest he might have in oil
matters. He explained that he had made some investments
of a speculative nature in some oil prospects or ventures,
but that there was absolutely nothing wrong about it.
However, such interest might be susceptible to a false
interpretation.

Senator Walsh went into quite some detail seeking information as to Mr. Burns' and Mr. Daugherty's methods
of acquiring information when they were conducting investigations of this kind and whether such investigations
would be handled through the main office in Washington
or through investigators located in the West, etc.

After meeting Mr. Vanderlip at Senator Wheeler's house
I came in contact with him a great number of times,
both at Senator Wheeler's home, Senator Wheeler's office
and Mr. Vanderlip's office in the N. E. Smith Building in
Washington, and Mr. Vanderlip stated the thorough way
in which he had perfected his propaganda and press agent
work in order that all material could be "put over" and
that he would be compelled to make good on the public
statements he had made.

Between the time I met Mr. Vanderlip and the date I
appeared on the stand I was going over with Senator
Wheeler almost—if not every day—the changes in the
questions and the answers as he had prepared them from
my documents, files, records, etc. Virtually all of the docu-

/ ments had been retained by him and kept at his home
after my interview with himself and Pinchot when we
went over the records. Also bear in mind that they had
been in his possession previous to this. When I called to
his attention that all of the records did not confirm the
answer to any number of the questions that he was going
to ask me his reply was, "Look at your records now and
you will find that the material has been supplied to and
added to on which you can make good if pushed to it by
anybody, but you are not going to be 'pushed to it,' because I am not going to let the examination of you get
out of my hands at any time."

He showed me the records since he had made the
necessary alterations and changes and supplied the necessary documents and that was satisfactory to me because
I was covering an investigation to expose the situation
as it existed had Mr. Daugherty seen fit, through Mr.
Miller, to ascertain the facts.

(Note—I believe, although I never discussed it with
him, that Colonel Miller will confirm positively that between February 29 and March 14, 1924, on any number
of occasions he tried to make an appointment with Mr.
Daugherty to apprise him of the true situation.)

After I had testified on March 14th, 1924, Senator
Wheeler urged me because he said my testimony had
been a great success, to use every endeavor immediately
to get in touch with Mr. W. J. Burns and request him
to come to see him (Senator Wheeler), and, carrying out
this request I called to see Colonel Tom Miller and
urged him to put me in touch with Mr. W. J. Burns,
which he did, and we three—Colonel Miller, Mr. W. J.
Burns and myself, met at Colonel Miller's office, and
I requested and urged Mr. W. J. Burns to allow me to
make an appointment to take him to see Senator Wheeler,
and Mr. Burns declined to meet him. I did not go
into any details with Mr. W. J. Burns because Senator
Wheeler had asked me not to do this, but Senator Wheeler had told me that his object in meeting Mr. Burns was
to arrange for a confidential conference between Mr.
Daugherty and himself (Senator Wheeler), whereby their
differences could be adjusted without further publicity.

Later, I again met Mr. W. J. Burns at the urgent
request of Senator Wheeler at the Metropolitan Club,
where he had an appointment with Elmer Dover, and repeated my urgent request to him that he meet Senator
Wheeler in a confidential interview and that all of this

matter could be stopped, but Mr. Burns declined to see Senator Wheeler, and I so reported to Senator Wheeler.

Now if so instructed I will take up my testimony line by line and analyze it, and state exactly the facts covering the entire conspiracy as it developed, not only to destroy Mr. Daugherty, but several other members of the cabinet and the government and create a new party that would swing La Follette and Wheeler into power, and this situation developed on the part of Senator Wheeler as a positive plan after my failure to get Mr. W. J. Burns to call at a confidential meeting with him at his home in Washington.

(Signed) GASTON B. MEANS.
Sworn to before me this 15th day of April, 1925.

Signed) JESSE L. KNAPP,
Notary Public, Westchester County, N. Y., Clerk's No. 273, Register's No. 7248. Commission expires March 30, 1928.

APPENDIX D

The following affidavits and statements are made by reputable persons. Needless to say, that while they were in possession of the truth concerning the falsity of the gossip regarding Mr. Daugherty and the Department of Justice, they were not allowed to testify before the Brookhart-Wheeler-Ashurst, Extraordinary Investigating Committee.

These documents should prove not only interesting to the public, but also to the newspapers which were so terribly misled.

I formerly resided at 449 Richmond avenue, Buffalo, New York, having offices at 740-42 Bramson Building, same city, and having conducted a stock and bond business in that city for the past three years.

On February 18th I was in Cleveland, Ohio, registered at the Hotel Cleveland in that city, prepared to start a campaign for the sale of securities of the Ideal Tire & Rubber Corporation. I found upon investigating that morning that it would be necessary for me to spend a

considerable amount of money on this campaign and did
not feel that I had sufficient funds to go ahead with it.
I remembered reading in the papers that Roxie Stinson,
an old sweetheart of mine of twelve years ago, had
fallen heir to a great deal of money, and so I called
her on the telephone and asked her to meet me in
Cleveland. She immediately agreed and came over to
Cleveland from Columbus, Ohio. * * * We went to the
Hotel Hollenden, where we registered as man and wife,
under the fictitious name of A. L. French and wife, of
Pittsburgh, Pennsylvania. * * * So upon going to Room
452, which was assigned us, I immediately started to
talk to her about my business proposition, when she interrupted and said, "I have a far bigger deal on right
now and you ought to come in on it." I asked her what
it was and she told me that she was being defrauded
out of her just portion of Jess Smith's estate by Harry
M. Daugherty and that she wanted revenge upon
Daugherty because he refused to recognize her or allow
Jess Smith to have her in Washington all the time that
they were in office and that she was prepared, if necessary, to invent stories and piece stories together that
would incriminate Daugherty to such an extent that he
would be forced to resign from office; also that she expected to sell her story for $150,000.00, which she felt
she was entitled to, and she asked me if I would get
some strong Democrat to purchase her story which she
concocted and also to pay her $150,000.00. Upon talking
to her for some time I realized that the woman knew
nothing positive herself, but was depending purely upon
hearsay and gossip. I left her at 12:30 that night and returned to my room at the Hotel Cleveland, where I met
one of my salesmen and had luncheon with him. The
following morning I called a former associate of mine,
one Henry O. Ellis, of Cleveland, Ohio, and told him
of this information that Miss Stinson had given me. He
said, "I would like to talk to the woman and see how
vicious she is." So we met her at the Hotel Statler for
luncheon and after introducing Ellis and going into
her story she said that if we would help her to find
some strong Democrat who would slander Daugherty and
use the statement that she would make and also pay her
$150,000.00 that she would pay us twenty per cent of
that amount. Upon leaving her and assuring her that
we would do this we immediately went over to Samuel
Ungerleider, a prominent broker in Cleveland, Ohio, and

told him just exactly what Miss Stinson had up her sleeve. * * * So he says: "The public mind is in such condition today that it would not pay to have any slanderous statements so totally false as these coming out; that something must be done to keep this woman quiet." So he said, "I will go with you back to her room at the Statler Hotel and talk to her," and said: "If she is the same woman I think she is we will have no trouble in keeping her quiet." (Miss Stinson went over to the Statler Hotel after luncheon with us and said her baggage would be there. I paid our bill at the Hotel Hollenden at 5:30 the following evening and had her baggage sent over to the Hotel Statler where she was already registered.) So upon Mr. Ungerleider going into the room and meeting Miss Stinson with me he immediately recognized her. * * * Mr. Ungerleider then asked her if she had any positive proof of the guilt of Harry M. Daugherty, which she immediately said that she had nothing. "Well, then," he said, "the only thing you can do is to keep your mouth shut and go back to Columbus and behave yourself or I am going to have you locked up for malicious slander of a government official." Upon returning to Ungerleider's office I met Mr. Mal Daugherty, brother of H. M. Daugherty, and upon being acquainted with the situation he thanked me for the interest I had taken in the matter to squelch any false reports that this woman might start. I left for Buffalo, my home, on February 21, and decided to forget the entire incident. The following morning, on Washington's birthday, however, I talked to my attorney, Mr. Henry Stern, 706 Mutual Life Building, Buffalo, and told him what had transpired in Cleveland, and that I was worried over a possible felony in registering with this woman. He then assured me that the worst I could be charged with would be a misdemeanor which was not extraditable, and to forget the whole transaction. Nothing more was said until the evening of March 7th, on which day we were moving our home. I received a telegram from my office—our telephone had not been installed—stating that Mr. Stern desired to see me at his office. The following morning, March 8th, I met Mr. Stern at his office and he was very much excited. He said, "Al, there is a federal warrant for you for conspiracy against an official of the United States Government * * * but due to my friendship * * * and upon my agreeing to have you go to Washington to testify against Daugherty this warrant will be withheld until you are safe in Washington if you go at once." I turned to his partner, Aaron Fybush, who was present, and said, "Aaron, I think the thing for me to do is to go over to the District Attorney's office and see if there is a warrant," and he said, "I agree with you." Upon his agreeing with me Stern jumped up in a rage and said, "You are just putting your head in a noose, because they will spirit you away from here and nobody will ever find you, and this is your only way out, to do as I tell you to do." He forced me to buy transportation to Washington, and we left that evening for Washington, arriving in Washington on Sunday morning. We stayed that day at the Hotel Washington and the following morning went to Senator Brookhart's office. Upon hearing Stern's information he immediately called Senator Wheeler. Wheeler became very much excited and said, "At last we have got something to go on, because up to now we haven't had a damn thing." He turned to me and said, "Fink, I want you to go to Columbus, Ohio, and bring this woman back." I said, "Not by a damn sight." He stepped out of the room for a moment and spoke to Mr. Rankin, Brookhart's secretary, and returned with a subpoena for me and also for Henry Stern and a letter addressed to me and signed by Brookhart, stating that I was under subpoena and was in the service of the committee functioning for the government, and was instructed to go and bring the party mentioned before the committee. Wheeler then said to me, "We want to leave just as quick as we can for Columbus." "But," he said, "we don't want to let anyone know where I am going; have you got any money?" I had about four or five hundred dollars with me, and he said, "Let me have $100.00. I don't dare go to the Senate paymaster and draw any money because they will immediately become suspicious of my taking a trip at this time." I gave him $100.00. He handed it back to me and told me to buy transportation for three on the 7 o'clock train to Columbus, Ohio. I did so. Stern, Wheeler and myself left and arrived at Columbus the following morning at about 10 o'clock. On the way out Wheeler tore the tags off from his baggage so that he could not be identified and checked them in the depot at Columbus, Ohio. We there got into a taxi and drove out to Miss Stinson's home. Wheeler handed me the subpoena and said, "You go in and serve her. We will wait for you." I went in and handed the sub-

poena to her and she said, "Why, Sander, you have
certainly got me into an awful mess." She said, "You
know I don't know anything, just as I told Ungerleider,"
and said, "here I am dragged into this mess." Well, I
told her that I was forced into it and that Senator
Wheeler was outside in the taxicab, and she said, "Let
them come in." So they did. She made the same statement to Wheeler, and he said, "I want to talk with you
alone." Stern and myself went out on her front veran-
dah. A few moments later Wheeler called us in and
said, "I have persuaded the little lady to return to
Washington with us." We took her dog to a dog hospital,
and left on the train for Pittsburgh, Pennsylvania, for
Washington, there being a four hour layover in Pittsburgh before the train continued on to Washington. We
arrived at Pittsburgh at 7 o'clock that evening, and all during the afternoon Wheeler spent in the drawing room
with Miss Stinson talking with her. He came back to Stern and
myself in the smoking compartment several times and said,
"My God, this woman doesn't know anything and I can't
get her to loosen up, but I think we can fix that when
we get to Pittsburgh". * * * He and Miss Stinson, Stern
and myself had dinner together. * * * Upon going to the
train later that evening, after staying at the table until
after ten o'clock, at which time Miss Stinson became
very affectionate towards Wheeler and proceeded to loosen
up the way he wanted her to. After boarding the train
and starting for Washington Wheeler spent several hours
with her * * * talking. The following morning Wheeler
came back to the smoking compartment and said, "At
last I have gotten this girl to testify the way I want
her to, and I had better get her right before the committee before she gets a change of heart." He said, "You
and Stern go to the hotel and then come over to Room
410 Senate Office Building, and we will start the hearings
at once." The hearings started that morning. After she
had started her testimony, at the end of the first day
I went to Wheeler and said, "I don't for one moment
propose that she is going to lie about this hotel episode
because it will ruin my family if it comes out," and
for several days she was kept off the stand on that
account, until Wheeler sent to Buffalo for my wife to
come to Washington so he could talk to her. She came,
accompanied by my secretary, Howard S. Edmonds, and
immediately came to Senator Wheeler's office. He remained alone with her in the office about three hours

and finally succeeded in persuading her that she should not feel any bitterness towards me and that I would be amply rewarded, as he had in mind that he was going to see that I received the appointment as Collector of Internal Revenue in Buffalo if I would go along with his plan to oust Daugherty from office, and that if I didn't, there would be dire consequences for me. He also told her that Stern was slated to receive the vacant Federal Judgeship that would be created in that section of New York State. He had previously told this to both Stern and myself in conversation on the way to and from Columbus. He also promised Miss Stinson that if she would play the game as he wanted her to, he would form a pool among his Democratic senatorial friends and give me the money to go to New York and sell the market short in advance of the news of Daugherty's resignation, which he would immediately enforce, and that Miss Stinson would immediately receive twenty-five per cent of the profits of this pool. A couple of days later Wheeler came to me and said, "I have made arrangements for you to meet Frank Vanderlip. Between you and me, he is the 'angel' of the committee. I have fixed things up for you to be properly taken care of." I was instructed to go to Room 509 at the Hotel Shoreham and meet Mr. Vanderlip. * * * Upon going to Mr. Vanderlip's room he was very much interested in anything that I might have to offer and said that he had decided to place me on his payroll, as he was prepared to spend his fortune in cleaning up the Department of Justice "in all of its rottenness." He said, "I have decided that you would be the man to go to Paris and get Howard Mannington. You can radio me after you get there and find out how much it will cost to get him to testify our way. I can arrange your passports so that you can sail from New York in 24 hours." He discussed several more phases of the investigation with me and wanted to know if I wouldn't help him pin something onto President Coolidge, mentioning a large sum of money that was forwarded last May from the Chase National Bank of New York City to the Riggs National Bank to protect Warren G. Harding's short account, in care of Ned McLean. I told him I knew nothing of this and of course would not swear to a falsehood. I returned to the Hotel Washington and talked Vanderlip's offer over with my wife and my secretary. She was very loath for me to accept it, and I called Vanderlip and told him that I

could not see my way clear to go for him. I visited
Mr. Vanderlip several times in the next few days and
he told me that his plans were to organize a third party
with Senator Borah as President, Wheeler as Vice President
and himself "the power that pulls the strings." From
conversations had with him I was under the impression
that he was very anxious to organize a third party, for
the reason that some time ago Vanderlip received some
very valuable oil concessions in Russia and that until the
Soviet government could be recognized here they would
be of no value to him. He said that he had always been
able to make plenty of money when he was on the inside
and that was one of the reasons he was conducting his
"citizens' research bureau" as he termed it, and that he
was prepared to spend fabulous sums of money to further
his own interest. My hotel bill had gradually been creeping
up and my money had been borrowed by Senator
Wheeler and also by Mr. Henry Stern, who made a trip
to Cleveland on the Sunday above mentioned, until I was
practically strapped. I went to Wheeler and told him that
I would like to be reimbursed and paid for expenses and
he said, "Why, we have not as yet passed any resolution
to the Senate paymaster authorizing these expenditures,
and you will just have to get along the best you can." I
complained of this to Stern, who by this time was very
intimate with Vanderlip and he said, "You will be taken
care of tonight or tomorrow." Stern came to me that
night and said, "Al, there is only one thing you got to
do." He said, "You are going to get paid for what you
have done for Vanderlip, and you are going to get a job
out of this thing, but we have got to have a hold on
you. We can't afford to have you in a position where you
can kick over the traces. So here's what you are up
against cold. I am your attorney in this Rochester affair,
and the evidence that will acquit you is in my posession;
also the bondsman on your bail is my particular friend"
(one Charles Jacobsen, of Buffalo, New York), "and unless
you can see that you must do exactly as we say I
promise you that you won't have any chance in this case
and that you will be committed to jail." He accordingly
spent about three hours going over a statement which
he wanted me to sign and swear to. He also told me that
the hotel would have me arrested for non-payment of the
hotel bill unless I did so. He also told me that he would
procure a letter for me from Senator Wheeler stating
that I was still under Government subpoena and act-

ing for the committee. He and Wheeler both told me
that this would protect me against the serving of any
warrant any place and that I could return to Buffalo
forthwith. After signing the false statement which he had
compiled I was told to go to his room in the Hotel
Washington, where I met Mr. Boyd Fisher, Vanderlip's
right hand man, who said: "I understand that you have
acquiesced to our wishes and we want to do the fair
thing with you." He said: "I am going to pay all of
your hotel bills and give you the difference in cash up
to a thousand dollars." He personally paid this hotel bill,
which can be proven by the management of the Hotel
Washington, after having gotten a check from Mr. Vanderlip cashed and brought back the difference, up to a
thousand dollars in currency, and threw it on the bed and
said, "This is yours." I said, "No, not yet." So I went
in to my secretary, who was in the room three or four
doors away, and told him that I was receiving this money
from Vanderlip, and took it in his presence and also in
the presence of Henry Stern. I then turned to Fisher
and said, "Mr. Fisher, you know that I have sworn to
a falsehood," and he said, "There are some cases where
it pays a man to perjure himself like a gentleman to protect a woman's reputation, and this is one of the cases."
"But," he said, "don't talk about it to me." Upon returning to Buffalo my bondsman, Charles Jacobsen, insisted
that we go immediately to Rochester at which time he
would arrange new bail, upon my pleading to the indictment, which had been found. Upon arriving in Rochester he immediately turned me over to the authorities
and returned to Buffalo. I have spent the past forty-four
days in jail, my wife receiving several communications
by telephone from Mr. Stern, she having talked to Senator Wheeler as well, and also receiving telegrams, one
that I attach here. (The Mr. Vee referred to is Mr.
Frank Vanderlip, who spoke in Rochester at the Western New York Press Association, and incidentally did not
come near me, as was stipulated in the telegram, which
you will notice was sent from the Senate at government
expense, by Henry Stern as well as others, which I can
produce.) The charge against me in Rochester was that
of grand larceny in connection with a stock transaction.
The complainant in this transaction has stated to several
people that she desired to withdraw the charge as it was
made under a misapprehension; that she had received full
value for every dollar invested. Upon arriving in Wash-

ington today I saw Senator Wheeler and he was very much perturbed to think that I had been able to effect my release. I also saw Gaston B. Means, who expressed himself to be very anxious to talk with me. I also talked to Mrs. Mabel Weitzman, Mr. Stern's friend, who was staying here in Washington, and she begged of me today when I told her that I was going to expose this whole rotten outfit, to do nothing until Mr. Stern could return from Atlanta, Georgia, where he was making a speech for Mr. Frank Vanderlip, and that she was positive they would be able to take care of me in every way if I would not expose them. I can furnish corroborating witnesses for every statement made in the above affidavit.

(Signed) A. L. FINK.

A. L. Fink being duly sworn, upon his oath says that the foregoing statement was dictated in whole by himself and is in all respects true.

(Signed) A. L. FINK.

Sworn to before me and subscribed in my presence at Washington, District of Columbia, this 14th day of May, 1924.

(Signed) HENRY J. ROBB,
Notary Public in and for District of Columbia.

STATEMENT OF HOWARD S. EDMONDS

I received a telegram on March 13th, 1924, from Henry Stern, who is attorney for the Wheeler-Brookhart United States Senate committee, in which he requested me to bring Mrs. A. L. Fink from Buffalo to Washington and to come myself. The message in substance was "bring Mrs. Fink to Washington at once. Al needs you desperately. Wire time of arrival."

We left that night for Washington. The next day I went with Mr. and Mrs. Fink to Senator Wheeler's office in the Senate Office Building in Washington. Senator Wheeler took Mrs. Fink into his private office alone and talked with her for some time and when she came out she was crying. We three then went back to the Washington Hotel where we were stopping.

After a hearing of the committee one morning I saw

Mr. Fink conversing with Frank A. Vanderlip in one of the corridors of the Senate Office Building. At this time Fink came over to me and handed me some money, saying take this and take my wife to lunch. Mr. Vanderlip has invited me to lunch with him.

I was called on the telephone in Mr. Fink's room a few days later by Mr. Boyd Fisher, chief counsel for Frank A. Vanderlip. He told me to get a bill for the expense which had been incurred by Mr. and Mrs. Fink and myself, as he was going up to Mr. Vee's. He told me to get Fink on the telephone and find out the amount. A few minutes later he knocked on the door of the room and cautioned me not to use any names over the phone, saying in substance, "Refer to me (Fisher) as Mr. F. and to Mr. Vanderlip as Mr. Vee."

A little later he came to the door and asked me if I had found out the amount of the expense and I told him I had not been able to locate Mr. Fink. Then he said he could not wait any longer and left.

A few days later I was told by Mr. Fink to get the bills from the hotel. I went to the office and got them and brought them up to Mr. Fink, who was in a room along with Boyd Fisher and Henry Stern.

(Signed) HOWARD S. EDMONDS.

Howard S. Edmonds being duly sworn, upon his oath, says that the foregoing statement was dictated in whole by himself and is in all respects true.

(Signed) HOWARD S. EDMONDS.

Sworn to and subscribed in my presence at Buffalo, New York, this seventh day of June, 1924.

(Signed)   JOHN W. CRYER,
Commissioner of Deeds, City of Buffalo, N.Y.

On February 21st, 1924, my husband, Alexander L. Fink, returned to our home at Buffalo, N. Y., from a business trip to Cleveland, Ohio. He informed me that he had succeeded in preventing Miss Roxie Stinson, a Columbus, Ohio, woman, from blackmailing Attorney General Harry M. Daugherty. He said that in his judgment she was just a disappointed woman who had expected to receive all of Jess Smith's estate at his death and was very unhappy over the fact that she had been willed only twenty-five thousand dollars. My husband said that he was sure he had succeeded in talking her out of this malicious idea.

On the night of March 8th, 1924, my husband received a telegram from his stenographer, Emma Ritzloff, saying that Henry Stern, his lawyer, desired to see him on an important matter the following morning. He came home about noon on March 8th much perturbed, saying Stern had told him that there was a Federal warrant for his arrest, charging him with conspiracy against the then Attorney General of the United States, Harry M. Daugherty.

My husband and Stern left for Washington March 8th and I next heard from my husband from Pittsburgh, Pa., on March 11th. In this telegram he advised me that he was in that city on government business. Several days later H. S. Edmonds, my husband's secretary, advised me that he was in receipt of a telegram from Washington sent on Government "frank" and signed "Henry," telling him to bring me at once to Washington, that my husband was desperately in need of me.

Mr. Edmonds and I arrived in Washington Friday morning, and I was led to Senator Burton K. Wheeler's office, Room 440, Senate Office Building. Upon meeting him, he asked me to come into his private office. He appeared very much worried and said to me in substance, "Mrs. Fink, your husband is a very foolish man. He is holding up the Committee hearings by threatening to refute Roxie Stinson's testimony. Now, I want you to be sensible and tell him that he has to allow her to continue to testify. He is going to be given a splendid appointment in Buffalo as Collector of Internal Revenue if he does what I want him to do. I am also going to make Mr. Stern a Federal Judge if we are able to make Daugherty resign. You should not be jealous over this woman and you should prevent your husband from throwing away this opportunity. Mr. Stern tells me that unless you urge him to help us to 'get' Daugherty he will destroy the evidence that will exonerate your husband in the case in which he is representing him in Rochester. So you see, little girl, it is up to you to do this to save your husband."

By this time I was crying and I finally promised Senator Wheeler that I would not desert my husband because of this episode with this woman. Mr. Stern then took me out into the corridor and then said: "You'd be an awfully foolish girl to hold Wheeler back as Wheeler has promised Al a big Federal job and also to make me a Federal judge. And if you can't see things our way, I can tell you now that it is in my power to send your husband to jail even though he is absolutely innocent in this Rochester matter. He'll be arraigned on a word from me even though the indictment has been pigeonholed for six months. So why don't you use some common sense. Wheeler is going to 'get' Daugherty one way or another and make a big name for himself."

Senator Wheeler then took my husband and me back into his office and continued to explain to us how valuable it would be to us if we would consent to join him in his "frame-up" on Daugherty. As a further inducement he told me that he was raising a sum of money among the Democratic Senators who were his friends for the purpose of playing the stock market as soon as he learned, as he would in advance, that Daugherty would resign. That he intended to reimburse Miss Stinson to the extent of 25% of this fund to make up for the $150,000.00 that she had originally demanded for her story. Senator Wheeler said that he would send my husband to New York to place this money and that he would receive a share of the profits for himself.

My husband told me a few days later that Wheeler had informed him that unless he testified to a certain matter pertaining to President Coolidge that he would not receive his expense money and that he, Wheeler, would not pay back the money he had borrowed from my husband. As my husband had expended all his money for the benefit of the committee and had no money left we were in a desperate plight. I advised my husband not to commit perjury even if he had to go to jail for a hotel bill. Later my husband told me that Wheeler had told him that Frank Vanderlip would pay my bill if he, my husband, would sign an affidavit that Miss Stinson was telling the truth. He told me of the two evils he had chosen the lesser. That he had signed the affidavit.

On March 19th Boyd Fisher, confidential secretary for Frank A. Vanderlip, came to my husband at the Washington Hotel and gave him, I am not sure of the exact amount, but something over $600.00 and agreed to pay our hotel bill, which was then in excess of $300.00.

My husband had been introduced to Frank A. Vanderlip and I saw him meet and converse with him in the corridor of the Senate Office Building.

(Signed) FLORENCE FINK.

Florence Fink being duly sworn, upon her oath, says that the foregoing statement was dictated in whole by herself and is in all respects true.

(Signed) FLORENCE FINK.

Sworn to before me and subscribed in my presence at New York City, New York, this 5th day of June, 1924.

(Signed) WM. J. MILLER,
SEAL   Notary Public in and for the State of New York.
My commission expires Mar. 30, 1926.

STATEMENT BY GASTON LECOLLIER

I, Gaston Lecollier, have been a waiter in Pittsburgh, Pa., for thirty-five years. On or about the 11th day of March, 1924, at about 8 o'clock in the evening, I served three men and a woman. Two men came in first and sat at my table. Then a lady and gentleman who were sitting at another table came over to the two men and sat at their table. I remember the incident well because I re-marked there was not enough room for four people. In serving the dinner I was asked to bring ginger ale and glasses with ice. I brought them.

I do not know the names of any of the party but a gentleman who says his name is A. L. Fink is a person I recall having seen before. I cannot remember whether the man whose photograph you show me (Burton K. Wheeler) was at that particular table at that time. I do, however, remember his face and having at some time seen him.

I do not know what was poured into the glasses with the ginger ale.

As I remember the woman sat facing the window. The photograph of the woman (Miss Roxie Stinson) which you show me I remember having seen but I cannot say she was the woman in the party.

(Signed) GASTON LECOLLIER.

Gaston Lecollier, being duly sworn, upon his oath, says that the foregoing statement was dictated in whole by himself and is in all respects true.

(Signed) GASTON LECOLLIER.

Sworn to and subscribed in my presence at Pittsburgh, Pa., this sixteenth day of June, 1924.

(Signed) C. B. LUCAS,
Notary Public in and for the State of Pennsylvania.

STATEMENT OF SAMUEL UNGERLEIDER,
Cleveland, Ohio.

Some time during February, 1924, Mr. Henry Ellis, a broker of this city whom I knew only as a customer of our office, called me on the 'phone and asked if I could see him. I told him to come over, and he did so. He stated that he understood that I was a friend of Mr. Harry M. Daugherty, the Attorney General, for a long time and for that reason he felt that he should advise me of some things which had just come to his attention: he then stated that he ran into an old acquaintance of his by the name of Fink from Buffalo, N. Y.; that Mr. Fink introduced him to a woman claiming that she had a lot of documents and information that would be harmful to Mr. Daugherty if they should be made public. Mr. Ellis said that he hadn't seen any of the documents, and from what he could learn Miss Stinson and Mr. Fink contemplated selling this information and that in his judgment they were trying to blackmail the Attorney General of the United States. I told him that I felt that it was a very serious matter and that it should be reported immediately to the Attorney General. He stated that Mr. Fink had accompanied him and was in the board room watching the stock quotations, and that he would call him in. Ellis stepped out of the office and shortly thereafter came in with a man, whom he introduced to me as Mr. Fink.

I told Mr. Fink that Ellis had advised me of their proposed scheme. Mr. Fink stated that he represented Miss Stinson, who had certain information detrimental to the Attorney General, and that unless Mr. Daugherty's friends would pay $150,000.00 for it she would make it public. I told him that I was very greatly incensed at such conduct and that it looked to me as though they were attempting to blackmail the Attorney General of the United States, and if they were, it might have very serious consequences for them. I told him that I thought he was doing a great injustice to himself and his family to engage in such a venture, and I asked him whether he stopped to think what the consequences might be to him if they attempted to go through with their program. I told him that I would immediately communicate with the Attorney General and report this matter to him, and advise him what they contemplated doing, and that I felt that it was a matter that should be reported to the County Prosecutor for immediate action. Mr. Fink seemed to begin to realize the situation, and said he hadn't looked at it from that angle at all, and that it was more dangerous than he thought and agreed to drop the matter.

Aside from my personal friendship for the Attorney General and my sympathy for him when threatened by injustice, I felt it my duty as a citizen to protect and uphold a government officer who was being attacked, and I immediately called up the Attorney General and talked to him on the long distance telephone and I told him what I had learned, and asked him if he could send someone here to investigate the situation for him. He told me that his brother, Mal Daugherty, was returning from Washington and that he would have him to go by way of Cleveland and that he would see me in the morning. I then informed Fink that I had advised the Attorney General of their plan and that Mr. Mal Daugherty would come to Cleveland on the following morning, and I asked him if he would be willing to tell Mr. Mal Daugherty just what he and Miss Stinson had planned to do. He agreed to do so, and I told him to come back the next morning.

The next morning Mr. Mal Daugherty and his attorney, Mr. Holcomb, Mr. Fink and Mr. Ellis had a conference in my office. Mr. Fink told Mr. Daugherty and Mr. Holcomb about the matter, stating that at first he and Miss Stinson had contemplated selling this information, but since talking to me last evening he decided that so far as he was concerned he was through and the matter was closed, and that he was going to urge Miss Stinson to abandon her plans and go back to Columbus. This conversation lasted quite some time. Part of the time I was present, on several occasions I was called out of the office. On one occasion I came in and I heard Mr. Holcomb say to Mr. Fink, "You say that you have determined not to go ahead but why do you think this woman will not go through with her proposed plan?" Fink put his hand in his pocket, pulled out what appeared to be a receipted hotel bill, threw it down on the table and said, "I know this will prevent her from attempting to do this because she is afraid of publicity, as we registered as man and wife and occupied the same room." Mr. Holcomb examined the bill

and asked Fink if he realized that this was a violation of
law and punishable by imprisonment; this seemed to scare
Fink still more, and he asked Mr. Holcomb whether it was
his intention to prosecute. Mr. Holcomb answered he was
not in a position to say just what they would do; he would
have to see just what the whole thing was about and de-
termine later. It was quite evident that Mr. Fink was terribly worried about the whole situation and about the
hotel episode. He said he wanted to go back to the hotel
and have a talk with Miss Stinson and see if he could not
prevail upon her to drop the whole proposition; that he
did not want to get any publicity out of this; that he was
afraid that his wife and family would find out about his
scheme and his relations with Miss Stinson, and felt this
would cause him a lot of trouble. Mr. Holcomb told him
that he had no desire to cause him any trouble but he felt
that the only trouble that was coming out of this was
what trouble he was making for himself. Mr. Fink asked
us to wait until he went to the hotel and talked with Miss
Stinson.

In fifteen or twenty minutes Fink called up Mr. Holcomb, and I heard Mr. Holcomb say he had no desire to
talk to Miss Stinson and there was nothing he felt he
wanted to talk about. In a short while Fink came back,
and said he had talked the matter over with Miss Stinson
and told her of the predicament they were in and had
persuaded her to drop this matter, but stated that she mis-
trusted him and insisted on talking to some of the people
who were at the meeting. Mr. Holcomb and Mr. Mal
Daugherty asked me to go to the hotel with Mr. Fink to
speak to her, which I did. When we came into the room
she said, "Where is Mal Daugherty? Why doesn't he
come up here?" I told her he didn't care to see her. She
then said she must see Harry Daugherty. I told her in
that case, she could no doubt reach him in Washington.
Mr. Fink was pacing up and down the room, very nervous,
and said, "Roxie, there is no use, if we attempt to go on
we will both go behind the bars." Miss Stinson answered
she did nothing that would put her behind the bars and
she was not afraid of anyone. She asked me what it was
all about and I told her, briefly, what Fink had said. She
denied the whole thing and Fink became very angry and
said, "Roxie, you know you are only putting me in bad.
Didn't you say that you had letters from Harry Daugherty to Jess Smith in your possession, and that the letters
would be very damaging to him, and that you wanted to

sell them and the other information you had about Mr. Daugherty?" Miss Stinson said she was not selling any information she had, as a representative of one of the newspaper associations called on her in Columbus offering to pay her for what information she could give him and she said she was not selling any information she had. I turned to Miss Stinson and said that this looks entirely different from the statements made by Fink. Fink then argued with Miss Stinson that she was trying to make it appear that he alone was the guilty party, and she said, "Well, I have the information we talked about, but I am not thinking of selling it. We made no plans or arrangements about selling it, we just talked about it. Whatever information I have, I will do with it as I see fit."

I left the room and went back to my office and in about half an hour Miss Stinson called me up, asking me whether she could see me, as she desired to talk to me. I told her I didn't care to see her and considered the incident closed.

STATEMENT OF HENRY O. ELLIS

On Monday evening, February 18th, after concluding dinner at the Hollenden Hotel, as I walked into the lobby from the dining room, I recognized Mr. A. L. Fink of Buffalo. He was accompanied by a woman. Mr. Fink appeared to me about to register at the hotel and saw me but did not seem to want to recognize me. The next day Mr. Fink called me on the telephone at the office of a friend in Cleveland and asked me whether I could see him immediately on a matter of great importance. I suggested that he state his business on the 'phone. He said that he had a proposition out of which there was a chance to make a lot of money and was very desirous to see me and talk to me about it. He asked me whether I would discuss this matter with him if he came over and I told him to come ahead.

A little later Mr. Fink came in and then told me that he knew a woman that had knowledge of a number of different transactions in which some prominent officials in Washington had been interested; he said that this woman wanted to sell this knowledge, and that both she and he thought that they could get a considerable sum of money for what she knew. He went on to say that this woman had had an account with the office of Samuel Ungerleider & Company, at Columbus, Ohio, and that she was very well acquainted with a Mr. Hays, the manager of that office. Mr. Fink asked we whether I could secure some information from Ungerleider & Company relative to certain accounts that this woman and other people had had with their office at Columbus. He further said that he had promised this woman to secure this information for her and that she expected him to return with the information within the next hour or so. I told Fink that I did not believe I could get this information, as it was not customary for brokerage houses to give out information relative to dealings or transactions that had taken place between them and their customers. I told Mr. Fink that I might try to get the information he wanted but was not hopeful of any success. Mr. Fink said to me: "There is a chance to make a lot of money and if you will help me to get this information I shall be glad to cut you in on this deal." I told Mr. Fink that if it was possible to help him secure the information he wanted, I might be able to serve him in this matter, but I did not care to go any further in the matter that he talked about, nor would I care to participate in any money that he or anyone else might make out of it. He said to me: "Now this is a wonderful opportunity to make a lot of money and I would like to have you meet this woman." He said, "She was with me last night at the Hollenden Hotel and we are still registered there as A. L. French and wife, of Pittsburgh." He further said that he was supposed to take lunch with her at the Statler Hotel and was very anxious to have me join them. After quite a little talk, I finally consented to lunch with them, as it was then time for lunch.

At the Statler Hotel we met the same woman that I had seen with him the previous evening at the Hollenden Hotel. He introduced me to her as Miss Brown. We went into the dining room and during the luncheon he repeatedly asked Miss Brown to tell me some of the things that she had told him. Miss Brown went on to say that she was very well acquainted with Harry Daugherty; also that she was intimately acquainted with Mal Daugherty, his brother; she also said that she had known Mr. and Mrs. Harding and that she was the former wife of a man who was very close to Harry Daugherty. She did not mention this man's name. She was very vindictive in all her references to both Harry Daugherty and his brother, Mal Daugherty. She said that she would go to any extremes to injure either or both of them. She claimed to have knowledge of certain transactions which, if they became public, would be very injurious to both of the Daughertys.

In reply to a question of Fink's, she said that before she would part with this information that she claims she had, she would have to be paid very highly. Fink asked her to name a figure that she wanted, and she finally said that she wanted to have $150,000 net to herself. It seemed that Fink and she had discussed prior to this time the division of money that they could get for this information and that Fink was to share in the proceeds of the total amount that would be received. The woman appeared to be reluctant to divulge any definite information; in fact, I stated to her several times during the conversation that I did not want to be made a confidant in this matter. To me she appeared to be haphazard and nervous. I was under the impression that she was laboring under delusions or possibly that she was addicted to drugs. Her statements were rather random. She said several times that Mal Daugherty was responsible for depriving her of certain properties; these properties, it seemed, had in part or whole belonged to her former husband, who, it appeared in the conversation, had committed suicide some time last year. She further said that Harry Daugherty was responsible for taking her husband away from her.

After leaving this woman, the thought suggested itself to me that in view of the fact that she had mentioned Ungerleider & Co., a number of times, and in further view of the fact that Mr. Ungerleider was known to me, I took it upon myself to telephone Mr. Ungerleider and ask him if he could see me. He said he could and I went over to his office and we talked for perhaps fifteen or twenty minutes. I told Mr. Ungerleider that I had met this woman and Fink. Mr. Ungerleider asked me what I thought of them, and I told him that in my opinion it was a case of blackmail as well as of vindictiveness.

It later developed that Fink had told this woman that I could be instrumental in helping them get the information that she desired from Mr. Ungerleider. She said that if she had this information that she would be better equipped in so far as evidence or proof was concerned. It seemed that what she had was nothing definite but could be made more definite if she knew of these various accounts at Columbus.

Mr. Ungerleider stated that in view of the fact that so much publicity was being given to the investigation at Washington, that anyone coming out with accusations, no matter how false they might be, would at this time receive attention. Mr. Ungerleider further stated that the matter should be brought to the attention of the Department of Justice immediately. I told Mr. Ungerleider that Fink was in the board room watching the stock quotations, and that it might be well for Mr. Ungerleider to talk to him. Mr. Ungerleider said, "All right, bring him in," and I went out and got Fink to come into Mr. Ungerleider's private office and introduced one to the other. Mr. Fink told Mr. Ungerleider that in his opinion this woman had a lot of very important information and data; he also said that he could control the woman and that she would do whatever he told her to, due to the fact that they had been intimate for a number of years. He further told Mr. Ungerleider that this woman was the wife of a Jess Smith, whose home had been in Washington Courthouse, Ohio, and who afterwards lived at Washington, D. C., and who was very friendly with Harry Daugherty. Mr. Ungerleider asked Fink what the woman wanted and Fink said "about $200,000.00." Mr. Ungerleider grew very angry and said that it looked to him like a pure attempt on Fink's part to blackmail the Attorney General, and that he would immediately report the matter to Mr. Daugherty and that the matter should be placed in the hands of the criminal authorities immediately, and that Fink had better drop the matter at once as he was very apt to get himself in jail, and his family would suffer, and Fink got pretty well scared. It seemed that he hadn't thought of what might happen, and got cold feet.

The following day Fink came to see me again and said that he was through but that he was going over to Mr. Ungerleider's office where he was going to meet Mr. Mal Daugherty, and that he was going to make a clean breast of the whole thing because he was afraid of a come-back. He asked me if I would go along and I did.

We met a Mr. Holcomb and Mr. Mal Daugherty at Mr. Ungerleider's office. Mr. Daugherty asked me to tell him what I knew and I did so. He interjected remarks at various times to the effect that he knew the woman was very vindictive and further that she was a tremendous liar, and he felt as if she would go to any extreme to injure either his brother or himself.

Fink then told Mr. Daugherty that Miss Stinson had told him that she had a lot of letters from the Attorney General to Mr. Jess Smith that were very compromising, and that she knew a lot of other matters about the Attorney General, and that the Attorney General and his friends would either have to buy this information, or else she would try to sell it to some prominent Democrat who would not be afraid to use it against Mr. Daugherty, and that she was interested in getting about $150,000 out of it; that at first he was interested with Miss Stinson in the matter, but that after the talk Mr. Ungerleider gave him the day before, he decided that he wouldn't have anything further to do with the matter and was going to help along by trying to persuade Miss Stinson to drop her plans. Someone at the meeting stated that she was so vindictive against Mr. Daugherty that they didn't think that Fink would have enough influence with her to drop her attack, but Fink pulled out a receipted hotel bill and said that they had registered as man and wife and had spent the night together at the hotel, and that he would use that as a club over her. Mr. Daugherty and Mr. Holcomb both said that it was not necessary to use any club to keep her quiet, as nothing that she knew could in any way be damaging. Mr. Holcomb then said that in his judgment the registering in the hotel and staying there as man and wife was a criminal offense and that he thought that both were subject to prosecution. Fink got scared and said that he didn't want any prosecution, that it would give him a lot of publicity, his family would find out about his situation, and begged that the whole matter be dropped, that he would go to the hotel immediately and do what he could to have Miss Stinson drop the matter and go home.

Fink then left us and I went away shortly afterwards.

(Signed) HENRY O. ELLIS.

APPENDIX E

George Remus, known as "the biggest boot-legger in the United States," from his cell at Atlanta issued the affidavit which follows, in August, 1924. Remus was indicted, convicted and sent to prison by Attorney General Daugherty.

During this writing Remus was released from Atlanta and is now engaged in going to trial at St. Louis on other indictments brought by Mr. Daugherty. Upon his release, Remus repudiated his repudiation. That he lied about his payment of money to Jess Smith has already been shown in this book. There is no question about this lie as Smith was dead at the time Remus said he paid him bribe money.

The other affidavits by fellow prisoners allege how Remus was conspiring to ruin Mr. Daugherty; the man who put Remus in jail.

And on the testimony of two criminals, Remus and Means, both convicted by Attorney General Daugherty, both liars by their own mouth and pen, they "got Daugherty."

STATE OF GEORGIA
COUNTY OF FULTON, SS:

I, George Remus, of lawful age, a citizen of Cincinnati, Ohio, of my own voluntary will and accord, without promise of reward, directly or indirectly, and for the sole purpose, so far as possible, of correcting a great wrong and injury, and for no other purpose, make this affidavit:

On or about the 10th day of May, 1924, one Harry Stern, an attorney for the United States Senatorial Investigating Committee, popularly known as the Wheeler-Brookhart Committee, came to me here in Atlanta, and represented to me that he had as much power as any member of the Committee, in as much as he was an attorney for the said committee, and the committee would act on his advice and suggestions, and he was sent here by them.

Stern informed me that his mission was to find out for the Committee if my testimony was such as they wanted. He began by telling me that the Senate Committee would "throw themselves behind me," and that they would get me out of here as soon as possible. He told me that I had better get in with them if I wanted to get out of here. He said that they (the Senatorial Committee) were out to "get" Attorney General Daugherty, and that it was common knowledge in Washington that I had paid someone between $250,000 and $300,000. He said he wanted me to make a statement that would directly implicate Harry M. Daugherty, as United States Attorney General, in "graft money." I then told him that I had never even met Daugherty, or talked with him, and that I knew of no illegal transactions in which he (Attorney General Daugherty) was implicated. Stern said that they were out to "get" Daugherty; that if I helped the Wheeler-Brookhart Committee to "frame" some of these transactions on

Daugherty, personally, they, the Senate Committee, would help me to get out of the penitentiary. I again told Stern that I had never met Mr. Daugherty, who was then Attorney General of the United States.

I now state the fact to be that I never met Harry M. Daugherty before he was Attorney General of the United States, while he was Attorney General of the United States or since he has ceased to be Attorney General of the United States, nor have I ever communicated with him by word of mouth, or on paper, either directly or indirectly, except that I have retained reputable attorneys, whose names will be furnished if it becomes necessary, who, as my attorneys, and in my behalf, and before I was incarcerated here, attempted, as my attorneys, to get Attorney General Daugherty to do, or permit to be done, something that would prevent my incarceration here, and that all of said attorneys each reported back that Attorney General Daugherty would in nowise interfere, or ask anyone in his department to interfere in my behalf, saying in substance that the law must take its course. The records bear me out when I further state that without fear or favor he prosecuted me and my associates most vigorously through all the courts of this country, and successfully defeated my every effort to avoid conviction and the serving of a sentence. The records further show that twice in the United States Supreme Court he, with his assistants, defeated me in my efforts to escape conviction and sentence. In one set of cases I had won in the nisi prius court on a question of law, and notwithstanding my conviction and sentence in the other case, the Attorney General prosecuted error on these cases in which I had won on a question of law, which the records show is not a common practice for the Attorney General, and succeeded in these cases in having the lower court reversed, to my injury. The obvious purpose of the Attorney General, who disagreed with the finding of the lower court, was to have the law established once and for all by the Supreme Court of the United States, and this he did.

The public has already been advised, through the press, of the unhesitating and vigorous prosecution in my case, at all times, and at all stages, by the Department of Justice.

When Mr. Stern called to see me, I had then been an inmate, for five months, of the United States Penitentiary at Atlanta, Georgia. There had been no favors shown me, and like all men in my situation, I craved liberty and caught at every chance that suggested a possibility of any relief from imprisonment, and so, after repeatedly saying to Mr. Stern that I knew nothing against Attorney General Daugherty, and being urged and promised as I have set forth herein, I did then finally consent to go to Washington and testify before the Senate Committee, and did there testify to many meetings with the then deceased Jess Smith.

I testified to meeting Jess Smith in Indianapolis, Indiana, Columbus, Ohio, Washington, D. C., and New York City. I named the hotels and places where I had met Jess Smith, and I substantially fixed the times when I had met him, and I testified that I gave him on these occasions tens of thousands of dollars, for the purpose of enabling me to obtain whiskey permits, also to continue to operate without molestation or interference by the Department of Justice, and to enable me to escape the serving of a sentence on the charges pending against me in the United States District Court, the Court of Appeals, and in the Supreme Court of the United States, which were being prosecuted against me by the Department of Justice, of which Harry M. Daugherty was then Attorney General.

I now state the fact to be that I never met the said Jess Smith in my life; that I never communicated with him, directly or indirectly; that I never tried to communicate with him, directly or indirectly; and that I never directly or indirectly gave him any money for any purpose, nor ever tried to give him any money for any purpose and that I made the statements to the Senate Committee under the circumstances above set forth. The fact that I never met Jess Smith will not be disputed by any person.

With reference to the alleged two hundred and fifty or three hundred thousand dollars that Attorney Stern said it was common knowledge in Washington that I paid to someone, I have this to say: I never did pay this amount of money to anyone in Washington, for any purpose, and the only possible basis for such a story is that:

Ten (10) days prior to my case being turned down by the United States Supreme Court, Gaston B. Means came to me and told me that for the sum of two hundred and fifty thousand ($250,000) dollars, he could have my case certified and considered on its merits by the United States Supreme Court, and have a decision favorable to me handed down by a majority of that Court, as a petition for animus curae had been allowed by the Supreme Court, and that in the consideration of the aforesaid petition he would have the influence of the Supreme Court to have a favorable vote upon said petition obtained, so as to certify the record from the lower court to the Supreme Court, and that he further could secure for me the return of my Bar Association membership. Three days prior to an adverse decision being rendered by the supreme court in my case, Gaston B. Means, in Washington, told me that for the sum of one hundred and twenty-five thousand ($125,000) dollars he could do the same thing. I told him "No," because I knew that it was impossible for any one man, or combination of men, by bribery, to accomplish any such thing, and I further, at this time, knew that Gaston B. Means was, and has been, trading on the names of his superiors without warrant and without their knowledge.

Means told me, upon my questioning him closely, that the money he wanted me to pay him was to be divided into four parts, one-quarter to the Chief Justice of the United States Supreme Court, one-quarter to the Attorney General of the United States, one-quarter to the Chief of the Bureau of Investigation of the Department of Justice, and one-quarter to be retained by Means himself. This, I knew, was impossible and this Gaston B. Means is the same Gaston B. Means who appeared before, and worked with and for the Wheeler-Brookhart Committee.

I further state that my testimony before the Wheeler-Brookhart committee was not a fair statement of what I intended to testify to, for the reason that, as the record will show, I was repeatedly stopped in my testimony when I started to say anything in favor of the Department of Justice, and I was further promised by Senator Wheeler that I would be given an opportunity to continue my testimony, which opportunity was not granted me. Senator Wheeler, both prior to and after my testimony before the Wheeler-Brookhart committee, attempted to induce me to testify positively that I knew that the Attorney General got one-half of the money I was supposed to have paid. I told him then that I could not so testify.

Further affiant sayeth not.

(Signed) GEORGE REMUS.

Sworn to before me, and subscribed in my presence, this 28th day of August, 1924.

                    (Signed) H. F. FRICK,
SEAL   Notary Public.

STATEMENT OF GEORGE CONNERS

I, George Conners, knowing of my own knowledge that George Remus testified falsely before the Brookhart investigating committee of the United States Senate, at Washington, D. C., May 18th or 19th, 1924, and I feel it only just to state herein the basis of the aforementioned knowledge and facts leading up to and concerning such false testimony, particularly in regard to Remus' testimony wherein he claims to have given one Jess Smith money, now deceased.

I know that the testimony of Remus before the aforementioned committee to be false and without foundation because I was present at various conferences with Remus and Mrs. Remus, where it was decided to have Mrs. Remus arrange with the Brookhart committee, or a representative thereof, to have Remus called before such committee, and also to have myself called. At these conferences it was decided that Remus was to tell the story which he did, and I was to corroborate the same. I said to Remus and Mrs. Remus at the time, "I am afraid to go on the stand and testify falsely, these men are smart men and will trip me up." Remus said, "They can't do that. Jess Smith is dead."

Remus told me that if I would corroborate his testimony at Washington, D. C., before the committee, he would either be commuted or paroled. He said that Mrs. Remus had made a deal with the committee, or its representative, to the effect that if he testified, as he did, that he, Remus, and his men, would be commuted.

Following are the statements Remus wanted me to corroborate: Statements which had no foundation, that Remus himself knew to be untrue, but which he claimed, if he made them, would get us all out of prison here. Remus claimed he wanted me to corroborate the statements he was going to make, as he said his statements alone would not hold. Also that everyone knew how close I was to him and that my testimony would bring about the desired effect. He, Remus, described to me what Jess Smith looked like, every day for about three weeks, and coached me on what to say on the stand, as I had never seen Smith and had never done any business with him. Remus wanted me to testify as follows:

1. That I had drew the money out of the bank for him and secured other moneys from the sale of whiskey, and had driven him to Indianapolis at the time he was supposed to have met Jess Smith at the railroad station there in the company of Judge Goff and other men; that I handed him the money, and that I saw him give the money to Smith. I never drove or accompanied Remus to Indianapolis, and neither did he go to my knowledge at the time mentioned or for the purpose mentioned. I never knew or saw Jess Smith.

2. Remus wanted me to say on the stand that I drove him to Columbus, Ohio, where we were supposed to have met Jess Smith in the lobby of the Deschler Hotel; that I had gotten twenty-five or thirty-five thousand dollars, part from the Lincoln National Bank at Cincinnati, and part from the sale of whiskey; that I saw him hand this money to Smith. I never went to Columbus or drove Remus there; never saw him meet Smith at Columbus or elsewhere and never saw him give any money to anyone at the time or place mentioned.

3. Remus wanted me to testify that on several occasions that he went to New York and Washington and other places where he was supposed to have met Smith, that I drew out of the bank and secured large sums of money from the sale of whiskey, and gave same to him for the purpose of his giving same to Smith. This is not true. I did not ever secure any money for him in any way for this purpose. The largest amount of money I ever drew out of the bank for Remus when he was about to take a trip was one time when I secured thirty-eight hundred dollars for him when he was about to take a trip to Washington.

4. I was Remus' confidential man, having been connected with him since 1920, and associated with him in several enterprises, and knew of practically all of his dealings. I knew who he gave money and for what purpose, and I know that he never at any time gave anyone, or rather he never gave anyone the amounts he mentioned. I cashed a great many of the checks Remus wrote for cash, and at no time were checks cashed for the amount or purpose mentioned.

5. Our arrangement, I mean the arrangement existing between Remus and the men associated with him, was to split pro rata all expenses regardless of what they were. If a certain deal was about to be consummated, or money paid out for any purpose, a conference would be called and a decision made. I know that Jess Smith's name or the payment of money to Jess Smith was never mentioned at any time. I would have known as an associate and I would also have known otherwise if Remus had ever paid any money to Smith, as his confidential man. There is absolutely no question but what I would have known the facts if Remus ever contemplated paying any money to Jess Smith.

6. I have handled hundreds and have seen thousands of checks written in Remus' office and elsewhere, and know positively of my own knowledge that there was never any notations or initials or marks of identification placed or written thereon. This was done purposely so that no identification would ever be possible.

7. Remus also had coached Harry Brown, his brother-in-law here at the Atlanta Penitentiary, along the same lines that he wanted me to testify. Brown told me that he was afraid to get on the stand. He said he did not know Smith, had never seen him, and that he knew nothing.

I had agreed, or rather I had not dissented from Remus' proposition, for the reason that Remus held some valuable property belonging to me that I was trying to get him to return, and while I had never intended to take the stand and perjure myself, I was keeping him in the dark as to my real purpose, as I wanted my property back. On March 28th I wired my wife to send my clothes at Remus' behest so that I would be ready when called. He said that he would state on the stand that some of his men knew of the transactions with Smith, and then would mention my name, so that they would call me to verify his testimony. He also had me arrange to get the New York Times every day so that I could follow his testimony so that when I was called it would be familiar.

(Signed) GEO. J. CONNERS.

Subscribed and sworn to before me this 3rd day of July, 1924.

(Signed) H. F. FRICK,

Notary Seal.   Notary Public.

SUPPLEMENTARY STATEMENT

Remus approached me daily in the kitchen of the prisons where I am clerk, and in the presence of Harry Raub, kitchen steward. He told Raub I had been his confidential man and was going to Washington to corroborate all his statements. He told Raub I had known all his business from the time he started in business in Cincinnati and knew of the moneys he paid Smith.

Remus had me arrange with Guard Curtis, in the kitchen of the prison, whereby Guard Curtis was to secure for me daily a copy of the New York Times to follow Remus' testimony. Remus claimed that the Times was the only reliable paper for such testimony. I so made the arrangement as Guard Curtis can testify.

Remus also was going to wire from Washington and have Guard Curtis accompany me to Washington, as soon as he could arrange to have me appear before the committee. He also told Harry Raub that Guard Curtis would accompany me.

Harry Brown, brother-in-law of Remus, was also coached by Remus as to what to say on the stand before the committee in Washington in the event that he, Remus, decided to have Brown called. Brown told me he was scared of the proposition, as he never saw or knew Jess Smith, and never knew anything about him. Brown knew as well as I that Remus never saw or did any business with or through Smith.

(Signed) GEO. J. CONNERS.
Subscribed and sworn to before me this July 3rd, 1924.

(Signed) H. F. FRICK,
Notary Seal.   Notary Public.

STATEMENT OF HARRY RAUB

I am assigned to work as kitchen steward in the U. S. Penitentiary at Atlanta, Ga., and in that capacity have become acquainted with George Conners, kitchen clerk, as my work naturally brings me into contact with him.

About the latter part of April and the first of May George Remus stated to me that: "Conners will be a very important factor in my testimony before the Brookhart

Investigating Committee in Washington, D. C., and it is essential that he be called before the committee to substantiate my testimony and statements." He said that he and Conners would be gone two or three weeks and would go to several states in order to get some papers bearing on the case. He further made the statement as follows: "When I get before the committee I will mention Conners' name and arrange to have him called as a witness to back me up." He further stated that "George Conners is my right hand bower and will make a dandy witness. He is straightforward and knows all about my business, having been connected with me almost since I started in the liquor business, and he knows all about the testimony I am going to give. We should have no trouble in making parole or being commuted after this matter is over." Remus further told me that Guard Curtis would get the New York Times every day and bring same into the prison to Conners so that he, Conners, could familiarize himself with the statements he, Remus, was to make, so that when Conners got to Washington he would know just what he, Remus, had testified to.

Remus talked with Conners, to my own personal knowledge daily for a period of not less than three weeks, part of the time in my presence and part of the time when I was not present. He was continually telling me that Conners had been his right hand man and knew all about his dealings and to whom he paid money. He said Conners knew all his business.

(Signed) HARRY M. RAUB.

Subscribed and sworn to before me this 3rd day of July, 1924.

(Signed) H. F. FRICK,

Notary Seal.   Notary Public.

STATEMENT OF E. A. BRADY

STATE OF GEORGIA
COUNTY OF FULTON, SS:

Myself and Mr. Clem L. Herbes were in a conversation with Mr. George Remus in regard to Mr. Harry M. Daugherty trying to fix our case so that we wouldn't have to go to the Penitentiary.

Mr. Remus came back to Cincinnati from Washington, and told Mr. Herbes and myself that Mr. Daugherty absolutely would not have anything to do with the case, and that he said that Mr. Remus and all of his associates would go to the penitentiary as far as he was concerned.

Mr. Remus went so far as to ask me to ask my friends to go to Washington to see if they couldn't do something in our behalf. This I refused to do.

This took place about a month and a half prior to our conviction in Cincinnati, and I refused to have anything to do with the affair.

Mr. Clem L. Herbes will sustain my statement about this.

(Signed) E. A. BRADY.

Subscribed and sworn to before me this 26th day of June, 1924.

(Signed) H. F. FRICK,

SEAL   Notary Public.

STATEMENT OF WALTER DEMARQUIS MILLER

I, Walter DeMarquis Miller, being of lawful age and a resident of Washington, D. C., without hope of reward directly or indirectly, make the following statement.

Shortly after the convening of the Wheeler-Brookhart investigation, I visited the Capitol one day and was trying to get into the committee room to hear the testimony, when I met Mr. Harvey Phillips, whom I had known a long time. He asked me what I was doing and I said I was out of work, that I had been working for the Attorney General, but I had lost out. He immediately said that if I would come round to his room that night he might be able to get some money for me out of it. At that time I had no idea that he was connected with or interested in the investigaiton. I told him I had no money for car fare. He said he had not much money himself but gave me $2.00.

That night I went to the Harrington Hotel, 13th and E Streets, N. W., where we had a drink, and he then told me if I would go to New York with him and make a statement involving the Attorney General, I could earn some easy money. I want to say here that I had not the least idea that anything I might say about the Attorney General would be taken seriously and as I was entirely out of funds and my room rent due, I was willing to do anything that promised easy money.

The statement was framed entirely by Mr. Schindler and his assistants, I merely agreeing to the details as they were suggested to me. The statements about the visits of women to the rooms of the Attorney General was not my work; I simply agreed to it in order to get money.

Before agreeing to this statement I exacted a promise that I would not be put on the stand at Washington. This they agreed to, yet I was called upon to take the stand and testify.

Each and every detail of this statement was made up by Mr. Schindler and his assistants and the words put in my mouth, and after going all the way to New York and believing that I would receive a large amount of money for the statement, I agreed to everything they prepared.

I have seen the Attorney General only once since I made this statement and then I met him on the street. He has not communicated with me in any way, and I make this retraction of my own free will. I had plenty of whiskey in New York and I had a fine time. * * *

No lump sum was mentioned, but I was to be paid at the rate of five dollars per day and was to be taken care of, which, of course, I understood as meaning that when the day service ended I would receive some substantial sum or at least profitable employment. I was paid for three weeks and then dropped and since have been unable to find any kind of employment because of the position I placed myself in by allowing these people to use or rather misuse me.

Early one morning a large and expensive limousine, which I believe belonged to Mr. Vanderlip, drove up to the house where I roomed and Mr. Fisher, Mr. Vanderlip's secretary, came to the door and asked for me; when I appeared he said Senator Wheeler wanted to see me. I objected to going to see Senator Wheeler but he said it would only require a moment, so I got into the car and went with him to the Capitol. When we arrived there we went at once to see Senator Wheeler, who asked me if I would go on the stand and testify to the things said in the statement. I refused, and for an hour a heated argument ensued; at the end, however, I was persuaded to testify, although I knew the statement was untrue.

(Signed) WALTER DEMARQUIS MILLER.

Subscribed and sworn to before me this 2nd day of September, 1924.

(Signed) OLLIE M. COOPER,

Notary Seal. Notary Public, D. C.

STATEMENT OF ARTHUR L. BRENT

On the morning of March 23, 1924, it being Sunday, Mr. A. W. Wells, a former Special Agent of the Bureau of Investigation, Department of Justice, accompanied by a gentleman who was introduced to me by Mr. Wells as a Mr. Arthur, but who I have reason to believe was Mr. Harvey Phillips, both of whom, I have since learned, were then employed by Mr. Frank A. Vanderlip as investigators, drove to my home in Vienna, Virginia, to interview me concerning the death of Jess W. Smith at Wardman Park Hotel, Washington, D. C., on May 30, 1923; it having been intimated by Roxie Stinson, divorced wife of Jess W. Smith, in her testimony before the Wheeler Investigating Committee, that he had been murdered. Mr. Wells asked me a great many questions, particularly in reference to the death of Mr. Smith, and also in an effort to obtain any information I might have regarding Honorable H. M. Daugherty. While no money was offered me on this occasion, Mr. Wells stated plainly that I could demand and would receive payment for any information I might be willing to give.

On March 27, 1923, in my capacity as Special Agent of the Bureau of Investigation, Department of Justice, it became necessary for me to visit the law office of Thomas Beckett (colored) at No. 507 D Street, N. W., where I unexpectedly met Mr. Wells again, and another agent of Mr. Vanderlip's, whose name I do not know. While there I was informed that Beckett and Wells had been discussing the possibility of securing a statement from me that would reflect upon the character of the Attorney General, Mr. Daugherty; I was informed by both Wells and Beckett that Mr. Vanderlip would pay me well; that he was a man who would not let anybody work for him for nothing. I explained that I was in a great hurry but would see them again. I immediately reported to Mr. W. J. Burns, Director of the Bureau of Investigation, who suggested that I keep in touch with them and see how far they would go in their efforts to get the statement referred to.

I had several interviews with Beckett and Wells thereafter, in Mr. Beckett's office, and Mr. Beckett also called me on the telephone several times. At one of these interviews I met Mr. Schindler, who was at that time assisting Mr. Vanderlip in his work here. Repeated efforts were made to procure a statement from me and also to bring me face to face with Mr. Vanderlip himself, but the latter course was opposed by Mr. Burns and I never met him. Beckett showed me the statement or affidavit made by Walter D. Miller, which I read and signed as a witness, disclaiming, however, all knowledge as to the truth of its contents, as the events chronicled therein were supposed to have taken place prior to my connection with the Department of Justice and before I knew Attorney General Daugherty. On the morning of April 4, 1924, Mr. Beckett, in his office, informed me that I could get $2500.00 in cash if I would make a statement similar to the one made by Walter D. Miller, and added that he would guarantee that I would get that amount, and, in fact, could name my own price. I refused to accept this offer, and on April 7, 1924, I again saw Beckett, in his office, he insisted upon placing me upon Mr. Vanderlip's payroll at ten ($10.00) dollars per day; my duty would be to develop such facts and information as would be of interest to Mr. Vanderlip. During all these interviews their object was to get information regarding Mr. Daugherty and Mr. Smith, and notwithstanding I told them time and again that I knew nothing of interest to them, they continued to make offers to me and endeavored to obtain information. Following Mr. Beckett's offer to place me upon Mr. Vanderlip's payroll I advised him that I would consider the matter and let him know in twenty-four hours. Just at this time, however, the investigation that was bringing me in touch with Mr. Beckett and Mr. Vanderlip's men, terminated, and thereafter I avoided them.

The statement as set forth herein is correct as to the facts and dates, and is made of my own free will and volition, and may be regarded as an example of the methods employed by Mr. Vanderlip in securing witnesses for the Senate Investigating Committee.

(Signed) ARTHUR L. BRENT.

Arthur L. Brent, being duly sworn, upon his oath says that the foregoing statement was made in whole by himself and is in all respects true.

(Signed) ARTHUR L. BRENT.

Sworn to before me and subscribed in my presence at Washington D. C., this 22nd day of May, 1924.

(Signed) WILLIAM R. NAGEL,
Notary Public in and for the
District of Columbia.

INDEX

244